W9-AJO-886

PRINTS

Michel Melot
Director of the Cabinet des Estampes,
Bibliothèque Nationale, Paris

Antony Griffiths
Assistant Keeper of Prints and Drawings,
British Museum, London

Richard S. Field
Associate Director and Curator
of Prints, Drawings, and Photographs,
Yale University Art Gallery, New Haven, Connecticut

André Béguin
Painter, draughtsman, engraver
and writer, Brussels

SKIRA
RIZZOLI NEW YORK

© 1981 by Editions d'Art Albert Skira S.A., Geneva
Reproduction rights reserved by A.D.A.G.P. and
S.P.A.D.E.M., Paris, and Cosmopress, Geneva
Published in the United States of America in 1981 by

RIZZOLI INTERNATIONAL PUBLICATIONS, INC.
712 Fifth Avenue/New York 10019

All rights reserved. No parts of this book may be
reproduced in any manner whatsoever without permission
Part I translated from the French
by Helga Harrison and Dennis Corbyn
English adaptation of the Glossary by Giulia Bartrum
Library of Congress Catalog Card Number: 81-51310
ISBN: 0-8478-0392-9
Printed in Switzerland

Table of Contents

5

I

THE NATURE AND ROLE OF THE PRINT

Definition, function and language of the print

Product and work of art

An art of the bourgeoisie

Industrialized pictures and their effect on the print

Michel Melot

Translated from the French by
Helga Harrison and Dennis Corbyn

DEFINITION FUNCTION AND LANGUAGE OF THE PRINT

The Buddhist Priest Hui-teng.
Rubbing of an inscription in the
Lung-men cave temples, Lo-yang, Honan province (China).
6th-7th century. (110 × 90 mm.)
Reproduction slightly enlarged.

Portrait of Mao Zedong,   ▷
after a drawing by Andy Warhol, 1973.
Set of 300 copies made from
a photocopying machine.
(215 × 292 mm.)

APPROACH
TO A
DEFINITION

The field of the print, in art history, is a kind of no man's land. Whoever ventures into it has to carve out a territory of his own. We shall try here to give a general idea of the lie of the land. Seen from a distance, it might easily be confused with the field of the printed image. Today, however, the latter extends far beyond the field of printmaking proper. Printed images are to be found all around us in unexampled numbers. The print is distinguished from them by the artistic connotation attaching to it. This distinction has next to be situated in historical terms, for its scope and force varies according to the period and social circumstances. The English collector Andrew W. Tuer tells how he dispatched his servant one day to a print dealer to fetch some fine states of a Bartolozzi print: the man did his errand promptly and brought the sheets back carefully folded in four![1]

We may begin by analysing the concrete qualities that go to define prints as a specific category of works of art. The concept that can be thus sifted out will help us to understand how these works originated, how and why the making of them has continued to the present day, and also the sometimes heated differences of appreciation which they have occasioned.

The smallest common denominator is to be found in the root meaning of the term "print," which conveys the idea of impressing a design or image, of transferring it from one surface to another. An early form of printing or rubbing is to be found in ancient China, where students thus took an impress of the lessons engraved on stone tablets. The decisive element in what we call printmaking was the taking of impressions on a soft material, on paper. It was in the fourteenth century that paper was introduced into Europe. Its use spread when the textile industry was developed enough to supply the linen and cotton rags that served as raw material. Sometimes the impression was made directly on fabrics, such as the large altar frontals which could not be replaced by paper.[2] At the present day screenprints have been made on aluminium. So the material medium of the print is not necessarily paper; but it does require a supple, light, readily portable ground.

The print is distinguished from the rubbing by the fact that the ground is not moulded but simply printed with ink. The three constituent elements of the print are: a design or pattern, a plate or block from which the design is to be transferred, and a more pliant ground on which it is to be impressed. Thus defined, the print is seen to include postage stamps, banknotes, pictures in the newspaper, official stamps, and even finger-prints. Such a definition takes us far afield from the work of art, but materially speaking there is little or no distinction between an official rubber-stamp and the ones used by certain artists, a large collection of which has been made by Hervé Fischer.[3]

Print,
woodcut,
woodcarving

Paul Gauguin (1848–1903):
Manao Tupapau (She thinks
of the spirit of the dead).
Woodcut, 1st state. (223 × 527 mm.)

Going beyond printing, Gauguin reworked his woodblocks as low-relief carvings

At this degree of generality the concept of the print has to be distinguished from that of the engraving. Rubbing presupposes engraving, incising: the design can be transferred because it stands in relief, and every printed image called for engraving until 1798, when lithography was invented. Engraving is opposed to designing rather as adding is to subtracting. To engrave means to incise. To design is in essence a matter of writing; a matter of adding a pigment to a ground or modifying this ground surface by means of chemical reactions. Since 1798 "designing" procedures have multiplied and spread to such an extent that it is now impossible to equate printmaking with engraving. This distinction becomes fundamental when the print is confronted with the photograph and the photo-engraving, which raise two distinct problems with respect to the print. A print is not necessarily an engraving. Engraving remains a cutting process, in relief or intaglio, which for the most part does not involve the taking of an impression. It was widely practised by the Greeks and Romans in the form of gem-engraving and goldsmiths' work, but not in the form of printmaking. Like the industry of metal-stamping, the arts of gem-carving, glass-cutting and metal-chasing extend far beyond the simple workshops where engravings are made with a view to printmaking.

It is, nevertheless, from goldsmiths' work that printmaking owes its origin in part, when the goldsmith conceived the idea of filling his incised lines with ink or lamp-black and printing the design before inlaying it with niello. The engraved object was then independent of the print, which was a later derivative of it. The engraver, whether goldsmith or carver, used the same

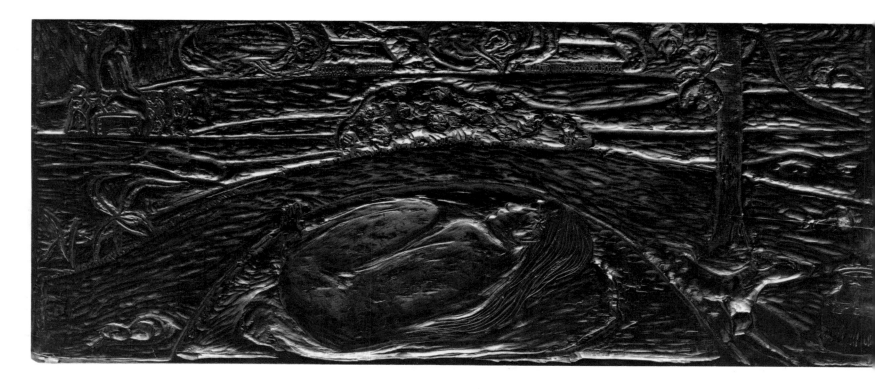

Paul Gauguin (1848–1903):
Manao Tupapau (She thinks
of the spirit of the dead).
Woodblock, recut by the artist
after printing of the first state
(see opposite page) and transformed
into a low-relief sculpture.
(223 × 527 mm.)

Hokusai (1760–1849):

Worship at the Hour of the Ox.
Preparatory drawing for the
woodcut. Brush and Indian ink.
(190 × 265 mm.)

Worship at the Hour of the Ox.
Woodcut from the book
Hokusai Onna Imagawa, c. 1830.
(190 × 265 mm.)

Eileen Lawrence (1946): ▷
Scroll (detail), 1977.
Watercolour on/and handmade paper.

◁ Rodolfo Krasno (1926):
Paired and Perforated Forms, 1967.
"Neo-gravure." (490 × 320 mm.)

tools: the graver or burin, the gouge, the scorper. But he did not use the same metals: his ground surface could neither be hard like gold and silver, nor too soft like tin. The work carried out with a view to a print thus became a specific medium of its own, as explained by Jean Eugène Bersier: "the unincised areas of the plate, the white areas if the engraving was printed, would not have the sense of 'light-givers' in the decoration of the object."[4] The "handwriting" was therefore quite different. The copper plate, too, in the engraver's hands, was not necessarily polished but only flattened; it might be left with the marks of hammering, with its roughness and burr, thus giving the impression the woolly outlines which are unacceptable to the goldsmith. The incised block or plate may however be a work of art in its own right, thus creating at times an unsurmountable ambiguity; this is perhaps the case with some of the woodblocks engraved by Gauguin in Tahiti–low-relief carvings made with a penknife from which impressions were subsequently pulled. On the other hand, when the plate is deliberately cut with a view to pulling impressions, it tends to lose its value as an object of art and becomes a mere tool. The copper plates often exhibited alongside the impressions are shown for their documentary interest, or as mummified relics like those which Dunoyer de Segonzac caused to be gold-faced after usage. Officially at least, such plates are not an object of aesthetic appreciation or market

value. We have however seen one engraver (Paoli Boni) offer his clientele a box containing both the plate and the impressions under the title "graphisculpture," and another (François Portelette) pull impressions from thin sheets of copper and aluminium with strong relief, thus obtaining a print which looks very much like a metal bas-relief. When the rubbing remains an uncoloured imprint, it may be classed as either print or carving. What seems to incline it to one or the other of these categories is its autonomy and pliancy. One hesitates to classify as prints the "markings" made by Hajdu and other works on paper often executed by sculptors. On the other hand, the three-dimensional sculptures moulded in paper pulp by Rodolfo Krasno have nothing of the print except the raw material, but between the two one can find all the intermediary stages in the work of this former engraver turned "paper sculptor." [5]

The taste for hand-made paper, produced slowly sheet by sheet from a thick grainy pulp whose surface in itself has a strong appeal for the public, has led recently to the production of prints of a new kind [6] in which the image is not impressed upon the paper but incorporated into the pulp in which the artist-papermaker has combined various ingredients: dried flowers, translucent plastics, old photographs, etc. In so far as these sheets can be framed, collected and preserved like prints, they are scarcely to be distinguished from the latter–which amounts

Print
and
drawing

Vicomte Ludovic-Napoléon Lepic (1839–1889 or 1890):
The Lake of Nemi, 1870.
"Mobile" etching (same plate with
four different inkings). (240 × 315 mm.)

Edgar Degas (1834–1917):   ▷
Female Torso, c. 1885.
Monotype, brown ink on Japanese
rice paper. (500 × 393 mm.)

to saying that the essential characteristic in the concept of the print is the material ground
supporting the image. But it must then be distinguished from a drawing.
Connected with goldsmiths' work, the origins of printmaking are also bound up in complex
ways with manuscript illumination, of which it took over certain functions. The earliest
hand-press of which we have record is known to have been in a monastery (perhaps in the
scriptorium?). What the earliest engravers offered their clientele was considered as a substitute
for miniatures, a cheap picture coloured by hand and passed off as an illumination. The hand-
colouring of prints has always been a standard practice; it was the principal means of producing
colour-prints until, in the eighteenth century, techniques were worked out of obtaining them
with coloured inks. But even then such elements as fine lacework, highlights or the sparkle
that gives life to the eye were often added afterwards with touches of white gouache. As soon

as the print was no longer oriented towards mass production, we find artists hand-colouring or "illuminating" the impressions, which then revert to the status of drawings. By means of inking the two arts were combined. This became a common practice with certain Impressionists like Vicomte Lepic and their printer, Auguste Delâtre, a craftsman of great skill who justifiably called himself an "artist-printer." Whistler in early days also relied on Delâtre to print his etchings but later came round to the view that the printmaker must do his own printing, so great was the importance Whistler attached to inking effects.

With the stencil technique,[7] drawing links up again with printmaking. Without pressure, but with a large brush, and without ink, but with watercolour or gouache, the artist can colour his design by covering the paper with a whole series of cardboard or metal stencils, even obtaining the most delicate effects of shading. The only point in common with printmaking is

James McNeill Whistler (1834–1903):
Nocturne, first plate of the set
Venice, Twelve Etchings, 1880.
Etching, with two different inkings.
(200 × 295 mm.)

that the image can be multiplied. Not so with the monotype,[8] which yields only one impression. Degas's famous *Female Torso* stands on the borderline not only of drawing but also of sculpture, for the figure was created by modelling the greasy ink with a rag and the fingertip. Since the image is obtained by running the plate through an etching press (and so crushing away the design), the monotype comes into the category of prints. But some of Degas's monotypes (like the *Dancer Taking her Bow* in the Louvre) baffle definition: "There is not enough monotype ink left on it to categorize it as a monotype," writes Eugenia Parry Janis.[9] Is it a counterproof (i.e. a proof taken not from the plate but from an impression on paper while the ink is still damp, giving a pale reflection in reverse of the impression just pulled) or a drawing with the lithographic crayon having nothing in common with a print except the use of this tool? Françoise Cachin has aptly described the monotype as "a perversion of printmaking," for the crushed ink is often no more than a background for the design, as she explains: "Degas initially conceived of the monotype as a supporting surface for colour, and the dancers and café-concert scenes he made between 1874 and 1878 are mostly pastels on monotype."[10]

It would be by no means paradoxical to view the history of printmaking as a succession of efforts to break away from the laborious process of engraving and move towards drawing: etching would mark the first stage and lithography the final break. But, with this break, attempts were promptly made to dispense with the stone and Géricault made a lithograph with pen and ink on plaster-coated paper. With the increasing use of transfer paper, and today's practice of transferring drawings photographically, the frontier between drawing and printmaking remains wide open, forming a free-trade zone to the great chagrin of would-be protectionists.

So it is that the term "graphic arts," comprising both drawings and prints, is more generally used for exhibitions and œuvre catalogues, just as drawings and prints have always been kept side by side in collections, and most print rooms include drawings and vice versa. It is true that drawing paper is available in a greater variety than the paper intended for printing, especially today with the prevailing fashion for thick fine-arts papers. This would not justify a differentiation between drawings and prints on the basis of the paper used; while, as we have seen with sculptures made of paper pulp, this initial element is absolutely necessary, it is by no means sufficient. A *print* necessarily involves a *transfer* of the image. This transfer is meant to permit—and does permit, except in the case of the monotype "perversion" mentioned above—the duplication of the image. It is this possibility of multiplication which gives its peculiar status to the print and prevents it from ever being confused with drawing.

Two inking effects by Whistler

Print,
photograph,
photo-engraving,
photocopy

Jean-Charles Troutot (1945)
and Christian Cavadia (1933):
Blue Symphony No. 2, 1979.
Drawing on tracing table connected
with a micro-computer. (225 × 345 mm.)

Gerhard Richter (1932):   ▷
Seascape, 1970.
Colour offset. (675 × 530 mm.)

A daguerreotype, unique and rigid as it is, has nothing in common with a print. The calotype, invented in 1841 and giving a series of impressions on paper, regained the qualities of the print. The enormous industry brought into existence by photography left the print in a small niche of its own, yielding to it the honours of art – usually, if not always. These two sectors, representing two rival economic systems, long remained quite distinct from each other; the relation between them has been like a love-hate relation, and so it remains to this day.

For the printmaker, photography was useful at first as providing a repertory of images taken from nature and real life. Then it was taken up as a technical device facilitating transfers and offering a useful substitute for tracing paper or the camera lucida, chiefly in lithography and screenprinting. Finally, in the last two decades, Pop Art has made extensive use of the photographic image, bringing it into the domain of the print.

The absence of a press and of ink is enough to distinguish the photograph radically from the print. No such distinction holds with photo-engraving. Here survive the printmaker's techniques of intaglio and relief engraving. Most of the time, but only after the 1880s, the existence of a screen for the printing of photographic images (half-tone block, photogravure or offset) offers a ready means of distinguishing a photomechanical reproduction from any other. The line block, however, as used for example in reproducing drawings for the press, derives ultimately from the black-line method of wood engraving.

A high level of facsimile reproduction can be achieved by means of costly photomechanical processes, such as photogravure retouched by hand, or non-screen offset, or, still better, collotype. But oddly enough, while these sophisticated techniques are hard put to maintain themselves against the flood of cheaper reproductions, the coarse halftone screen characteristic of pictures published in the newspapers has taken on a symbolic value from the great success of Pop Art. The fact is that the photomechanical image is perceived today as being pregnant with symbolic meanings and utilized as such by artists, thus reinvesting the very sector of art in which the print had taken refuge in self-defence.[11]

The debate or quarrel between printmaking and photography is therefore fast becoming academic now that other reproduction techniques are invading the market. Several artists have already demonstrated that a photocopying machine can produce picture sheets which, whether we like it or not, have to be assimilated to prints. Computer drawing, which has now taken over the field of mapmaking and drafting, has also attracted artists, who explain the advantages of it and feel entitled to call the result an original print, inasmuch as they have done the programming themselves. The paradoxical thing about it is that this *nec plus ultra* of mechanization permits the production of an almost unlimited number of prints, each different from the other, programmed to be all unique: it is a printmaker's dream, or his nightmare.

Print,
illustration,
poster

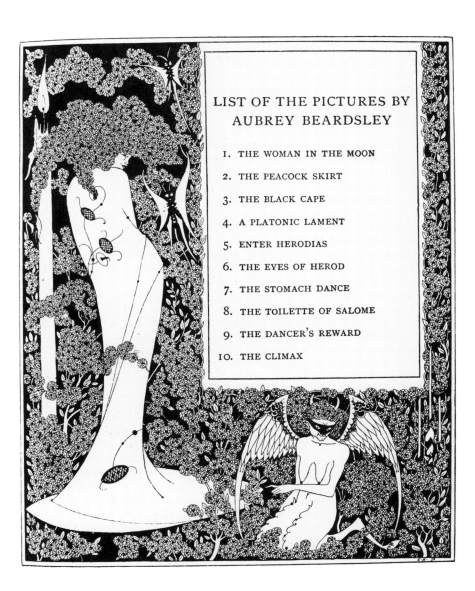

Aubrey Beardsley (1872–1898):
Contents Border Design from
Oscar Wilde's *Salome*, London,
Elkin Mathews and John Lane, 1894.
(177 × 141 mm.)

After this overview it is time to single out certain enclaves within the field of printmaking and consider to what extent they actually form part of it. One such enclave is book illustration. Some catalogues and collections carefully distinguish illustrated books from single sheets, some assimilate them to prints. An illustration is normally characterized by its dependence on a text; but once it is removed from the book it becomes a print. All too often, indeed, in the case of de luxe illustrated books, the text is only a pretext, as in a much-unread eighteenth-century edition of the French poet Jean Dorat, memorable only for its fine plates. French publishers of the Romantic period, after 1830, worked on the same principle, and in the twentieth century it is notorious that illustrated books designed for bibliophiles seldom amount to more than an album of prints, the latter in fact also being sold as a set without the text or even singly as "waste sheets." For all that, the production of prints and/or illustrations has given rise to careful distinctions, for the reason referred to here at the outset: into the concept of the print there enters the idea of a loose, independent, easily handled sheet incompatible with its being included in a text or bound up in a book. It will be found that the greater the independence shown by a printed image within a book, the more it moves away from the category of illustration and comes under the heading of a "print."

One finds the same things happening with posters. The oldest ones, posted up in the sixteenth century in the course of the controversies provoked by the Reformation, have long been filed away in the portfolios of the print rooms. During the vogue for illustrated posters in the 1890s, the lithographs of Toulouse-Lautrec and Mucha were both posted on hoardings and sold singly in the offices of literary reviews like *La Plume*, which also served as an exhibition gallery for the Salon des Cent. Poster collectors, who are often print collectors, set great store by some of these modern posters and may go to great trouble to obtain them in a proof before letters. This vogue has been popularized by the production of "posters," or more often reproductions, which are not meant for public display but for private usage; and so, since they are not posted up, they come readily into the category of prints.[12] On the other hand, when one speaks of prints, one does not normally think of the publicity sheets posted on the hoardings across the way or on the walls of the Métro station. Here again the concept of the print seems inseparable from the loose, independent sheet.

But any image can become a print. Such is the case with labels, for example, of which there are innumerable collectors, and which together with postcards, menus, concert and theatre programmes, cigar bands, etc., form the "side lines" of print collecting. But when the label is painted with a stencil directly on a wall or a package, or when Ernest Pignon-Ernest executes a unique screenprint on the wall of the gallery where he is exhibiting, there is no longer any question of prints;[13] or rather the print, by way of the poster, reveals its kinship with the fresco.

Henri de Toulouse-Lautrec (1864–1901):
Miss Loie Fuller, 1892.
Lithograph heightened with watercolour.
(370 × 260 mm.; with passe-partout 407 × 270 mm.)

Anonymous (15th century):
Christ on the Cross between the Virgin and St John.
Hand-coloured woodcut pasted
inside a chest. (150 × 105 mm.)

Anonymous (15th century): ▷
Pilgrimage Badge of
Our Lady of Hal (near Brussels).
Coloured woodcut.
(200 × 285 mm.)

FUNCTION
AND
FORMATION
OF A LANGUAGE

From the foregoing review of printmaking and its scope and possibilities emerges an overall definition of the print which, if it is to take all its concrete forms into account, must be restricted to its abstract qualities. What constitutes a print is not the medium or the technique of the image, but an aggregate of aptitudes to which it must answer. The first, as with drawing, is the independence, the light and ready handling of the image. If these qualities are required of the print, it is because it must be easy to carry and easy to keep at home, either in a portfolio or on the wall. The print is a portable work of art, one that travels easily. The period that invented the print, the fifteenth century, also invented the credit system enabling money to travel easily. This quality made the print an object which could readily be appropriated by the individual, in contrast with the pictures known till that time: frescoes and altarpieces.

The second characteristic, distinguishing it from book illuminations and drawings, is transferability, which makes it an object of substitution. This quality is actually a drawback, since it condemns the print to be the offshoot of another art work which remains its archetype. By this very fact the print falls into the category of fiduciary objects, somewhere between the bill of exchange and the "indulgences" of Pope Leo X. If this drawback is accepted, it is because it is the necessary prerequisite of this second basic quality: the possibility of duplication. The print thus becomes an interchangeable work of art, one that can be multiplied and distributed. As such it goes its way alone and can be appropriated by anyone. It can be manufactured by means of the production processes worked out between the fourteenth and sixteenth century. Adapting itself to the modern world, the print has become a work of art which changes hands easily from seller to buyer and one which lends itself to industrial production.

When, at the time of the Reformation, the doctrine of transubstantiation became a point of discord between Protestants and Catholics, the controversy over "representation" reached its height. Opponents of religious imagery denounced as a superstitious practice the assimilation of a picture to its referent, while others saw in the new techniques of image-making a means of illustrating and disseminating religious faith. Erasmus held up to ridicule those "who imagine that the sight of a statue of St Christopher... will guard them against death during the day."[14] But the belief persisted and there are plenty of St Christopher prints by Meckenem, Dürer, Beham and Aldegrever inscribed with captions like "Whoever looks at the image of St Christopher will feel no weakness during the day" or "Look daily upon Christopher's face and you are sure not to die a violent death on that day." On one side we have Pope Leo X selling indulgences in the shape of woodcuts bearing the monogram of Christ—treasury bonds drawn on the bank of Paradise; on the other we have Luther denouncing churchmen who lived on the income of monasteries inhabited by one monk whose main business was selling images.

Some curious early coloured woodcuts have survived, representing the Virgin or a saint, which were pasted inside the lid of small chests or strong-boxes (late fifteenth and early sixteenth century), probably containing valuables like jewelry and title deeds.[15] Curious not for their style but for their purpose, which was protective, these images were not intented to be seen, and so long as they were out of sight they served their purpose. Other examples are known of pictures pasted on doors, and in 1841 some old woodcuts were found pasted inside some tombs in the cathedral of Saint-Sauveur in Bruges.

The Chinese origins of printmaking seem to be no different. "With woodblocks the priests make charms on which they engrave constellations and the Sun and Moon. Holding their breath they take them in their hands and print them. Many of the sick are healed" (*History of the Suy*, first quarter of the seventh century). The charms representing Buddha figures printed side by side on a sheet (c. eighth century) discovered in 1906–1909 by Paul Pelliot in the Tun-huang caves[16] are explained by the texts, which tell how in Japan, from 764 to 770, the Empress Shotoku had the magic formulas of Buddhist prayers printed in millions of copies. According to Jean Fribourg, "the charms and amulets of religious origin were followed by a profusion of popular astrological charts, New Year's wishes, and auguries of happiness and male children, which were sold in large numbers among the people and which have never ceased to be produced down to the present day."[17]

Originally, then, the print was an object endowed with symbolic value and a power of appealing to the imagination. Even in Europe such prints have never ceased to be produced; the weakening of the connection—once a physical connection—between the image and its referent has not done away with them. These prophylactic images hanging on the wall in the Flemish interiors which served as the setting for the "Annunciations" of Robert Campin or Joos van Cleve had the value of a crucifix.[18] Craftsmen hung up in their shops the "guild images" representing their patron saint. Pilgrims, in their wayfarings, wore a "pilgrimage badge" designed both to identify them and protect them. The framed print hanging today in many middle-class homes may be considered to "represent" a Picasso or a Dali. One begins, then, to understand why the print is so insistently asserted to be "original" (assimilated to its referent). It has now been enlisted in the service of another belief.

An object
of
substitution

△ German master (early 15th century):
St Christopher, 1423.
Coloured woodcut from
Buxheim (Swabia). (290 × 206 mm.)

◁ Israhel van Meckenem (before 1450–1503):
St Christopher.
Engraving. (170 × 105 mm.)

◁◁ Buddhist Charms.
Chinese woodcut.
7th-8th century.
(280 × 300 mm.)

Mould, module, model

It is the nature of the print to adapt itself, whatever the medium, to one and the same usage, as an object of substitution sufficiently linked to its archetype to be described as the direct emanation of it, but sufficiently independent of it to satisfy the new laws of production and distribution. The block or plate then becomes the "module" or, as it was called in the fifteenth century, the "mould" which delivers up the same object for all but for each an object of his own. Thus the only early print to have come down to us in its original frame[19] was meant to receive the individual prayers of the nuns of the convent of Yerres, after the reform of the convent in 1515: it was a new object of devotion, clearly exteriorizing the practice of private prayer, and probably much used in religious houses where new channels of spiritual life had been installed, sometimes forcibly installed.

From the idea of a module providing an interchangeable object, one passes readily to the idea of a model. While the exact repeatability permitted by the mould still preserves a close and even spiritual connection with the archetype, it also contains within it the seeds of degeneration and secularization, in the sense which the latter term bore in the fifteenth century: the image brought knowledge out of the religious and scholarly world, which then were one, and disseminated it. This is clearly stated in the preface of an *Ars moriendi* blockbook (i.e. with text and pictures cut in the same woodblock): "In order that this matter may stand everyone in good stead, it is placed here before the eyes of all, both in writing, which will serve only for

Parisian Master (late 15th century): △
The so-called Vérard *Danse Macabre*
(Dance of Death), Paris, 1492.
Illuminated woodcut, detail.
(Whole page 560 × 395 mm.)

French Master (late 15th
or early 16th century):
Dance of Death inspired by the
Vérard *Danse Macabre*, between
1492 and 1540.
Fresco, detail.
Nave of the church of
Saint-Orion, Meslay-le-Grenet,
near Chartres (Eure-et-Loir).

Matthäus Merian (1593–1650):
Death and the Pope, and
Death and the Emperor, Basel, 1649.
After the Dance of Death in the
Dominican Church of Basel.
Engraving, details. (Whole page 202 × 152 mm.)

Hans Bock (c. 1550–1624):
Death and the Pope, and
Death and the Emperor, 1596.
After the Dance of Death in
the Dominican Church of Basel.
Pen and Indian ink wash.
(192 × 313 mm.)

clerks, and in pictures, which will serve for both clerks and laymen." The medieval *Dance of Death* thus came down from the frescoed wall to be put into the hands of all, and in some cases the popularity of these prints prompted the fresco painters to take up the theme anew.[20] Once reproduced, the image brought its content into the public domain, where it was destined to provide models for work in still other media. This new function of the print is referred to already in the sixteenth century in the preface to albums of prints, like Léonard Thiry's *Story of Jason* in which the publisher expresses the hope that the pictures may be taken up "in a tapestry and one day adorn the halls of royal palaces." Pattern books or *livres de pourtraicts* for decorators began multiplying in the sixteenth century; one of them, for example, is entitled *Pourtraicts divers destinés aux lingères, maçons, verriers et autres gens d'esprit,* supplying patterns for needlewomen, masons and glassmakers. Pictures of workshops show prints hanging on the wall, as in the manuscript of Piccolpasso intended for potters. In Antwerp in 1564 Hans Liefrinck published a pattern book for "painters, goldsmiths, image-carvers and other artists" *(Divers compartiments ornementaux inventés par J. Floris, profitables aux peintres, orfèvres, tailleurs d'images et autres artistes).*

27

△ Niccolò Pellipario (c. 1480–1540/47):
Warrior struck down and throttled
by Death, c. 1520–1530.
Maiolica dish.
(Diameter 280 mm.)

Hans Burgkmair (1473–1531):   ▷
Lovers Surprised by Death, 1510.
Chiaroscuro woodcut in
three tones. (214 × 153 mm.)

◁◁ Diana and Hounds,
second half of 16th century.
Pendant after a design
by Etienne Delaune.
Gold, enamel, jewels and
chalcedony. (Height c. 90 mm.)

◁ Etienne Delaune (1518/19–probably 1583):
Diana and Hounds.
Engraving. (40 × 30 mm.)
Reproduction slightly enlarged.

Art historians and scholars are often called upon to trace the print on which a Limoges enamel·
or a Castelli maiolica was patterned. The list of such discoveries would fill a whole book or
more. Printmaking at its beginnings was closely connected with goldsmiths' work and jewelry.
Etienne Delaune, goldsmith and armourer to Henri II (1547–1559), produced engraved designs;
with him, and others, designing, printmaking and metalwork went together. Prints were
likewise connected with woodcarving and sculpture, also with cabinetmaking, embroidery and
tapestry. Even easel painting, fresco painting and book illumination, if more rarely, were by a
curious reversion led to copy prints.

It is not the accumulation of examples that interests us here, but rather the transformation
brought about by prints in the methods of producing works of art. The print was a picture
continually on the move, but in one direction: from the workshop that made the model to the
craftsman who copied it. By way of certain correspondences, one can follow through the
sixteenth century the paths of that movement. As an object of the widest diffusion, the print
in fact centralized the places where models were produced. It became the vehicle of a
prevailing taste catered for in the great economic centres (Antwerp, Lyons, Nuremberg) and

political centres (Rome, Fontainebleau). The editions published by a Plantin or a Jean de Tournes were a commodity of international trade, and so were the "moulds" used for the illustrations–those woodblocks which made their way from one workshop to another, and which turn up now on the Rhine, now on the Rhone.

As prints spread and appealed to an ever wider variety of men, there occurred a reverse tendency towards a unification of taste through style, as copied and recopied by one craftsman after another, and towards a narrowing down of the subject matter, reduced to a repertory of stereotyped motifs, as shown by the catalogue of the sets of prints offered by a leading Paris publisher, Philippe Galle: 43 plates of allegories *(Prosopographia)*, Seven Virtues and Sibyls after Blocklandt, the Four Ages of Man after Aegidius Quinetus, the Four Evangelists after Blocklandt, Portraits of Famous Men, 17 plates of Water Gods, 17 plates of Nymphs, and 17 plates of Gods; these last served as models for the carvings on some furniture now in the Musée des Arts Décoratifs and the Musée de Cluny, Paris.[21]

The print thus became a channel of transmission between two sectors conventionally described as "major art" and "minor art." The providing of models for both remained one of the most common functions of the print, which thereby became a powerful upholder of tradition and academicism. In the nineteenth century more and more "miscellanies" of lithographed motifs and figures were published. A pupil of Gros, Bernard Julien, made his living after 1840 by publishing innumerable compilations of this kind. Nineteenth-century art school teaching was largely based on prints and casts. Reproductions of old master paintings were even sold in the form of lithographed outline drawings to which the student was expected to add the colours.[22]

The print was not only a means of diffusing models: it was the vehicle of a veritable codification of images, with a view to fixing a univocal language of art. Generations of artists were schooled by "standard works" on classical mythology illustrated with engravings, such as Giraldi's *De deis gentium* (1548), Cartari's *Imagini* (1566), Conti's *Mythologiae* (1581) and Ripa's *Iconologia* (1593). In addition to the practical interest for artists intent on copying the fashionable imagery

The coded image

◁ Rosso Fiorentino (1494–1540):
Ignorance Cast Out, 1534–1537.
Fresco. (1.67 × 2.55 metres)

René Boyvin (c. 1525–c. 1580): ▷△
Ignorance Vanquished, after
Rosso Fiorentino.
Engraving. (300 × 405 mm.)

Antonio Fantuzzi da Trento ▷
(c. 1508–after 1550):
Ignorance Vanquished, after
Rosso Fiorentino, 1542 (?).
Etching. (300 × 425 mm.)

and respecting conventions, the Neo-Platonic movement showed a great theoretical interest in the reproduction of pictures as a tangible manifestation of concepts. Thus, in the wake of Andrea Alciati's *Emblemata* (1531), there arose a whole literature of pictured "mottoes," "emblems," "hieroglyphs" and "iconologies." These were used as dictionaries of imagery. They were based on the idea that the image established the concept in standard form and fixed a standard interpretation of it.[23] All this was only made possible by printmakers and the printing press. Long after Lessing in his *Laokoon* (1766) had refuted the theory of "Ut pictura poesis," the assimilation of pictorial language to written language, these practices remained active, even in a degraded form: it was not until 1791 that appeared the iconology of Cochin and Gravelot, *Traité complet des Allégories, Emblèmes, etc. Ouvrage utile aux artistes et aux amateurs, et pouvant servir à l'éducation des jeunes personnes.* One finds the same phenomenon occurring after the publication of Lavater's *Physiognomische Fragmente* (1775–1778), which standardized the physical portrayal of people in terms of their moral nature, linking the face with the soul. In France Le Brun published his recipes for codifying the visual expression of emotion in painting (*Méthode pour apprendre à dessiner les passions,* 1698); based on the theories of Descartes, it remained in use in art schools down to the nineteenth century.

The increasing number of these image books, with their standardized types of design, resulted from a natural aptitude of the print: as a light, loose, easily manipulated sheet, it lent itself to collections and compilations. More will be said later about collectors, but it may be pointed out now that prints by their very nature were easy to accumulate, to classify, to conserve. They permitted a ready accumulation of "treasures" in the economic sense of the term, but above all a methodical accumulation of knowledge. This faculty of the independent print sheet constituted an irresistible attraction for the scholars of the sixteenth century, each intent on some particular "corpus" or "thesaurus"; an even greater attraction for those of the first half of the seventeenth century, with their taste for encyclopaedias and systematic classifications of knowledge.

By way of emblem books, medal books, series of famous men, etc., the print diffused the spirit of encyclopaedic knowledge. The biography of a humanist and antiquary like Jean-Jacques Boissard (1528–1602) can be followed from one compilation of his to another: *Habitus Variarum Orbis Gentium* (1581), *Vitae et Icones Sultanorum Turcicorum* (1596), *Icones Virorum Illustrium* (1597), *Romanae Urbis Topographia* (1597–1602) and so on. In the seventeenth century Galileo's friend Cassiano del Pozzo devotedly brought together all the remains of Roman civilization in 23 volumes of drawings and prints and a series of medals and carvings. Before being collected for its own sake, the print proved a better medium than any other for the collecting of pictures; it might have been supposed that it was invented for this express purpose. It was the ideal medium for portrayals of the world in atlas form, also for galleries of portraits. Jacopo Filippo Foresti's *De claris mulieribus* was published in Ferrara in 1497; Andrea Fulvio's well-known book of portrait medals, *Illustrium imagines*, appeared in 1517.[24] Possibly these portraits were imaginary; before all else they offered a vision of History. Much the same might be said of the popular books of "Physiologies" or of "Frenchmen Painted by Themselves," fanciful encyclopaedias in which society is classified in the manner of Cuvier and which reveal a Balzacian awareness of the fabric of modern societies. Our present-day systems of micro-photography and data processing have done no more than multiply this use of the print as an "image bank."

Photography too gave a new dimension to the use of the print as a "museum without walls." For it had been one of the key functions of the print to feature not just a particular work but a whole collection, thereby reflecting a halo of glory on the collector himself. A contemporary of Cassiano del Pozzo, the wealthy Genoese banker Vincenzo Giustiniani commissioned the publication of two volumes of prints (1628–1631) reproducing his collection of antiquities. A similar undertaking by the brothers Reynst was broken off in 1658, the same year in which were published the 230 plates of David Teniers' *Theatrum Pictorum* after the collections of

"Portraits of some famous men who have flourished in France from the year 1500 to the present," c. 1600. Engraving (entire and detail) known as "La Chronologie collée." (Each sheet 370 × 240 mm.)

An object of accumulation

1.	2.	3.	4.	5.
Phil. de Commines. S.ʳ d'Argenton.	Charles d'Amboise. S.ʳ de Chaumont.	Gaston de Foix. Duc de Nemours.	Arthus Gouffier. S.ʳ de Boisy.	Pierre du Terrail. S.ʳ de Bayard.
19.	20.	21.	22.	23.
François de Bourbon. Duc d'Anguyen.	Henry d'Albret. Roy de Nauarre.	Iean de Bourbon. Comte d'Anguyen.	Pierre Strozzi. Mareschal de France.	Charles de Coßé. S.ʳ de Brißac.
37.	38.	39.	40.	41.
Guy de Laual.	Anne de Ioyeuse.	Henry de Bourbon. Prince de Condé.	Henry de Lorr. Duc de Guyse.	Bern. de la Valette. Admiral de France.
55.	56.	57.	58.	59.
Guillaume Viole. Euesque de Paris.	Iean de Moruilliers. Euesque d'Orleans.	Iacques Amiot. Euesque d'Auxerre.	Nicolas de Thou. Euesque de Chartres.	Claude Despence.

Archduke Leopold Wilhelm. This taste for engraved picture galleries and prestige operations reached its height with the *Cabinet du Roi* of Louis XIV. The patron or sponsor had to finance a whole workshop of engravers, as did the great dealer Jean de Jullienne who between 1721 and 1734 set out to have 750 Watteau drawings engraved and printed; in this he was copying the aristocratic fashion for "engraved galleries." In the Dresden print room are documents concerning the steps taken by its keeper Heinecken "to engrave and bring out a series of prints after the famous pictures in the Royal Gallery." On 9 April 1749 a contract was signed with Lorenzo Zucchi, who engaged to engrave and publish a hundred prints in five years' time, while the king agreed to pay 4,000 livres a year "to maintain the necessary people." Heinecken applied to Mariette for the commentaries on the pictures, sent out a prospectus to the learned world, wrote to Laurent Cars (then engraving Le Brun's paintings in the Grande Galerie of Versailles, published in 1753) asking him to recruit some good engravers, and hurried forward the second volume so that it would be ready for the Leipzig fair of 1755.[25]

Acting as an encyclopaedia or a "museum without walls," the print served to reproduce an impressive number of works, vouching for the power, usefulness and importance of the medium. Whether in the case of the *Cabinet du Roi* or the great picture series of the French Revolution by Grasset de Saint-Sauveur, the print provided the artillery for ideological offensives.

The Triumph of Galatea *as transposed by the print*

Raphael (1483–1520):
The Triumph of Galatea
(detail), 1511.
Fresco in the Farnesina, Rome.

1

According as the reproduction is considered as a technique or a channel of meaning, the distance placed by the press between the plate and the impression will be seen as a degradation or as a reinforcement of the representation.

At any rate, one might say that the print is a "second-degree" image, meaning by this that, being degraded, it becomes a "second-hand" image or, being reinforced, an image raised "to the second power." These contradictory notions may arise quite spontaneously in the spectator. The idea of degradation has been well conveyed by Marcel Proust: "But at the moment of making the purchase, and though the thing represented had an aesthetic value, my grandmother felt that vulgarity and utility too obstinately held their own in the mechanical medium of representation: photography. She tried to use guile, and if not to eliminate commercial banality entirely, at least to reduce it, to substitute for it something still of art, to introduce into it several 'thicknesses of art'... But while the photographer had been removed from the representation of the masterpiece or of nature and replaced by a great artist, he regained his rights in order to reproduce that very interpretation. Seeing its vulgarity loom up before her, my grandmother kept trying to fend it off. She asked Swann whether the work had not been engraved, preferring whenever possible old engravings which still had some interest beyond themselves; those, for example, that represent a masterpiece in a state in which we can no longer see it today (like Morghen's engraving of Leonardo's Last Supper before its deterioration)."[26]

The idea of reinforcement is conveyed both by the *engraving* (the rootedness of it, the indelible mark) and by the *impression*. In the mind, too, one's keenest recollections are "graven" or "impressed" on the memory. The workings of the print have something in common with the practices of land art (the furrows and trenches marking the earth) or body art (the scars or tattooings marking the body). We have hardly moved from the domain of magic practices in which the early engravers of Buddhist charms carried out their work; one might say that the print has done no more than change its gods. The making of a print is thus justified over and above any concern for reproduction, and artists take to it because they find in the print an idiom unlike any other. This purist notion of printmaking (which in fact seldom exists in the pure state and only in well-defined periods) is found for example in certain Minimalists who lay the whole weight of meaning on a single stroke (on the incising of that stroke) or on the texture of the inking. The work is susceptible of two interpretations: one wholly materialistic (the work reduced to its concrete trace gives itself out only for what it is in its actual matter), the other wholly spiritualistic (this concrete trace remaining a form stripped of meaning and referring only to the mind of its "creator"). Artists who thus wish to release themselves from any expressionistic pretext speak now the language of matter, now the language of spirit.[27]

2

3

4

5

6 7

Engravings after Raphael's fresco by:
1. Marcantonio Raimondi, 1511.
2. Hendrick Goltzius, 1592.
3. Nicolas Bocquet, 1690.
4. Nicolas Dorigny, 1693.
5. Bernard Picart, 1734.
6. Domenico Cunego, 1771.
7. Joseph-Théodore Richomme, 1820.

The image multiplied

Camille Pissarro (1830–1903):
Twilight with Haystacks, 1879.
Etching and aquatint,
3rd state. (105 × 180 mm.):

Impression in black and white
and three impressions pulled on
different coloured papers in
different coloured inks.

The perfect vehicle for presenting a series of pictures at once materially independent and intellectually connected, the print affords many possibilities of accumulation, repetition and transposition. It offers a further advantage which printmakers continue to make much of today. Contemporary prints are frequently presented in sets or portfolios. One may even say that some of the most famous contemporary prints, like Andy Warhol's *Marilyn Monroe* or Robert Ryman's *Six Aquatints*, are suites, each element of which has meaning only in relation to the others and amidst the others. Which is to say that the possibility of "collection" already has a semantic value for the artist and that he exploits that possibility.

By its very nature, as we have seen, printmaking takes an invariant (the master design or certain elements of it), and from it produces a series of variations due to effects of inking, to hand-colouring of the impression, to differences of paper and ink. By pulling the same print with different inks, Pissarro obtained a series of impressions comparable in their effect to that which Monet obtained by painting his sequence of *Haystacks* and *Rouen Cathedral* at different times of day. Here there is no question of duplicating and diffusing an image. The print is used to get not a reproduction but a differentiation. The prints of a painter like Henri

Goetz, such as his *Explorations* in which the motif is "explored" from sheet to sheet as in a film sequence, or his *Variations* in which he plays on the mutation and transformation of motifs from one plate to the next, are significant examples of this practice, which explains in part why the print transcends its ordinary function of duplicating and disseminating an image. It offers a specific process to which the artist can respond even if duplication is no part of his purpose. Printmaking in itself is already an artistic language which precedes the symbolic values attached to its content. That printmaking was bound up with the commercial development of a capitalist economy is obvious, even before 1530. As a saleable commodity it was part of that economy, it reflects its workings, it even contributes to it as a tool. The oldest extant printseller's catalogue, that of Alessandro di Francesco Rosselli of Florence, dating to 1528, consists chiefly of maps and town views. Similarly, the "catalogue index" which has come down to us from a leading publisher, Antoine Lafréry (Rome, 1571), contains 112 maps out of a total of 461 prints. In the expanding economy of the later Renaissance, when cartographers were kept busy remeasuring the world and redrawing their maps, the print obviously had an important part to play.

The print
and
the representation
of time

Georges-Henri Manesse (late 19th century):
Madame Vigée-Lebrun, after Jacques-Louis David.
Etching, 1st and 7th states. (275 × 200 mm.)

It is more important to explain in detail how the print served to reinforce the new measurement of time, and not only by the fact that the voyages of discovery involved the measurement of space with time units. The printed image evokes two attitudes towards time. First, the idea that the print should preserve for eternity the traces of past or passing civilizations: pictures of Roman ruins are the second largest category of prints listed in Lafréry's catalogue of 1571, and we know how intent the intellectuals of the Renaissance were on immortalizing the glory of man's achievements. Secondly, the printed image, by the fact of being printed, and by way of its technical constraints, reveals the act of the artist as a process of manufacture. Hence the importance of the notion of *state* in printmaking (unknown in the other graphic arts), since the print permits the pulling of proofs from the plate *in the course of the work*, each proof marking its progress and preserving a token of it. The printmaker's work is thus divided up into stages like a time sequence, and each *state* materializes this work in progress. This notion of the print as a self-recording image, as both work and a record of work, played a decisive role in the first half of the sixteenth century, with artists who were intensely, proudly, aware of their historical importance. It has been plausibly suggested that the etchings of the School of Fontainebleau, which cannot be explained as an attempt to diffuse the works in question, may have been made with the idea of recording for posterity a series of paintings which the artists themselves valued very highly.[28] This is not so far from the view of Jean Adhémar: from the fact that the prints were conserved by the "concierge" charged with the upkeep and conservation of the Château de Fontainebleau, he concludes that they were intended as archive material recording a particular "moment" in the history of art.[29] From this point of view one can better understand these rapid and confidential etchings, so very different from the deeply cut engravings made after the same paintings and printed in several thousand copies by Paris publishers.

Once the print had been replaced by photography as a means of recording and disseminating pictures, there arose a totally different notion of the "state," one that enjoyed an enormous success with both artists and art lovers. Instead of marking a stage on the way to a final work, the state became an image of fleeting time applied to the design itself, which was no longer the permanent and stable design of the Renaissance, but the vehicle of values continually renewed and reinterpreted, as with the Impressionists. At the impressionist exhibition of 1880 Pissarro exhibited in the same frame different states of the same print, as if each state was a finished work in its own right, or rather as if the work as a whole consisted of all its states. Like the inking effect, which varied with each impression and gave rise to the fashion for what Lepic aptly called "mobile" etchings, this multiplying and featuring of carefully numbered states came into its own at the end of the nineteenth century, shortly before the old concept of time, which had regulated economic life since the Renaissance, was seen to be at an end in music, in philosophy, and in science.[30]

Edgar Degas (1834–1917):
In the Louvre, Painting, Mary Cassatt,
1879–1880.
Etching and drypoint,
1st, 10th and 20th states. (301 × 125 mm.)

PRODUCT
AND
WORK OF ART

French Master (16th century):
Crucifixion with Emblems of
the Abbey of Yerres (Essonne),
south-east of Paris.
Hand-coloured woodcut in
black wooden frame.
(105 × 75 mm.: with frame 157 × 132 mm.)

Anonymous (15th century):
The Last Supper, 1463.
Dotted manner.
Hand-coloured impression
pasted into a prayer book.
(69 × 50 mm.; with painted frame 143 × 90 mm.)

The rise of the print was conditioned on the one hand by the new ways of producing and distributing goods and the new purposes to which they were put, and, on the other, by the traditional use that was to be made of it in the ideology of art. "In that way," writes Richard S. Field, "the woodcut engendered the beginning of a new coherence in the masses of a feudally splintered society. On the other hand, the image on paper was also a new form of private object, available to an expanding population with a growing ability to purchase." [31] The characteristics of this *product* – a transferred image, mass-produced by a printing machine – were very different from those of the *work of art* with its transcendence of creation and immanence of meaning. The two were mutually contradictory. If such an object was to be produced, society had first to produce its maker, the engraver, who had as yet no place in the social order. Indeed, it was in his personality that this initial contradiction had to be resolved, and that is why such composite qualities were expected of him: he had to be both "creator" and "craftsman," both "intellectual" and "manual" worker. The personality of the engraver would always oscillate between workman and artist, and even today, when the artist alone dominates, there are "archaeological" traces of the workman in every printmaker.

In 1452 the carpenters' guild at Louvain claimed jurisdiction over an "image-maker" on the grounds that he worked on wood. To begin with, if the engraver was to be recognized as such, he had to be fitted into the rigidly structured world of the craft guilds; in Florence it was not until 1571 that painters were exempted from compulsory membership in the guild of physicians. The Louvain image-maker, called Jan van den Berghe, refused to be assimilated to the carpenters, arguing that the "singularity" of his art belonged to "the realm of the clerks [intellectuals] rather than the craftsmen [manual workers]." [32] But it was the carpenters who won the case. This documented incident shows that the earliest woodcuts may well have been produced by craftsmen who were aware of the aesthetic qualities of their product and of their own status as "artists." Subsequently, however, the success of woodcuts and their international dissemination at fairs, festivals and pilgrimages led to organized mass-production of them, and their makers were absorbed, beyond all question, into the ranks of craftsmen.

The production of woodcuts followed the rise of a paper-making industry, which developed from 1360 onwards: the first paper-maker in Nuremberg set up his mill in 1390, the first Flemish paper-mill was operating in 1405. In 1403 the painters of Bruges were already complaining of unfair competition from local calligraphers, who bought picture sheets in Utrecht to illustrate their manuscripts cheaply and even ventured to sell them separately. This violated both the guild rules and the monopoly which medieval artists had on their local market. In 1426 the magistrates of Bruges prohibited the importation of picture sheets; so did those of Venice in 1441. But these were futile measures, unenforceable in the face of the economic trend that was sweeping the new product into the swelling flood of international trade.

It is worth quoting Jacques Le Goff's description of the historical setting in which woodcuts made their appearance: "The crisis of the fourteenth century... created a new clientele, mainly middle-class, for products and an art form which may have tended towards mass-production – what printing would make possible in the intellectual field – but which, on the average, still achieved a very respectable standard of quality, because of a rising standard of living enjoyed by new social classes and a broadening base of prosperity and taste."[33] At the end of the fourteenth century, Le Goff goes on, "the traditional manufacture of fine cloth, the 'old cloth trade,' was badly affected by the crisis, and its old centres began to decline; but, at the same time, new centres arose, devoted to the manufacture of cheaper cloth intended for a less rich and less exacting clientele." The same, no doubt, applies to manuscript illumination. As for the early woodcuts, they were confined almost exclusively to religious uses, but a religion profoundly affected by the same historical developments: the intenser spirituality that followed the Black Death of 1369, making its impact on the new urban centres through the Mendicant Orders and the Preaching Friars. "Piety was more conspicuous, more demonstrative than ever. Popular preachers unleashed the enthusiasm of crowds and called forth the most physical expressions of devotion."[33] It was in the merchant towns of Flanders and the Rhine valley, in

◁ Master of the Playing Cards
(Upper Rhine, active c. 1430–1440):
Playing Card with Five Birds.
Engraving. (135 × 98 mm.)

Bernhard Merckle ▷
(Nuremberg, active c. 1560):
Two Playing Cards of the
"Ansbach" type, c. 1560:
Two of Acorns, and
Knave of Leaves.
Hand-coloured woodcuts.
(Each 97 × 70 mm.)

Bohemia and Bavaria, that the production of picture sheets, often monastic in origin, spread. Richard S. Field has suggested that the blockbook of the *Sick Lion* must have been commissioned around 1458 by the Preaching Friars of Basel, the same Dominicans for whom two sets of frescoes of the *Dance of Death* in that city had already been made.[34] In connection with Quentin Massys, Van Mander recalls that at Bruges in 1486 "it was an old custom for the fraternities who cared for the sick, the Lazarists, to parade through the town carrying a big wooden torch... distributing woodcut pictures of saints. A great many of them were therefore needed."[35]

These picture sheets, woodcuts made from blocks cut along the grain, must not be confused with the skilful metalcuts which appeared in the mid-fifteenth century and which have a quite different history. The latter are of course also prints, but might be described as a different breed of the same species. There is a certain amount of interaction between these two art forms, typical of an experimental period: thus we have the "dotted manner," engravings on metal in which the plate could sometimes be inked for either intaglio or relief printing, and which we find being used at the end of the fifteenth century in the place of miniatures. It is even possible that some plates were engraved for their own sake, as unique pieces of goldsmiths' work. This shows that, before 1500, prints might be intended for a wide range of different uses. Metal engravings, based on the same system as woodcuts but not meant for the same purposes, did

Designing and making

North Italian Master (late 15th century):
The World (?), card from a Tarot pack.
Hand-coloured and embossed woodcut. (189 × 90 mm.)

not all aim at the same public. They could be found in the goldsmiths' workshops in the Piazza del Duomo in Florence and in other towns, like Nuremberg, which were governed by a middle class oligarchy whose economy was founded in part on luxury handicrafts catering both for the aristocracy and the higher clergy. The difference between the northern and the Italian towns, according to Frederick Antal, was due to a rather less intense religious sentiment in Italy, a tradition of art industry in its towns, and a more sophisticated middle-class clientele. "It was a sign of the economic decline as well as the political insignificance of the masses in Florence, that the popular illustrated manuscripts of the fourteenth century did not give rise here, as they did in northern countries, to block books and to the production of countless woodcuts to satisfy the needs of the less well-off among the middle class and of the artisans. At the beginning of the fifteenth century, it appears that only a very few woodcuts were produced at all."[36] Yet we know that in 1430, in Florence, one Antonio di Giovanni di Ser Francesco referred in his tax declaration to "woodblocks for playing cards and saints," and we have evidence for a card painter in Bologna as early as 1395. Playing cards demonstrate the ambiguity between the "luxury" object and the "popular" object. Although they figure among the earliest woodcuts, along with devotional pictures, the first playing cards—traceable not to the towns, but to the courts—in fact had a didactic and even scholarly character.[37]

The metal engravers:
goldsmiths
or
painters

Maso Finiguerra (1426–1464):

The Coronation of the Virgin.
Impression on paper from the
engraved silver plate before
the plate was inlaid with niello.
(130 × 88 mm.)

The Coronation of the Virgin.
Niello print, in 16th-century frame.
(130 × 88 mm.; with frame 220 × 153 mm.)

Antonio Pollaiuolo (c. 1432–1498):
The Battle of Naked Men, c. 1470.
Engraving. (405 × 613 mm.)

Different techniques (which also determined differences in price) were used to produce prints for these different classes of customers, "popular" or "scholarly"; and more important still they were produced by different kinds of makers. While the woodcutters generally came from the artisan class and perhaps from the monasteries, the metal engravers came from the goldsmiths' workshops and could vie with the painters or even stand on the same footing with them. All the early woodcuts are anonymous; likewise, it is impossible to identify the makers of the Florentine nielloes and early Italian engravings before the goldsmith-painter Antonio Pollaiuolo and his *Battle of Naked Men* (c. 1470). Thus the print did not spring from the heart of the art world, centred on painting, but evolved on the fringes, seen by some as a promise, by others as a threat. Most immediately threatened was the manuscript illuminator. There was not much connection in the fifteenth century between engraving and painting: it was rare for an engraver to work directly from painted models, and research in this direction in both Florentine and Flemish art has yielded very little.[38] But from the moment prints entered the artistic domain they inevitably rivalled painting and often won out over it. The print held a trump card: it travelled easily, and while it did not often copy painting, it was itself copied. Schongauer's engraving of the *Temptation of St Anthony* "so delighted Michelangelo when he was young that he copied it in a painting" (Vasari). In the work of even so independent an engraver as the Master of the Housebook, Max Lehrs has found echoes of Schongauer, who was widely copied in Italy, as Dürer would be later on. "Robetta and Nicoletto da Modena copied from Schongauer, and we find such masters as Gerard David, Geertgen tot Sint Jans, Mabuse, and 'the Bruges Master of 1500' borrowing from his engravings."[39]

The artist
coping
with reproduction

A Dürer motif taken over by four artists

◁ Albrecht Dürer (1471–1528):
Four Nude Women or The Four Witches, 1497.
Engraving. (190 × 131 mm.)

△ Wenzel von Olmütz (active c. 1480–1500):
Four Nude Women, after Dürer.
Engraving. (187 × 132 mm.)

Barthel Beham (1502–1540): ▷
Three Nude Women and Death.
Engraving. (77 × 54 mm.)

Israhel van Meckenem (before 1450–1503): ▷ ▽
Four Nude Women, after Dürer.
Engraving. (201 × 126 mm.)

The problems raised by this new practice became all the more acute as the domain of art, represented by painting, increasingly asserted its autonomy. At the beginning of the sixteenth century these problems were twofold: first, the control the artist had to retain over his work which, by its nature, tended to escape him in the form of reproductions; secondly, the workshop organization which set up an increasingly rigid division of labour to make the most of the print's commercial potential. This made it difficult for the print to be assimilated to a work of art; the latter, even if produced in a large studio by a team of assistants and pupils, came forth under a single master's name. In the great debate opposing the painter to the sculptor, the liberal arts to the mechanical arts, the engraver had moved steadily towards the painters; for though the goldsmith-engravers, like Jacques Callot, long continued active, from the beginning of the sixteenth century we find engravers like Lucas van Leyden who were oriented towards painting and were themselves accomplished painters.

Dürer synthesizes this attitude of the goldsmith-craftsman who strove for the dignity and autonomy of the artist-painter and used the print as a means to that end. His journey to the Netherlands in 1520–1521 shows the use he made of his prints: he sold whole sets of them (at least ten times his complete œuvre as a printmaker); he presented them to influential people, like the archbishop of Bamberg, the chamberlain of Charles V, and the regent Margaret of Austria, who, he hoped, would commission a portrait from him; and he exchanged prints with fellow artists, like the goldsmith Alexander and Lucas van Leyden. In his travel diary Dürer wrote: "Lucas van Leyden made me a present of an entire set of his engravings; in return he received a collection of mine, which I value at 8 florins." Or: "I am giving Polonius a complete set of my prints. Through the painter they are to be sent to Rome and I have been promised some Raphael drawings in exchange."

The most noteworthy anecdote about these early prints, related by Vasari, is that of the complaint lodged by Dürer against Marcantonio Raimondi, whom he accused of making copperplate engravings, complete with his monogram, after his woodcuts and selling them in the Piazza San Marco. This grievance may have been one reason for Dürer's journey to Venice in 1505. Embarrassed by this unprecedented action—the copies having doubtless been made "in good faith"—the Venetian Senate pronounced a guarded judgment: it authorized the copies but forbade Marcantonio to add Dürer's monogram to them. Marcantonio's own engraving of Dido was copied by others even more cunningly: "Such careful forgeries were made in the Renaissance because there was already a market of keen print collectors, and sheets of high quality fetched a good price." [40] In 1511, when Dürer published as a set his woodcuts of the *Life of the Virgin*, he prefaced it with this warning: "Woe unto him who ventures to assail us and lay hands on the toil and invention of another!" In 1512 the Town Council of Nuremberg issued the following notice: "In the precincts of the Town Hall, a foreigner is taking the liberty of selling pictures bearing Dürer's mark, but these are counterfeits; he shall be compelled to remove all the marks, or everything shall be confiscated." [41] The problem also arose in Italy: in 1514 a certain Zoan da Brescia, who had had some woodblocks of a Story of Trajan "cut by hand," complained that the cuts had been plagiarized and demanded exclusive rights to them for a period of ten years.

The prints thus pulled in larger or smaller numbers could be transformed into an "œuvre" only by means of a "secondary," essentially legal ideology without which they could not be treated as works of art. We know that, from 1475, the painter-goldsmith Mantegna was connected with an engraving workshop in Mantua, whose economic importance was such that

▽ Nicoletto da Modena (active c. 1490–1511): The Judgment of Paris (?), after Dürer, 1500. Engraving. (169 × 123 mm.)

two engravers who had decided to leave it and set up on their own account were assaulted, left for dead in the street, then accused and forced to flee to Verona. Mantegna, moreover, was long considered to be the inventor of engraving–as late as 1582 by Lomazzo. Raphael too was associated with an engraving workshop, an undertaking at once artistic and commercial, and he employed Marcantonio Raimondi to engrave his drawings, the sale of the prints being arranged through his factotum, Baviera.

After pursuing a protectionist policy to safeguard the interests of the illuminators, cities like Venice and Nuremberg realized the commercial importance of this new art and legislated to protect it locally, glossing over the contradiction between a "manufactured" product and a "creative" work by the novel notion of "intellectual property." Venice adhered to a firm policy in this matter, which helped to make it a great printing centre in the sixteenth century. In 1500 a monumental engraving in six plates, Jacopo da Barbari's *Bird's Eye View of Venice*, was published there by Anton Kolb, a Nuremberg merchant attracted to Venice by the grant of exclusive rights for four years. The expansion of the art market and the prestige acquired by major artists made the danger of fraud very real: between 1515 and 1525 the workshop producing woodcuts after Titian forged some of the master's drawings.[42] In 1508–1510 the publication of the *Triumph of Christ*, a woodcut after Titian printed from ten blocks with an overall length of ten feet, a "poor man's fresco" intended for exhibition and no doubt as anti-Roman propaganda, had a considerable impact,[43] as did the later publication by the same workshop of the *Crossing of the Red Sea* and *Abraham's Sacrifice*. The plate of the latter was printed in 1515 with the publisher's and engraver's signatures but without the painter's name. It was not until the third printing that a scroll was added, acknowledging it as a work "del

Titian (c. 1490–1576):
The Crossing of the Red Sea, 1549.
Woodcut printed from twelve blocks.
(Overall size 1.21 × 2.21 metres)

celebre Tiziano"; and in the fourth the artist's name alone is inscribed in the frame in capitals: "TIZIANO."

Around the great Renaissance masters, during the second decade of the sixteenth century, printmaking was thus drawn into the field of art and began to play a part in creating the artist's image. It is in this light that we must regard the appearance, around 1515, of new techniques calculated to bring the print closer to painting and drawing. In 1513 etching was first used for the making of prints, though the process had long been known to goldsmiths and armourers; they used it for the damascening of hard metals like those of sword blades. Etchers were no longer engravers in the strict sense but drew with the needle, leaving the actual engraving to a chemical process. About the same time, also in mannerist circles, the chiaroscuro woodcut was perfected: a woodcutting process which creates the illusion of a painting in grisaille. Vasari was persuaded by this mannerist movement, which set the seal of recognition on print-making both as a curiosity and as a modern art form, to include its history in his *Lives*, timidly in the first edition, and then in the shape of a "Life of Marcantonio Raimondi." Although prints may have been considered a marginal art form, a studio "by-product," this shows that they were nevertheless acknowledged to have an intrinsic, symbolic significance.

Vasari did not concede an equal importance to the woodcut; he acknowledged its merits, but it still bore the stigma of its popular appeal and wide dissemination. But within a few years this situation changed: the reversal, which took place mainly during the period of the Council of Trent (1545–1563), was due to the massive propaganda use of the print by the Counter-Reformation, which was, doctrinally and economically, a "reconquest of Europe by the image" (Emile Mâle).

The organization of printmaking

Hieronymus Cock (c. 1510–1570):

◁ Ruins of the Colosseum, Rome, 1550.
Preparatory drawing for
the set *Views of Roman Ruins*.
Pen and black ink. (217 × 325 mm.)

△ Fifth View of the Colosseum,
from the set *Views of Roman Ruins*,
Antwerp, 1551.
Etching. (302 × 222 mm.)

Antwerp in the sixteenth century was the commercial centre of Europe.[44] As part of the Spanish Netherlands, Antwerp had direct access to the Spanish-American markets, and the great publishing house of Plantin made a fortune not so much from its scholarly publications as from the thousands of Bibles and devotional pictures exported by missionaries. This period of prosperity continued until the slump of 1566, but since 1550 the print publisher Hieronymus Cock had been taking advantage of the favourable state of the market, and after 1558 his dealings with Plantin grew apace. Cock departed from the earlier system in which the engraver was his own printer and dealer−like the engraver Nicolas Hogenberg, at Malines, who did a brisk trade in religious prints. Cock separated the techniques of production from the techniques of sale and introduced a division of labour within the production processes. With him, prints begin to record the names of the draughtsman (*del.*), painter (*pinx.*) or inventor of the design (*inv.*), as distinct from the names of the manufacturer (*fec.*), engraver (*sculp.* or *inc.*) and publisher, whose *excudit (exc.)* seems to indicate that he owns the plate and with it the rights of reproduction. Nothing could be further from the modern idea of a work of art than this organization and division, all geared to the making of a consumer product. Admittedly, in the house of Cock, the workmen were still on occasion interchangeable with the artists, and Cock himself put his hand to all the different tasks; but by his working methods he separated himself from the domain of art, which now became a distinct field.

Whereas Vasari deals at length with Cock's prints in his "Life of Marcantonio Raimondi," the Dutch art historian Van Mander dismisses him briefly: "I have little to say of Hieronymus, for he forsook culture and art at an early stage to engage in trade. He commissioned and purchased oil and tempera pictures, published engravings and etchings… He grew rich and bought one house after another." The international print trade developed along these lines, initially publishing reproductions of famous works in Italy, ancient and modern, ranging from the ruins of the Colosseum to Raphael's *Loggie* in the Vatican. Cock engraved some of the "sights" during his stay in Rome in 1548–1551 and subsequently sent well-known artists there specially, like Bruegel in 1553, thus supplying models for the artists employed to propagate the triumph of Rome and the Catholic Church. The secretary of the bishop of Liège wrote to Titian: "I hope to receive by way of Antwerp a further six copies of the said prints, for his Lordship has kept those you sent me for himself. Master Hieronymus Cock, painter and printer of copperplate engravings, of whom Cornelis Cort was a pupil, has told me that a Bolognese promised he would bring some back from Antwerp around next May, having contracted with your Excellency to be the sole agent for your Excellency's works." [45] Workshops of reproductive engraving sprang up to supply this trade. At Liège the school of Lambert Lombard merged with the house of Cock in 1553. Van Mander tells us that the school of Frans Floris in Antwerp had over 120 pupils. All these workshops did copperplate engraving, although the accounts of the firm of Plantin show that engraving cost the publisher three times as much as woodcuts.

Hieronymus Cock (c. 1510–1570):
St Jerome in a Landscape with Ruins,
after a painting by
Maerten van Heemskerck, 1552.
Etching. (226 × 351 mm.)

Jan and Lucas van Duetecum
(mid–16th century):

△◁ Ruins on the Palatine, Rome,
perhaps after a drawing
by Hieronymus Cock,
plate II of the set
Views of Roman Ruins, Antwerp, 1561,
published by Hieronymus Cock.
Etching and engraving. (238 × 328 mm.)

◁ View of a Sculpture Garden, Rome,
after a drawing by
Maerten van Heemskerck,
plate V of the set
Views of Roman Ruins, Antwerp, 1561,
published by Hieronymus Cock.
Etching and engraving. (239 × 327 mm.)

Federico Barocci (c. 1528–1612):

The Pardon of St Francis
(Christ in Glory between the
Virgin and St Nicholas appearing
to St Francis in the chapel of
the Portiuncula at Assisi), 1581.
Etching and engraving. (535 × 324 mm.)

St Francis Receiving the Stigmata. ▷
Etching. (231 × 151 mm.)

The engraver earned much more than the draughtsman or designer: the publisher paid 12 to 20 florins for a drawing and over 70 florins to the engraver. How little importance was attached to the designer can be seen from the fact that his name is often omitted from the signature.[46] Numerous smaller shops grew up side by side with Cock's, run by their engravers, often subcontracting with other publishers for a wider sale. From 1562 on, the most prolific workshop in Antwerp, that of the three Wierix brothers, operating in the service of the Jesuits and their propaganda, contracted with at least twenty-three Antwerp publishers. Other dynasties of reproductive engravers sprang up all over Europe. The Van de Passe family, who published first in Cologne in 1589, then at Utrecht, opened workshops in Paris, London and Copenhagen. The Sadelers were to be found at Antwerp, Venice, Prague, Munich, Cologne, Frankfurt, Verona and Rome.

Submerged by this flood, what happened to the artist's engraving? Two apparently contradictory things: on the one hand, it became more marginal than ever and quantitatively insignificant; on the other, the widening gulf separating it from the prints market gave it a rarity value which attracted the first collectors. It is interesting to juxtapose two quotations, both showing how much interest in Dürer survived after 1560. In his *Discours admirable de l'art de terre* (1580) the master potter Bernard Palissy wrote: "Haven't you noticed how much the printers have damaged the painters skilful in delineation? I remember seeing the histories of Our Lady printed in thick lines after the work of a German called Albert, and the said histories came to be held in such little regard because of the large numbers made of them that each of these histories was given away for a farthing, and yet what a fine invention there was in the designing of them." [47] In 1567, when sending him some Dürer prints, Plantin complained to an Italian correspondent of "the various prices, differing greatly from each other, which difference comes from the judgment or state of mind of the painter or connoisseur of these designs, who sometimes charge for one item (though printed by the same hand, from the same plate, on the same day and at the same hour) twice, thrice or four times as much as for another, which is very disconcerting for those who are not used to this and who consequently might amaze those to whom they send them without warning." [48]

Raphael Sadeler the Elder (1561–1628): ▷ △
St Francis Receiving the Stigmata.
Engraving. (218 × 170 mm.)

Anthonie Wierix (c. 1555–1624): ▷
St Francis Receiving the Stigmata.
Engraving, 2nd state. (204 × 171 mm.)

Different versions of Guido Reni's Virgin and Child

1. Bartolommeo Coriolano (1599–1676).
   Chiaroscuro woodcut. (230 × 152 mm.)

2. Anonymous (17th century).
   Drypoint. (113 × 154 mm.)

3. Anonymous (17th century).
   Woodcut on grey paper. (117 × 151 mm.)

The state of the artist's engraving as described here–so different from what it had been around 1510–contrasted with the virtually complete domination of the reproductive print, generally a copperplate engraving, the work of a skilled practitioner, a laborious task but one that allowed the printing of large editions and even, when the plate was worn, the "re-engraving" of clear, regular cuts for a new edition. An engraver might spend several months on a plate; it was a costly investment. But then editions of over a thousand impressions might be printed off; a Paris inventory of 1557 lists a stock of 1,050 *Dancing Dryads*,[49] and we know that there were editions of 3,000 prints after Poussin.[50]

This system promoted the predominance of the famous painters and made for a uniformity of taste. It deformed the work of art by the very way in which it made it known. It has recently been shown how much the wide dissemination of such works as Guido Reni's owes to their deformation by the print. First of all, the selection of the work itself was determined by the technique of transcription, for a drawing or a small picture lends itself more readily to reproduction than a fresco or an altarpiece; but mainly because of the commercial selection made by the publisher who invested only in such subjects as would interest the print-buyer. Thus Reni has become above all the painter of stereotyped Madonnas, a stereotype created not by the taste of the public but by the printmakers. The Reni prints must be seen as reflecting not the actual paintings but "the growing privatization of religion and a middle-class culture

54

4. Anonymous (17th century).
   Etching. (178 × 162 mm.)

5. H. David.
   Engraving. (188 × 170 mm.)

6. Guillaume Vallet (1633/36–1704):
   Engraving. (390 × 310 mm.)

4   5

6

The workshop without the artist

Philip Joseph Tassaert (1732–1803):
The Martyrdom of St Stephen, after Rubens.
Impression and counterproof, both
heightened with wash and red chalk.
Engraving and etching.
(470 × 324 mm.; counterproof 477 × 324 mm.)

centred on the home."[51] Reni's work as transmitted by the print is in no way representative of his original body of paintings: it almost amounts to an "iconographic programme" selected by successive publishers from his works for this particular purpose and this particular culture. The consequences were magnified by the fact that the reproductive print became a handy and indeed an indispensable tool of the art critic's trade. This is a serious matter because of the way printmaking scales down the painter's work; all the more serious because some of the great art theorists, Vasari, Fréart de Chambray, Winckelmann, had to make do with prints for lack of originals. It has often been pointed out that intransigent Neo-Classicism was able to refer to antique art only through the already idealized view of it conveyed by academic prints. But the engraver in turn, who instinctively interpreted the forms according to his own views, saw antique art through the eyes of the theorists of his own time. So we find that a sixteenth-century engraver in reproducing a fresco described by Vasari has embodied errors in his copy that had slipped into the writer's description.[52] It is useless to ask who copies what when everyone shares the same convictions, but it must not be forgotten that the way a work became known through a reproductive print needs to be criticized and re-examined together with the process of that reproduction. Thus the same Guido Reni painting appeared in different versions as etching, engraving, woodcut and even chiaroscuro woodcut. These different "packagings" of the original image are as important as the image itself, and each gives it a different meaning.

In the seventeenth century the print became a commercial commodity, carefully diversified, even within the same firm, according to its market. This market was much broader than that of painting. Rubens, as we know, traded very efficiently on his "brand name" by circulating prints for which he supplied the designs, nor did he shrink from bringing an action against the Paris publisher Honnervogt, who had "plagiarized" him. The prolific print production of Rubens' studio consisted mainly of book illustrations intended for export. There are only six woodcuts, executed by Christophe Jegher. One of them, a *Head of Christ*, bears the signature of one *"Quellinus delineator"* (designer). But the same subject on a copperplate engraving by Paul Pontius, of the same size and also dedicated to the general of the Jesuits, bears the signature of Rubens. Hans Vlieghe in his study of Quellinus [53] rightly deduces that the latter must have been the designer of an intermediate model intended for the woodcutter, and he wonders why the name of Rubens appears only on the copperplate version. It was probably because of a difference in the price and public for "noble" as opposed to "popular" prints. For instance, when the engraver François de Poilly,[54] initially a follower of the prevailing spiritual movement, began work in Paris publishing devotional images for the cult of the saints and the Virgin Mary and the adoration of Christ, he did not sign his prints. He also made engravings after the classic Italian painters: Guido Reni, Giulio Romano, Raphael. Then from 1648 on, after a journey to Rome, he catered for a different public, engraving after the "moderns," Bernini and Pietro da Cortona. At that point he signed his prints.

The market at which the print was aimed determined the technique and, with it, the relative importance of engraver and designer—which, that is, could be regarded as the "author" of the print. One of the trickiest problems facing the print historian has been to evaluate the part played by Van Dyck in the preparation of his *Iconography*.[55] This series of eighty engraved portraits of famous men of his time was issued, undoubtedly on the painter's initiative, by the Antwerp publisher Martinus van den Enden. Like Rubens, Van Dyck had supplied preliminary drawings, and apparently for many portraits a model painted in grisaille, approximating even more closely to the print. But in the second edition, published in 1645, after the artist's death, fifteen new plates appeared, unfinished etchings signed by Van Dyck. Five of these were printed as he left them, the others more or less touched up by professional engravers. Van Dyck seems to have set great store by his own signature: he sometimes signed himself as painter, sometimes as draughtsman, sometimes as engraver-etcher. On one impression of the first state he has even written his signature by hand, *"Antonius van Dyck fecit."* It is difficult to assess what part exactly he played in the production of these plates, and we shall never know whether he executed these unpublished etchings in order to give the professional engravers an even closer model or whether he was engaged in a personal, parallel work with no thought of publication. His *Iconography* stands at the juncture of two diametrically opposed currents in printmaking: studio etchings and encyclopaedic publications. At this period both currents were equally strong, and after the supremacy of the artists (before 1530) and then that of the reproductive engravers (around 1560), two distinct yet complementary markets evolved.

The artist in the workshop

Sir Anthony van Dyck (1599–1641):
Portrait of the Painter
Jan de Wael of Antwerp,
between 1627 and 1632.
Black chalk drawing.
(159 × 124 mm.)

Sir Anthony van Dyck (1599–1641):

Portrait of the Painter
Jan de Wael of Antwerp:

1. Etching, 1st state,
   (227 × 178 mm.)

2. Etching and engraving,
   2nd state. (227 × 178 mm.)

3. Etching and engraving,
   6th state. (227 × 178 mm.)

S·ERASME ORA PRO NOBIS·

Allo spirito nobile del mio Benefattore il Sig.° Stefano Garbesi suo seruo Pietro Testa Dona et Dedica

Pietro Testa (1611–1650):
The Martyrdom of St Erasmus,
c. 1630–1631.
Etching, 2nd state.
(285 × 175 mm.)

In Italy techniques had become more widely diversified as the public they catered for became more diverse. Artists' prints coexisted with just plain printmaking. The first known connection between an "academy" (an institution that symbolizes the intellectualization of the visual arts) and printmaking is found in the inscription *"Academia Leonardi Vinci"* on engravings dating from the early sixteenth century.[56] But the doctrinal sweep of the Counter-Reformation contained the effects of this liberalism again, just as the Antwerp workshops had succeeded in establishing a hierarchy of tasks so as to impose the rules of productivity on the artist. The Frenchman Antoine Lafréry, the leading European print publisher alongside Cock, had settled in Rome in 1544, a year before the opening of the Council of Trent. With an even keener eye on trade than Cock himself, he never seems to have done any engraving himself; in 1572 he issued the first known catalogue of a print publisher. In Rome worked the most prolific reproductive engravers, like Enea Vico, of whom Mariette said: "His engraving aimed at obtaining a large number of impressions from the same plate." This situation lasted as long as the "reconquest" went on, and it was not until after 1630 that commissions from private collectors could rival those from religious institutions and communities, which led to a change in the engraver's status. In seventeenth-century Rome there were intellectual circles at the service of rich patrons for whom the print represented a modern and, we might say, "experimental" notion of the work of art. When Galileo defended realism against mannerism on the grounds of its scientific approach,[57] his arguments were grist to the mill of the younger school of painters who felt that etching offered a better solution to their problems than painting in the grand style. These artists found patrons among the intellectuals, like Niccolò Simonelli, an administrator in charge of the Chigi household during the papacy of Alexander VII. Francis Haskell has described Simonelli as "a man of independent and cultivated taste, for he was in very close touch with a number of interesting artists outside the main stream of fashion— Salvator Rosa whom he helped to launch, Pietro Testa to whom he lent money, Giovanni Benedetto Castiglione who dedicated to him a print of Diogenes searching in vain for one honest man."[58] Initially, Pietro Testa approached printmaking in a spirit unchanged since Dürer: he made his own prints, distributed them himself, and dedicated them to influential cardinals in order to make his reputation. But in 1677 his name appeared in the catalogue of the print business of the Rossi family, which seems to have acquired his plates after his death.[59]

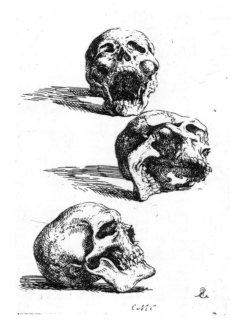

Salvator Rosa (1615–1673):
Three Human Skulls,
study for the painting
Democritus Meditating Amid Tombs.
Etching. (140 × 90 mm.)

Carlo Maratta (1625–1713):
The Martyrdom of St Andrew,
after Domenichino's painting
in the church of
San Gregorio Magno, Rome.
Etching. (297 × 437 mm.)

The reproductive engraver as artist

Michel Dorigny
(c. 1617–c. 1666):
Hercules.
Engraving.
(328 × 255 mm.)

Around 1630 a change also took place in Paris as a result of increasing demand, both from the middle classes, for whom the print chiefly catered, and from the newly ennobled who were investing some of their wealth in collections. The "cabinet of curiosities" became an indispensable part of the enlightened man's arsenal: its core was the portfolio of prints. Thus printmaking developed in two directions: it was both an object of curiosity and a record of curiosity. The interest in the strongly Italianized virtuoso etcher went hand in hand with a new image of the reproductive engraver, who asserted his own personality, no longer content to be a servile copier. He achieved a greater independence from the painters he reproduced, sometimes ranking as an equal or a member of the same family, like Michel Dorigny, who became Simon Vouet's son-in-law in 1648; together with his brother-in-law François Perrier, Dorigny acquired exclusive rights to the sale of prints after Vouet's paintings. Though still a manual worker, the printmaker as he grew more successful asserted his claims to the status of an artist. When the Académie Royale was founded in 1648, the engravers were kept out, but in a few years this ruling was reversed and in 1663 Dorigny became the first engraver to be admitted. In 1663 the "Cabinet du Roi" was initiated, a collection of engravings representing French monuments and the king's gardens, palaces and art treasures; and in 1666 Colbert, by purchasing the Marolles collection of prints, brought them for the first time into the royal collections. It was altogether a decisive period, since in 1660, after long and often stormy negotiations, Louis XIV had recognized the "freedom" of the engraver's craft, its character as work not only of the hand but of the mind: "It is the glory of France... to cultivate the liberal arts as much as possible, such as line engraving and etching, which depend on the imagination and must not be subject to any law but that of the artist's genius... This art cannot be likened to handicrafts and manufactures; none of its products form part of the necessities or means of subsistence of society, but serve only as ornaments, objects of pleasure and curiosity; their sale therefore, which depends on chance and inclination, must be entirely free." Besides prestige, this status conferred a formidable advantage, free trading in prints. Anyone could set up as a print dealer, but admittance to the Academy meant the renunciation of all commerce: the academician undertook "not to keep shop and to break his shop sign." The engraver had been ennobled, but now he had to live up to his new status. He left the class of tradesmen and craftsmen to become a member of the liberal professions. His dearly bought liberty did not always sit easily on him, for by its nature printmaking remains an "industry" and a trade. Because of the contradiction between a product and a work of art, this recognition was also something of a trap. The print as a work of art had to be exempt from controls and repression. But from 1642 on the centralized administration of the French monarchy insisted on the *dépôt légal*, the depositing of duty copies, as a means of surveillance exercised through the booksellers; and the engravers in their turn called for copyright laws to protect them from forgeries, the ransom they had to pay for their liberty.[60] In England engravers were not admitted to the Royal Academy, but an Act of Parliament obtained by Hogarth in 1735 forbade counterfeits. Many French engravers envied their colleagues in England, where printmaking was not recognized as an art but protected as an industry.

Jean Le Pautre (1618–1682):
Water God,
after François Perrier.
Engraving. (284 × 430 mm.)

So by the middle of the seventeenth century the print was a commodity that carried weight. In the Paris shop of François de Poilly seven presses were at work, and the 1712 inventory enumerates 2,189 plates and 54,960 impressions.[54] The price is still that of a "product": a *Nativity* after Mignard is priced at 400 livres, but seven plates after Guido Reni, Raphael, Annibale Carracci and Le Brun sold together for only 200 livres. The fame of the painter did not affect the price, the difference being due to the fact that some were plates commissioned from de Poilly for which he did not hold exclusive rights, while others were part of his own editions. There was also a third category: copies executed by his apprentices, which were added, unsigned, to the stock of devotional pictures or helped to popularize contemporary painting, as advocated already by the critic Roger de Piles.[61]

At that time there were three ways of classifying and evaluating prints; contrary to present-day usage, they were not mutually exclusive. In 1751 and 1752, almost simultaneously, appeared a catalogue of the engraved work of François de Poilly (a reproductive engraver), one of prints engraved after Rubens (a painter), and one of prints by Rembrandt (a painter-etcher).[62] None of these printmakers was then given any pre-eminence over the others by print fanciers; or rather the latter sought all three types of prints alike, while the price of most prints depended on the size of the copperplate or the amount of work it required. The Nanteuil workshop rarely brought out more than one plate a year, and Audran took six years to engrave the four plates of the *Battles of Alexander* after Le Brun.

For Rubens only the commercial aspect of prints mattered: in Antwerp the print was a reprocessed version of the picture aimed at a different market. The same image might be offered in different guises, more or less sophisticated, all referring back to an absent prototype. This approach was the antithesis of the painter-etcher's who felt that printmaking gave some scope to the creative process, which is the hallmark of a work of art. In the context of the first middle-class republic established in the Netherlands in 1648, Rembrandt's studio worked along both these lines. By producing fine etchings which were the printed equivalent of his great religious paintings of the early 1630s, Rembrandt was trying to make his name as an artist in the grand manner. He followed Rubens' example by accompanying one of these etchings, the *Descent from the Cross* of 1633, by a note prohibiting all reproduction. He followed the example of the Carracci by using the print to practise realist sketches and "popularized" genre scenes. But in both cases the important thing is that, by 1630, he was a painter and an artist famous for his paintings. His status as an artist–based on his reputation as a painter–vouched for the originality of the etchings he made after his paintings (which would otherwise have qualified as "reproductions"); and his rough sketches, which would normally have stood at the bottom of the hierarchy of genres, were raised in etchings to the rank of art. From then on, the same criteria were applied to prints as to paintings, and the print ceased to be the mere product of a skilled worker, even of a superior practitioner like Goltzius.

Nor was it any longer simply the miniaturization of an original–not even of a Rubens. In Holland in the mid-seventeenth century the synthesis was made by a middle class that had at last

Jan Lievens (1607–1674):
Portrait of a Man
with Fur Coat and Cap.
Etching. (271 × 223 mm.)

Pupils and collaborators

△◁ Jan Joris van der Vliet (c. 1610–?):
Man with Plumed Hat,
after a drawing by Rembrandt, 1631.
Etching. (148 × 128 mm.)

△ Ferdinand Bol (1616–1680):
Man with Plumed Hat.
Etching. (138 × 110 mm.)

◁ Rembrandt (1606–1669):
Oriental Head,
after Jan Lievens (?), 1635.
Etching. (155 × 134 mm.)

acquired political power and for whom the print was no longer a work with an inherent contradiction. The uncouthness that some connoisseurs of the time saw in Rembrandt's painting, which was described as "ridiculous" and "disgraceful," was accepted in his prints, which did not have the same function or the same public (just as for some people Daumier the lithographer excused the painter, while for others the painter ennobled the lithographer); so Rembrandt's etchings won a different or at times an "alternative" success from that of his paintings. It was largely through his etchings that Rembrandt came to be appreciated again in the eighteenth century. Prints, after their overall conversion into "works of art," came to be an integral part of an artist's output, both in their creation (for a work of art cannot easily be subject to a division of labour) and in the posthumous inventory of his work. They were acknowledged to have their due place in his œuvre catalogue. Rembrandt was the first painter-engraver whose prints were catalogued by a dealer—by Gersaint, in 1751. Since then there have been at least twenty-two catalogues of Rembrandt's etchings. Collectors have been more fervent in their endeavours to bring together a complete set of his prints than in the case of any other printmaker.

66

Copies, reprintings, facsimiles, forgeries

◁ ◁ Rembrandt (1606–1669):
The Large Raising of Lazarus, c. 1632.
Etching, 9th state. (326 × 238 mm.)

◁ Anonymous 18th-century copy, reversed (detail).
Etching. (357 × 252 mm.)

△ Anonymous 18th-century copy, unreversed (detail).
Etching. (360 × 252 mm.)

The concept of an "œuvre" cannot readily be applied to prints: it requires a vast effort of erudition to establish them as a credible unit. Rembrandt's "œuvre" as an etcher varies from 71 to 375 prints, depending on the cataloguer.[63] Single-handed authorship is even less common in the printmaker's workshop than in paintings executed with the collaboration of assistants and pupils. Houbraken and Sandrart have left descriptions of Rembrandt's crowded studio. Sandrart writes: "His house in Amsterdam was full of young people of good estate who came to him to study art. Each of them paid him a hundred guilders a year, not counting the profit he made from the paintings and prints of these apprentices, which sold for 2 to 2,500 guilders."[64] We know how difficult it is for the experts to distinguish between the works of the early Rembrandt and those of his friend and collaborator Jan Lievens, for whom an equally great success was predicted. Many etchings simply do not have the unity with which the master's hand, working alone, would have informed them. For instance, the *Raising of Lazarus* (c. 1632), though a famous plate, has long been suspect. Seymour Haden suggested Bol and Lievens, and Middleton suggested Van Vliet, as Rembrandt's collaborators on it. Coppier thought it was begun by Van Vliet and Lievens, then reworked by Rembrandt. Hind put the hand of Rembrandt's pupils at the end, not the beginning: "There are, however, a vigour and freedom in the central work, which incline me to regard only the later additions and rework as by an alien hand (which might

Rembrandt (1606–1669):

The Large Raising of Lazarus, c. 1632.
Printing of 1906 by Alvin-Beaumont
and Michel Bernard, Publishers, Paris.
Etching, 9th state. (370 × 250 mm.)

The Large Raising of Lazarus, c. 1632. ▷
Non-screen facsimile in photogravure,
made from the 4th printing by
Amand-Durand, Publisher, Paris, 1880.
(360 × 253 mm.)

have been Van Vliet's)."[65] The *Raising of Lazarus* is signed *R. v. Rijn. f.* Coppier, one of the most sceptical students of the etchings, suggested that Rembrandt's signature should be regarded as a collective trade-mark: "As prints were profitable and gave him publicity by multiplying his large compositions, he turned to the group of young artists who had come for training to his Bloemgracht studio and set them to printmaking under his guidance."[66]

By its wide dissemination, the print facilitated copying, and as it was already a duplicate it is difficult to distinguish the original print from the reproductions made from it. Some printmakers, especially in the eighteenth century, made a speciality of copying Rembrandt's etchings. It is fairly easy to recognize the copies made by hand, which were produced in their thousands by diligent amateur and professional etchers, although it was necessary to coin the term "deceptive copy" for the most successful ones. Thus Rembrandt's fame, spread by ever larger numbers of new prints copied from his work by men like Basan, Watelet, Novelli and Cumano, grew steadily. And the snowball effect did not stop there: for eighty-five of Rembrandt's original copperplates survived, and once he had become world-famous "re-impressions" kept being run off. New pulls were made from them as late as 1906, although by then they could only produce crude travesties of his etchings–Rembrandt "originals" that were less faithful than even the feeblest reproductions.[67] An impressive list has been made of the "falsifications" of Van Dyck's *Iconography*, due to fresh printings from the original plates, to the suppression of some features, the addition of new ones, substitutions, scraping, re-engraving, etc.[68] Finally, after 1880, when it became possible to make photogravure or collotype facsimiles that are practically indistinguishable from the original, it was the demand for the work of the most famous printmakers (Rembrandt, Dürer, Goya, Van Ostade) that made it worthwhile to undertake these costly printing ventures.

It is Rembrandt who has been the object of the subtlest and most accurate reproduction techniques,[69] which have often deceived the greatest experts,[70] when the utmost sophistication and cunning have been applied to print off the photogravure, touched up by hand, on a copperplate press, on Japanese paper, just like those Rembrandt used himself.

The elaborate study and scholarly analysis of prints make sense only if the specific identity of the author and the singleness of his work play an important part in our definition of the artist and the work of art. Prints are not a special case, but by their very nature they simply do not lend themselves readily to definition, as we have seen. Problems of attribution, which implies a personal authorship, and problems of authenticity, which implies the integrity of the artist's work, have little relevance when we are dealing with the composite and multiple character of the print, and a nagging doubt remains at the very moment the print is raised to the rank of a "work of art." The cases and conditions in which this has been done successfully are all the more remarkable.

AN ART
OF THE
BOURGEOISIE

Veshr les Nuds.

Par vn effet assez connu,
L'Homme, vray sufet de misere;
Sortant du ventre de sa Mere,
Entre dans le Monde tout nû.

Pour s'exempter de la froidure,
Il se couure contre ses maux
De la laine des Animaux,
Et s'eschaufe auec leur fourrure.

Mais comme par la Pauureté
Toutes choses luy sont contraire;
Il peut manquer des necessaires,
Et le voir dans la nudité.

Alors par vn soing veritable,
Il faut que charitablement,
Tu l'assistes de vestement,
Prenant pitié de ton semblable.

le Blond excud auec Priuilege du Roy.

Abraham Bosse (1602–1676):
"Clothing the naked," from
the set *The Works of Mercy*.
Etching and line engraving.
(254 × 322 mm.)

Jacques Lagniet (1620–1672):
"The nobleman is the spider ▷
and the peasant the fly,"
plate 45 of the first book of *Proverbs*, 1657.
Line engraving.
(190 ×170 mm.)

That the print is an art of the bourgeoisie is true in so far as it was born at the same time as the middle classes and in the same places, sharing in their growing prominence, as we have seen, in Antwerp, Amsterdam, the Paris of the 1630s, and eighteenth-century England. Its success in the United States and its recent triumphs in the 1960s would seem to confirm this broad judgment. It also seems to apply in the case of the Japanese print, as one may gather from the following comments by Richard Lane on the subject of ukiyo-e: "Like the era which nurtured it – the Edo Period (1600–1868) – ukiyo-e represents a unique development in Japanese art: a great renaissance based upon a largely popular foundation, whereas the earlier pinnacles of Japanese civilization had been due primarily to the aristocracy, the samurai or the priesthood." Further on we read: "Ukiyo-e... began in the sixteenth century. It was this period that first saw the rise of popular art and culture as a decisive factor in Japanese civilization." [71] This historical analysis fits in with that of the objective characteristics of the print in our first chapter. And yet it must be admitted that, on the whole, such a judgment qualifies as facile in European terms. The so-called "bourgeois" print imposed itself on popular taste with remarkable ease, and we cannot ignore the fact that it was taken up with enthusiasm by the aristocracy. It would be a little nearer the mark to speak of it as an art "that has a certain connection with the middle classes." This would be more in keeping with its appeal for the "enlightened" aristocrat and its drawbacks in the eyes of certain prominent but conservative members of the bourgeoisie.

Like the fresco and the drama, the print appeals to the "general public," but it is still a private thing. While it may remain within the prerogatives of an affluent class, its dissemination implies the desire for a broader basis. In the acceptance, or at least assertion, of that desire lies the whole social history of the print, and it is here that a certain discrimination is needed. In France, under the *ancien régime* (before 1789), the aristocracy addressed the bourgeoisie through the medium of the print. After the Revolution, the so-called "popular" print was actually a bourgeois print addressed to the people. To revert to the example of Japan and the account by Richard Lane: "The broad outline of ukiyo-e's development over three centuries appears to follow these lines: paintings for the aristocracy; paintings and prints for the cultivated upper-middle classes; prints primarily for the urban masses. Ukiyo-e was not, by any means, an essentially popular art. It was romantic, nineteenth-century Western collectors who imagined that it was." The same error was fostered by certain socialist historians in commenting on the rise of the western print. This is because in the print, as in ukiyo-e, the ranking order of the different genres is the opposite of what it is in painting; scenes of everyday life predominate, portraiture is vulgarized, and historical scenes are swamped by anecdote and caricature. This is why, although the Japanese print might as well have flowered on another planet, its subject matter has so much in common with that of the European print: portraits of courtisans and actors, street scenes, artisans at work. [72]

Popular taste
and
popular themes

Stefano Della Bella (1610–1664):
Frontispiece of his *Diversi Capricci.*
Etching. (84 × 98 mm.)
Reproduction slightly enlarged.

Cornelis Bega (1620–1664):
The Laughing Peasant.
Etching. (48 × 41 mm.)
Reproduction slightly enlarged.

The *Galerie des Courtisans,* issued in 1633 by the popular publisher Moncornet, was perhaps the first set of prints appearing in France to invite comparison in this respect with those of Japan. The development of the genre scene at that time went hand in hand with an expansion of the urban, non-clerical market. In Paris, in the 1630s, it coincided with a shift in the trading system whereby the printseller was no longer the actual craftsman and printer. Signs of a similar development were apparent in Italy from 1600 onwards with the invention of caricature, the Bologna set of *Cries,* and the work of Mitelli. In the first half of the seventeeth century, engravers like Matthäus Merian (1593-1650) and Wenzel Hollar (1607-1677) were prolific chroniclers; they turned out topical prints in abundance, tackling a great variety of genres, including those held in least esteem. Among the customers – and thus among the genres they purchased – can be distinguished a number of different levels, rather as in the corresponding literary genres, the novel and the drama. At the bottom of the ladder were the caricatures sold in Paris: "Below the cemetery of the Holy Innocents and at the end of the Pont-Neuf, you can find copperplate engravings of Spaniards who look more like devils or monsters than men, with hooked noses, moustaches curled up like hoops, ruffs with six or seven tiers, butter-pot hats, and

△ Pieter Jansz. Quast (1606–1647):
Plate 10 from the *Beggars
and Peasants* set, 1640.
Etching. (213 × 165 mm.)

◁ Adriaen van Ostade (1610– 1685):
Peasant with his Hand in his Cloak,
1638? Etching. (87 × 64 mm.)
Reproduction slightly enlarged.

△
Jacques Callot (1592–1635): △
Seated Vagabond Eating, from
the *Italian Vagabonds* set.
Etching. (138 × 87 mm.)

Rembrandt (1606–1669): △
Male and Female Beggar
Conversing, 1630.
Etching. (78 × 66 mm.)

swords with the guard at the feet and the point at the shoulders." [73] The *Livre des Gueux* published by Lagniet (1657) was considered contemptible by a serious collector, Michel de Marolles, but the same theme of beggars and tramps was treated by the most eminent engravers such as Callot and Stefano Della Bella. For Callot and Bellange, genre scenes in the Flemish vein were, according to Ternois, "one aspect of the production of Lorraine and the taste of Lorraine," [74] but from 1600 on provincial tastes of this kind merged to create a veritable European movement that, while it produced no memorable paintings, is familiar to us through its preferred medium of expression, the print. Frederick Antal has painstakingly traced this movement back from Hogarth, whose work from 1730 on, just when the English bourgeoisie was at its peak, carried on a whole tradition of engraving to which not only the Flemish and Dutch, but also the French and Italians, had contributed and which had catered for an urban public for more than a century.[75] Print publishers (for example, Guérineau and Isak in Paris) were popular figures and the poem *Paris en vers burlesques* (1652) includes a lengthy passage beginning: "Come and see this printseller/An illustrious personage..."[76]

Georges Wildenstein's research into tastes in painting at the beginning of the reign of Louis XIII in the early 1600s,[77] shows the important part played by prints in the interior decoration of Paris mansions belonging to eminent lawyers, court officials, and merchants. In the list of print collectors of his time that Michel de Marolles (1600-1681)[78] has left us, we find the same sort of middle-class figures: a third of them are churchmen (educated priests like Marolles himself), a third parliamentarians, and the remainder members of the liberal professions (teachers, doctors, businessmen, artists). Of the public for prints in the sixteenth century, little is known, apart from a few examples (consisting mainly of intellectuals) from which it is impossible to generalize; the nature of the public for which the print catered is difficult to pin down until the moment when it becomes politically coherent.

Francesco Villamena (1566-1624):
A Brawl.
Line engraving.
(350 × 500 mm.)

Jacques Bellange (1594–1638):
Two Beggars Fighting, 1614.
Etching. (312 × 210 mm.)

Claude Mellan (1598–1688):
Portrait of Nicolas Fouquet,
1660. Line engraving.
(330 × 231 mm.)

In the world that had emerged from the Renaissance and was gradually being taken over by the bourgeoisie, the portrait was, so to speak, an essential ideological product. It was also the most common and most widely collected of the genres practised by the engraver. Its rise can practically be followed with the naked eye, as its numbers increase and its format grows progressively larger, from Thomas de Leu's vignettes in the sixteenth century to Pierre Drevet's monumental copperplate engravings in the eighteenth. In the sixteenth century the portrait was like an item in an encyclopaedia showing the great of this world according to their rank. In the eighteenth century the sitters' faces are almost lost to sight, surrounded as they are by swathes of velvet and by attributes glorifying their particular functions. But, in every case, the portrait is of a notability. All the collections of portrait prints were classified according to the social status of the sitter, starting with the King. Claude Mellan "would only engrave portraits of illustrious persons distinguished either for their rank or for their merit, and he used to say that one shouldn't make engravings of any other people." [79] Gérard de Lairesse wrote: "This custom is nevertheless to be recommended among noblemen in order to stimulate them to uphold the glory of their honourable names and prevent them from doing anything to tarnish it... whereas it is only stupid conceit for the ordinary individual to seek to preserve his likeness with the aid of art." [80] The desire to have one's own portrait coincided with the beginnings of engraving. In François Villon's *Grand Testament* (1461) the following lines occur: "*Et afin que chascun me voye / Non pas en chair mais en painture / Que l'on tire ma pourtraicture / D'encre,*

Robert Nanteuil (1623–1678):
Portrait of Nicolas Fouquet,
1658. Line engraving.
(322 × 248 mm.)

s'il ne coustait trop cher." ("And so that everyone can see me, not in the flesh but in painting, let my portrait be executed in ink, if it doesn't cost too much.")

The point is this: the engraved portrait, with its wide diffusion, was of much greater interest socially than the portrait painting but, paradoxically, the former – aimed at a wide public – cost the client much more than did the luxury article. Thus there are hardly any engraved portraits of unknowns, apart from those with a comic flavour like Gérard Audran's *Guillaume de Limoges*, which is an allegorical representation of the populace rather than the portrait of an individual. It was only gradually that members of the bourgeoisie made their appearance in the realm of the portrait engraving – much more slowly than in that of painting. In the eighteenth century Largillière asserted that he preferred commissions from wealthy bourgeois to commissions from the aristocracy, since the former paid more. But they did not yet have their portraits engraved, which would have suggested a political motive on their part. In 1715 Louis Desplaces made an engraving, after Largillière, of a portrait of Marguerite Bécaille, a wealthy middle-class woman who had founded various charities. The fact that she was a private individual makes this engraving unusual for its time. Artists and intellectuals, however, had always had their portraitists, and in the work of Desplaces and Largillière a portrait of Mademoiselle Duclos of the Comédie Française precedes that of the worthy Madame Bécaille by a year.[81]

Portraiture had become so much the touchstone of the engraver's art that, from 1704 on, engravers seeking admission to the Academy had each to submit two portraits as their

Gerard Edelinck (1640–1707):
Portrait of the Printer Frédéric
Léonard of Brussels, after
Hyacinthe Rigaud, 1689.
Line engraving. (431 × 347 mm.)

Jean Morin (1609–1650):
Portrait of the Printer
Antoine Vitré, after
Philippe de Champaigne.
Etching. (312 × 211 mm.)

reception piece. Respectability was thus conferred on a genre that painters often dismissed as mere pot-boiling. Louis-Sébastien Mercier's *Tableau de Paris* gives an account of its growing vogue: "Everybody wants his portrait painted and engraved… A shrewd engraver who dealt in prints sold princes' portraits during their lifetime and authors' portraits after their death. Of one plate he said: 'Better run it off quickly for the prince won't live very long… People are so conceited that portraits are multiplying on all sides. Look at all these copper plates! Who needs portraits of nonentities like these? The painter and the stationer and the engraver and the printer are all having their likenesses engraved; no doubt it will be the turn of the printseller next...'"[82] Though the members of the bourgeoisie were slow to become the subjects of portraits, they had always counted among their purchasers. At each illustrious death or birth, publishers hastily refurbished well-worn plates and brought out the same faces again, under different names; some portraits of the Pope and the Dauphin served for several generations. The practice was so common that it has been possible to amass whole collections of these "apocryphal portraits."[83] Thus in the reign of Henri II, under the name of Ronsard, the new poet

Samüel Bernard.
Chevalier de l'Ordre de S.t Michel, Comte de Coubert.
Conseiller d'Estat.

Pierre-Imbert Drevet (1697–1739):
Portrait of Samuel Bernard,
after Hyacinthe Rigaud, 1729.
Line engraving. (619 × 421 mm.)

in favour at the Court, portraits were sold of his predecessor La Jessée, who had died prematurely
before the publisher had been able to get rid of his stock.[84] The aim of the portrait engraving,
then, was to make prominent persons familiar to the public, to popularize them: the link with
the people lay there. Every portrait constituted a bid for recognition, with a political motivation of
a kind whose importance it is difficult to imagine today. If one takes the trouble to examine
Robert Nanteuil's portraits from a historical standpoint, it will soon be apparent that not a date,
not an attribute, not a pose is insignificant. The face is the product of elaborate stage-management,
the attitude cunningly calculated. The ambitious churchman Retz had his portrait engraved when
no more than coadjutor to the archbishop of Paris. Condé, the great military leader, desiring to
make the people of Paris forget his acts of treason, had himself portrayed in ermine robes.[85] By
1750 prominent bourgeois were no longer satisfied with ceremonial portraits, which became
reserved for a few well-known writers and financiers. The vignette came back into fashion,
and miniaturists did a brisk trade. Later on, photography would take over, showing "the ascent
of broad strata of society to a greater political and social significance."[86]

Jacques Callot (1592–1635):
The Large Thesis, 1625.
Etching heightened with the graver.
(813 × 511 mm.)

The print was thus an instrument of power; hence its use by absolute monarchs and the taste for it in circles seeking the support of the bourgeoisie or of the people. In the seventeenth century both tendencies combined in complex fashion to foster a diversified taste for works such as those of Jacques Callot. The flourishing Court of Lorraine turned to engravers – Brentel of Strasbourg, Merian of Basel – to celebrate *The Funeral of Charles III* (1608) or *The Entry of Henri II* (1609). In Florence etchers like Cantagallina at the Parigis' workshop treated such subjects as *The Decorations at Florence for the Marriage of Grand Duke Cosimo II* (1608), operatic sets, and regattas on the Arno. But the glorification of the ruler was gradually submerged in the delineation of the crowd; the festival merged into the fair. Thus Callot could be at once the official chronicler of the siege of the Ile de Ré and the bitter narrator of the *Miseries of War*. Folksy Italian realism in the manner of Villamena alternated with grandiose, sometimes highly official subjects. Hence the "Theses," posters overloaded with allegorical figures and fulsome declarations, which were presented by suitors or artists to those in power to solicit their protection.[87] Similar

The print as an instrument of power

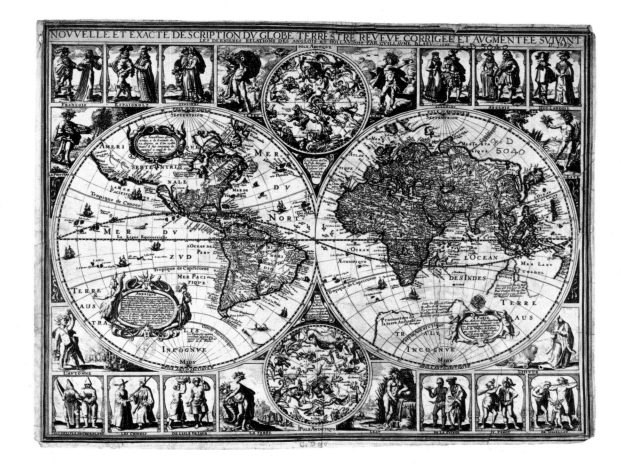

"New and exact description of the earth…
revised, corrected and augmented following
the latest accounts of the English and Dutch,"
by Willem Jansz. Blaeu, Paris, A. de Fer, 1645.
Line engraving reworked with etching. (427 × 555 mm.)

pompous adornments were also to be found on maps of the world. In the eyes of the middle classes, the engraving should betoken power. This was achieved, under Louis XIV, by the establishment of a royal workshop and the gradual publication of the twenty-three volumes of the *Cabinet du Roi,* made up of engravings celebrating his power. In a letter of 15 July 1675 to the French ambassador in Stockholm, Colbert explained the use of some prints he was sending him: "to see them and make them seen in the country where you are." But almost at once their plebeian character is reasserted: "and in case you should feel like making a gift of them, you must please be careful not to speak of the King, for they are mere trifles unworthy of association with His Majesty's name."[88] We also know that these rather ceremonial prints were sold cheaply, thus showing that they were intended to enable the less affluent to have a share of royal glory. One could trace the parallel development of the print as a political weapon in the hands of the opponents of power: caricatures and satires addressed to an even less affluent public and those used by the Dutch to discredit the enemy. But this is not our intention: the point here is to see how the battle of the prints was, as it were, transposed into another key in the domain of art, or rather how the recognition of the print as an art form was part of this battle.

Sébastien Leclerc (c. 1637–1714):
The Academy of the Sciences and Fine Arts.
Line engraving. (248 × 384 mm.)

What was merely a "trifle" to the King was considered by others as an article of the utmost interest and refinement, and it was not long before print lovers started to discriminate and establish an appropriate code of values. We have evidence that the engravings of Sébastien Leclerc, head of the Gobelins workshop, were an early subject of speculation, for we know that the collector Claude Potier had assembled a fine set of his prints but that Potier's friends considered them rather too common. Potier decided to commission from Leclerc an engraving of *Venus on the Waters* for his collection. He deliberately saw to it that only a few impressions were run off and triumphantly presented it to his critics as a rarity. In 1694 he ordered another engraving from Leclerc and – for the sole purpose of embellishing his collection – had a number of different states produced: eleven states are known for twelve impressions.[89] Such practices, then rare, became more and more widespread in France with the rise of the Third Estate. It is true, as we have seen, that print collectors existed in the sixteenth century, but they are mysterious figures and few of their names are known. Under Louis XIV print collectors of several kinds were to be found. Works by notable artists were collected, and Claude Maugis, chaplain to Marie de Médicis, took forty years to complete his Dürer collection. But in the printed catalogue of the Marolles collection of engravings in 1666 (the prototype of such catalogues), listings by artist are included alongside listings by subject. "Moreover," the Abbé de Marolles informs us, "the prints representing ceremonies, entries into towns, mottos, emblems, buildings, ancient and modern statues, medals, tournaments, engines of war, and machinery are of no less service to the history of the divine and human sciences and of all the fine arts than are the other prints representing battles by land and sea, animals and plants, likenesses of great men, as well as the customs of the nations, genealogical trees, maps, and the historical series of things both sacred and profane."[90]
This encyclopaedic notion of the print was, however, accompanied by a growing tendency to build up collections of engravings considered specifically as works of art. On his death in 1746 the Duc de Mortemart, an unconventional, free-thinking aristocrat "who knew no principle of religion and gloried in the fact," left a collection of 25,000 prints, classified entirely by artist.[91] In

1699 the first collector's "handbook" appeared; written by Florent Lecomte, it laid down the lines for an ideal collection. In 1727 the *Mercure de France* published advice for print collectors by Dezallier d'Argenville; this contains few specifically formal judgments, but bases taste on the balance of a collection rather than the choice of impressions. The engraving is valued as a means of reproduction with the role of giving "an idea of the good pictures and drawings of the great masters." Titian and Van Dyck are among the masters to be collected, along with Le Brun and Callot, and Della Bella and Leclerc. However, "arrangement by artist does not satisfy the scholarly amateur" who prefers to go by subject, and Dezallier finds the schemes adopted by Marolles and Florent Lecomte over-ambitious and "quite likely to put the amateur off."[92] Print collecting is thus brought within the scope of the simple amateur, and a classification by theme is suggested: portraits according to social rank, landscapes, etc., "chosen," he adds, "as good pieces." This as yet rather vague recommendation, reiterated by others, was to become of prime importance and later handbooks put forward the criteria for selecting "good pieces." It was the dealers who first took up this point, in connection with the public sales that became increasingly frequent with the growth in the market after 1730. The "prefaces" to these sales catalogues are essential documents. Printsellers had, in fact, ceased to be mere "dealers in picture sheets," or stationers and booksellers, and had become connoisseurs capable of amassing a complete collection for a customer or of compiling a "scholarly" catalogue. They developed their own aesthetic principles. At the Quentin de Lorangère sale in 1744, the art dealer Gersaint expressed surprise at "the singular fashion in which M. de Lorangère has arranged his prints... subjects and masters are all mixed together in the portfolios." The following year, in the preface to the catalogue of a mixed sale complementing the La Roque sale, Gersaint published a veritable manifesto in favour of what he called the "choice print."[93] He protested against "rag-bags," those accumulations of miscellaneous prints that made up the big collections of the seventeenth century, and he called for a careful selection based in the first place on the material quality of the impression: a good printing, preserving the purity and subtlety of the engraved line, and a uniformly high standard of printing in sets of engravings. He warned the novice against "false brilliance" and "black patches." In the opening sentence he asserts: "One does not become

Jean Berain the Elder (1640–1711):
Decorative design for the Galerie
d'Apollon in the Louvre, from
Ornemens de peinture et sculpture...,
Paris, 1660–1668.
Etching and line engraving.
(330 × 238 mm.)

The print as an object of connoisseurship

Canaletto (1697–1768):
The Piazzetta with the Piera del Bando,
Venice, 1744–1746. Etching (144 × 212 mm.)

interested in prints, nor should one seek after them, if not to examine their tastefulness, elegance, style of composition, or admire the variety of the different subjects they depict." For Gersaint, each print should be judged "in the purity of the first impressions." This idea of judging quality in terms quite divorced from "content" reappeared in the nineteenth century when Philippe Burty defended the original print against reproductions, in a preface entitled *La Belle Epreuve* ("The Fine Proof"), by which he meant the first impression pulled of a print, with wide margins.[94] In 1767 Basan published his *Dictionnaire des graveurs anciens et modernes*. His aim was a simple one: "I have observed," he writes, "for several years that the catalogues of print sales are eagerly sought after." But the most influential handbook of the period was Heinecken's *Idée générale d'une collection d'estampes* (Leipzig and Vienna, 1771), written by the curator of the Dresden collections. It was followed by several dictionaries of engravers, those of J. C. Füssli (Zürich, 1771), Strutt (London, 1785) and Huber (Leipzig, 1787). The *Réflexions sur la peinture et la gravure* (Paris, 1786), by the dealer Joullain, also demonstrates the extent of the theorizing that brought the print into the canon of art forms. Collectors were no longer just scholars and *curieux* but also connoisseurs. During a journey to Italy in 1650, Richard Symond from England had assembled a print collection in the spirit of an interested tourist. It was in quite a different spirit that, in Venice a century later, his fellow countryman Joseph Smith, the British consul, sought out Canaletto's etchings fresh from the press and had them bound in leather albums together with drawings by the same artist. With such collections, the print entered the museums, and in fact they form the nucleus of the great print rooms in London, Vienna and Dresden, where they are generally located in museums next to the drawings. By way of contrast, one can still point today to the older concept on which the *Cabinet des estampes* in Paris is based, stemming from the encyclopaedic interests of the seventeenth century, admitting every kind of picture, and attached to a library.

It very soon became clear that the royal collection in Paris and that in Vienna were based on entirely different concepts. In 1717-1718 Prince Eugene of Savoy assembled a print collection with the aid of the Parisian dealer Jean Mariette, whose son Pierre-Jean was called in to classify it according to a new system, i.e. by schools, with a note on each artist. The result was 290 volumes sumptuously bound in red leather and a methodical classification worthy of any history of art. In 1735 Pierre-Jean Mariette was called in simply to remount the prints in the royal collection in Paris, and in 1738 Prince Eugene's collection was purchased by the Emperor Charles VI. It was thus in Vienna that the work of classification was continued, this time by Adam Bartsch, who had entered the service of the Court Library in 1777. Visiting the Paris collection in 1784, he wrote: "The organization of this print cabinet, which was the first thing I studied, differs in several ways from that of the imperial collection, but it is certainly no better. There are no critical lists such as those Mariette attached to each volume and the similar ones I started to introduce."[95] He was accordingly opposed to the ideas of the Paris "custodian," Hugues-Adrien Joly, who mixed reproductions and originals together in portfolios arranged by artist and kept many portfolios arranged by subject. Whereas Quatremère de Quincy, the theorist of French Neo-Classicism, proclaimed in 1791 that "engraving is not and never can be an art," Bartsch promoted the idea of the "painter-engraver," enshrining it in the title of his monumental catalogue: *Le Peintre-graveur* (Vienna, 1803-1821).

This development went hand in hand with the progress of art criticism. As early as 1686 the *Mercure Galant* had made an abortive attempt to publish "the list of prints being engraved and the pictures on which they are based." In the *Mercure de France,* which started publishing art criticism in 1737, "articles on prints exhibited" are to be found after 1750. Earlier, in 1704, an advertisement for a newly published set of prints had asserted that "all these prints are originals by M. Perelle and other excellent engravers." The essay on art became a regular feature of Paris periodicals, giving a certain prominence to the role of the picture and probably having a decisive influence on Lessing and Diderot.

General View of Venice from the Grand Canal.
Peep-show picture of the 18th century.
Hand-coloured etching (265 × 398 mm.)

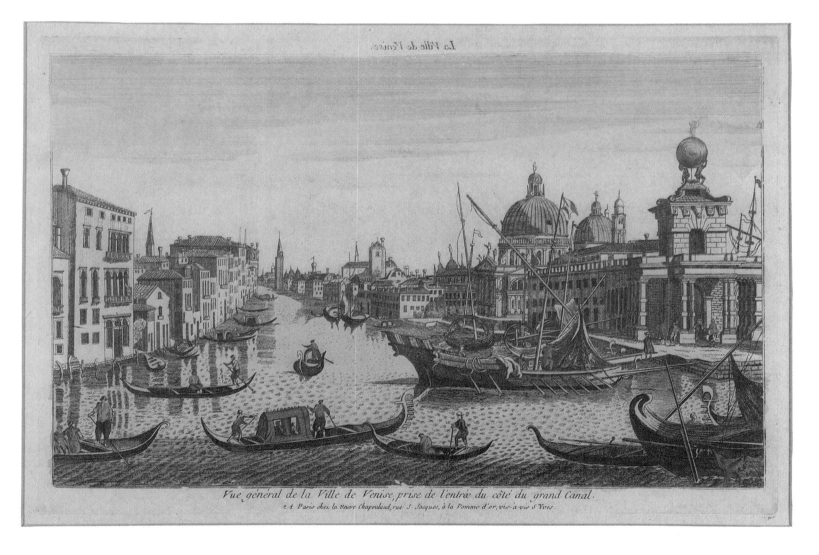

This trend may also be linked with the founding of art schools in France, from the Académie Royale des Beaux-Arts (1648) to the Ecole des Beaux-Arts (1795), by way of Blondel's Ecole Libre (1740) and the Ecole Royale des Elèves Protégés (1749) – all of them places where the reproductive print was to play a major part. In each case, the concept of the print was bound up with the key idea of "progress" in the minds of the moralists and educators concerned. It would, however, be absurd to conclude from this that the print was uniformly "progressive," for the idea of progress was far from being a homogeneous one, even within the bourgeoisie. For Diderot, the defender of Greuze, the print was no more than a means of popularizing models of the civic and moral virtues, using aesthetic means that were not specific to it but copied painting and sculpture. This is why Greuze, who attached great importance to the reproduction of his paintings, did not take the trouble of doing his own engravings, although he took a special interest in establishing a commercial system of distribution controlled by the artist himself.[96] The same consideration led Hogarth to attach special importance to the print, and he also used it as a weapon to challenge, with a new aesthetic that was closer to popular feeling and caricature, the taste of such aristocratic connoisseurs as Lord Burlington, whom he considered reactionary. On the eve of the French Revolution, the pressure of the bourgeoisie had resulted in a broad consensus of opinion as to the utility of the print, shared by enlightened aristocrats and revolutionaries alike. Duke Albert of Saxe-Teschen (1738–1822), a ruler with progressive ideas, made it his aim – one in which he succeeded, oddly enough with the aid of the French Revolution – to assemble a collection of prints with an avowedly educational purpose, a veritable history of art open to the public.

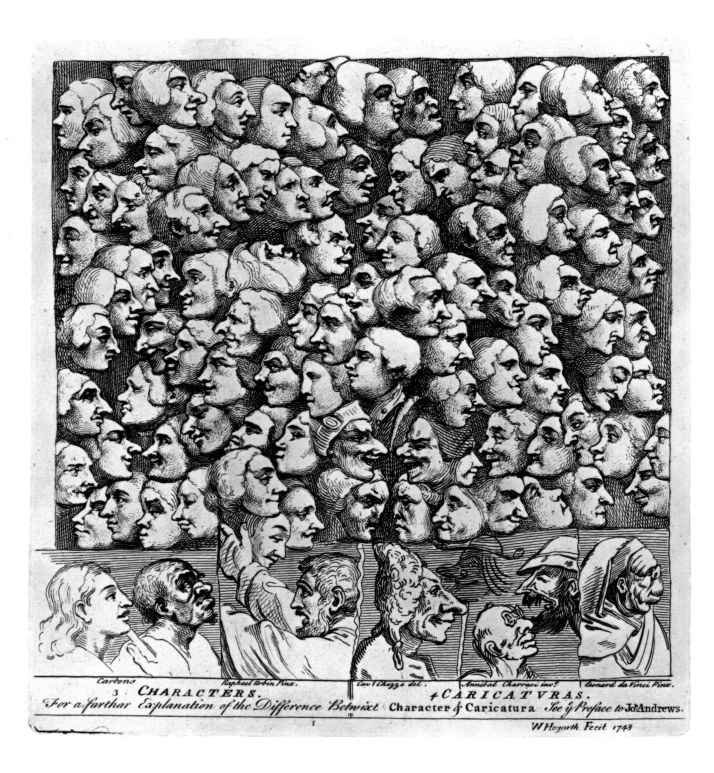

Characters and caricatures

Pierre-Charles Ingouf (1746–1800),
after Jean-Baptiste Greuze:
Two plates from the series
*Têtes de différents caracteres,
dédiées a M. J.-G. Wille…
par son ami J.-B. Greuze…,*
Paris, 1766.
Etchings. (Each 175 × 123 mm.)

◁ William Hogarth (1697–1764):
Characters and Caricaturas, 1743.
Etching. (204 × 200 mm.)

Such was the foundation of the Albertina in Vienna. This conception of "the general utility of the dissemination of fine works of art" was certainly – as the present curator, Walter Koschatsky, remarks – compatible with "a spirit of rationalism at once encyclopaedic and convinced of the progress of humanity." [97] Thus one need not make too radical a distinction between this venture and the projects of the French revolutionaries for the encouragement of engraving; for example, the plan by Laurent Guyot (the publisher of a series of plates on the fall of the Bastille among other things), which appeared under the title *Plan d'un conservatoire d'estampes et école nationale de gravure, à l'effet d'utiliser les arts, les artistes et le commerce sans occasionner aucune dépense au trésor public* (Paris, August 1796). The idea was that this "print museum" would be run by the artists themselves, who could register their engravings (thus protecting themselves against forgeries) and even print and sell them there. It is, however, worth noting that "the engravings which were to have right of asylum in the Conservatory were not the same as those on the Revolution that were distributed by Guyot himself, but dealt rather with patriotic themes: great republican deeds, national costumes, monuments of freedom." [98] Guyot's idea resurfaced in 1847 with the "print museum" proposed by the Schongauer Society in Colmar in order to "disseminate knowledge of the masterpieces of art, facilitate study, and develop a feeling for beauty"; and with the "museum of copies" that Charles Blanc wanted to found in 1848. [99] One of the last such undertakings that was private and aristocratic in origin was the "Lithographic Gallery" sponsored by the Duc d'Orléans – last descendant of enlightened princes and defender of the young Romantics – who died in 1842.

The print
as a
vehicle
of progress

SERMENT DU JEU DE PAUME.

On 31 May 1791 the Constituent Assembly received a deputation of engravers who made a speech on "the utility and importance of engraving," and on 8 December in the same year the Legislative Assembly was called to pronounce upon a draft decree, prepared in March 1791 by Basan, on the protection of engravers and publishers of prints.[100] Thus there can be no doubt about the revival by the new regime of interest in an art form highly valued by those strata of society on which it counted for support. The Jacobin Club had commissioned the large canvas entitled *The Oath of the Tennis Court* from David, but only a sketch of it appeared at the Salon of 1791, for the Club had not been able to pay for it and it was decided to raise the money by putting Jazet's etching of it up for subscription before the painting itself was finished. But the real graphic revolution is to be found in the avalanche of caricatures in which the bourgeoisie of London and Paris took so much pleasure. Boyer de Nîmes, a royalist, wrote a detailed history of the caricatures inspired by the French Revolution (*Histoire des caricatures de la révolte des Français,* Paris, 1792) which shows his disapproving interest in such works. That the Jacobins were no more tolerant of caricatures is demonstrated by the decree of 28 Germinal, Year II (17 April 1794) and the measures taken to "seize the various works that might be prejudicial to morals and public spirit." Although counter-revolutionaries, notably the English, drawing on Gillray's talent, were circulating hideous pictures of the *sans-culottes,* the "People's Republican Society of the Arts" and its members, such as the Neoclassicist J.B. Wicar, concentrated their attacks on engravings contravening morality and the typically bourgeois genre and boudoir scenes of Louis-Leopold Boilly.

Fragments du Temple de Jupiter Olimpien
d'Agrigente.

Jean Houel (1735–1813):
Fragments of the Temple of Olympian Jupiter
at Agrigento, from *Voyage pittoresque des
îles de Sicile, de Lipari et de Malte,*
Vol. 4, Paris, 1787.
Aquatint. (230 × 364 mm.)

The print had been one of the means of recording the history of art and making it possible to discuss it. At this point, the print itself became a subject for the historian, and a specific literature grew up around it to enhance its ideological influence. This literature, though going back as far as Vasari, did not become systematized until the middle of the seventeenth century with the appearance of essays like John Evelyn's *Sculptura: or the History and Art of Chalcography and Engraving on Copper* (London, 1662) and Filippo Baldinucci's *Cominciamento e progresso dell'arte dell'intagliare in rame* (Florence, 1686). It will suffice here to call attention to a question that was of vital importance from the standpoint of the art historian: that of the origins of the print, which was to be keenly debated both then and for a long time afterwards. The controversy got under way with the publication of Major Humbert's *Abrégé historique de l'origine des progrès de la gravure* (Berlin, 1752), in which German nationalism confronted the claims of Italian historians, and went on until H. Jansen's *Essai sur l'origine de la gravure* (Paris, 1808) and W. Y. Ottley's *Inquiry into the Origin and Early History of Engraving* (London, 1816). The main problem arose from the determination of eighteenth-century historians to trace the origin of the print back to antiquity, thereby establishing both its nobility and its longevity. Major Humbert considered it "surprising that the Ancients who engraved so many excellent things on hard stones and crystals… had nevertheless no idea of the woodcut or copperplate engraving." In 1766, in his important book on woodcuts, *Traité historique et pratique de la gravure en bois,* Papillon admitted that it began in the fifteenth century, but only after seventy pages of wild speculation about hypothetical ancient examples, all taken from Pliny: "It was the first of the arts to appear in the world, for if it is true that the children of Seth engraved stones and bricks, it may be conjectured that they had previously made engravings on wood since it is a softer material." [101] Caylus, too, glossing the word "Imprimerie" (Printing) in his *Recueil d'Antiquités* (Paris, 1752–1757), expressed surprise "that the ancient Romans did not invent it, since they made seals... and printing differs from this form of carving only in the mobility of the letters." There is one passage in Pliny's *Natural History* (XXXV, 2) that might well give rise to confusion. The large Paris edition promoted by Malesherbes was published in twelve volumes from 1771 to 1782. In his *Recherches philosophiques sur les Grecs* (1788), Cornelius de Pauw delves into it to confirm his conviction of the antiquity of engraving and, more specifically, of portrait engraving.

It is hardly surprising that such subjects attracted investigators, and that these came up with discoveries. In 1769, visiting the collection at the Carthusian monastery at Buxheim in Swabia, Heinecken found, pasted inside a *Laus Virginis,* a woodcut of St Christopher on which was engraved the date 1423. Here again, engraving on wood preceded engraving on metal, for it was not until 1803 that Pietro Zani published his "interesting discovery at the National Print Room in Paris of an original print by the celebrated Maso Finiguerra." During the nineteenth century, other discoveries sparked off polemics – frequently violent and exacerbated by chauvinism – about the origins of engraving. The earliest works found included the Passion series in Berlin on copper,[102] the Brussels Virgin of 1418,[103] and the Protat wood block,[104] all of which gave rise to bitter controversy and were thus condemned, in the words of Hymans, "to remain eternally dubious." Writing in 1766, Papillon admitted his ignorance in the matter, merely giving it as his opinion that engraving started in the fifteenth century and that woodcuts preceded metal cuts. Not much more is known on this question even today, but it only had to be raised for the print, too, to have a "history."

Heinrich Guttenberg (1749–1818):
The Eruption of Mount Vesuvius on 14 May 1771,
plate 33 of J. Volaire's *Voyage pittoresque
de Naples et de Sicile,* Vol. 1, Paris, 1781.
Etching. (218 × 372 mm.)

Nicolas De Launay (1739–1792):
The Swing (Les Hasards heureux de l'escarpolette),
after Jean-Honoré Fragonard, 1782.
Etching and line engraving. (515 × 425 mm.)

Francisco Goya (1746–1828):

Old Man on a Swing, 1824–1828.
Etching, burnished aquatint
and/or lavis.
(185 ×120 mm.)

Old Woman on a Swing, 1824–1828.
Etching and burnisher (?).
(185 × 120 mm.)

The original print, which art lovers were beginning to single out, still remained hidden away for the most part in private collections. When it did come out into the open in the form of caricatures, it was not recognized as something valuable. It was on the reproductive engraving, conceived as a major genre, that the partisans of progress placed their hopes. In fact, it was photography that ultimately gave them the kind of didactic, democratic picture they sought, inheriting at the same time the mortgage on the artistic nature of the product. As for the print regarded as a work of art, it is to the restricted field of the etching that one must turn to find out what was really going on. Forty years separate *Les Hasards heureux de l'escarpolette* (The Swing) by De Launay after Fragonard (1782) from Goya's *Old Man* and *Old Woman on a Swing,* etched at Bordeaux between 1824 and 1828. Painted in 1767, Fragonard's original picture was commissioned by the Baron de Saint-Julien, a typical rake of the *ancien régime,* who is shown favourably placed for peeping under the petticoats of his mistress. Goya's old man and woman date from the end of his life, a period of despair when the artist, deaf and in exile, saw his country fall once more into the hands of a dictator, after a terrible war. For him the print, being easily circulated, offered a means of denouncing the despotism and obscurantism of the old regime. But Spain did not have the enlightened bourgeoisie that existed in France and England: Goya's sets of etchings were cries in the wilderness and could not even be published.[105] The De Launay etching presents the image of a frivolous society heedless of impending ruin; Goya's two etchings reflect a society whose hopes have been crushed. The latter, like most of Goya's etchings, only found a public in the second half of the century, being printed in Madrid by the Calcografía Nacional in 1859.

The print
invades
the magazines

Frans Ertinger (1640– after 1707):
Woman of Quality Walking in Town Incognita,
fashion plate published by Nicolas Bonnart,
Paris, 1689.
Line engraving. (280 × 165 mm.)

Philibert Louis Debucourt (1755–1832):
"He fails to come! (Etruscan coiffure, cross-belt),"
1800. Plate 35 of *Modes et Manières du Jour*,
Paris, 1798–1808.
Coloured etching. (163 × 92 mm.)

Wenzel Hollar (1607–1677):
Woman seen from the front. (84 × 65 mm.)
Woman seen from behind, 1645. (86 × 61 mm.)
Etchings.

The nature of the print was such as to satisfy liberal demands on the political or aesthetic level in two complementary ways (indissociable for some, contradictory for others): through the democratization of art, and through its commercialization. With the print, it was possible to reach not only increasingly wide groups of urban dwellers but also the educated public in the provinces. This public grew in proportion to the rate of electoral reforms and the lowering of property qualifications for the vote. It was also closely linked with newspaper readership. One can trace the different stages whereby pictures came to feature in the papers, first on separate pages published in regular "series," then in parts accompanied by a text, and finally bound together with the text to form the earliest illustrated magazines. This process first affected fashion plates, in which certain publishers, such as Bonnart, started to specialize in the late seventeenth century. Impressive even today are those in the *Monument du Costume* series, commissioned by a banker and published irregularly in 1775, 1777, and 1783. These were imitated by the *Galeries des Modes et Costumes* sold in parts by the publishers Esnault and Rapilly. In 1785 appeared the first proper illustrated periodical, *Le Cabinet des Modes;* containing small coloured etchings, it was followed by *Le Moniteur de la Mode* in 1796 and La Mésangère's *Costumes parisiens* in 1797.

To satisfy the growing market, techniques had to be brought up to date. Speedy execution was essential, and this went along with liveliness of style. One symptom of the change in attitude towards engraving was the fashion for etching among amateur artists wishing to work on a small scale in a medium combining ease of execution with pleasing effects: Thus, in certain cultured and fashionable circles where drawing was already popular, etching became the thing. Naturally, the amateurs concerned were recruited from the ranks of the well-to-do, with connections among the nobility and the upper middle class, and enjoyed plenty of leisure.[106] They also included art patrons and collectors such as the Comte de Caylus and the Abbé de Saint-Non. The taste for etching went along with a taste for miniatures, pastels, and gouaches. Miniatures and pastels made

Pietro Antonio Martini (1739–1797):
"The Lady of the Queen's Palace,"
after J. M. Moreau the Younger, 1777.
From the series *Monument du Costume physique et moral… ou Tableaux de la Vie*, Neuwied, 1789.
Etching. (268 × 218 mm.)

La Dame du Palais de la Reine.

The demand for colour

Francesco Bartolozzi (1727–1815):
Lady Smyth and her Children, 1789,
after Sir Joshua Reynolds.
Stipple engraving in colour.
(510 × 425 mm.)

their appearance at the Salon of 1739, gouaches in 1759. Professional painters in gouache were so popular that etchings of their intimate and sentimental scenes were circulated by the reproductive engravers: Moreau the Younger engraved the works of Baudouin, De Launay those of Lavreince, then those of Mallet. There was thus a whole social and stylistic movement favouring the development of the colour print. The technique of printing chiaroscuro woodcuts had been known since the early sixteenth century; that of printing a copperplate engraving in colour from several plates was much the same; so it was not because of any technical obstacle that the appearance of the colour engraving was delayed until the middle of the eighteenth century. It did not appear earlier because there was no demand for it. The earliest experiments seem to have been made in the mid-seventeenth century, notably by Hercules Seghers, who, we are told, "sought to transform his prints into paintings." [107] But his technique, which produced only single impressions (a fact that fascinates today's artists), was considered by his contemporaries, and perhaps by Seghers himself, as a failure. However, from the early eighteenth century, beginning with J. C. Le Blon's

Coloritto; or, The Harmony of Colouring in Painting (London, 1723-1726?), three-colour and four-colour processes multiplied. The "letters" in the *Mercure de France* and the controversies about the priority of the different inventions bear witness to the importance of the issues and the public interest in them. Starting in 1727, they reach a climax between 1747 and 1756 with the improvements brought about by Gautier d'Agoty. In preference to line engraving, the mezzotint was employed; this had the advantage of permitting modelling and was developed in England in the first half of the eighteenth century for the reproduction of portraits. Another half-tone process, the aquatint, made it possible to create the illusion of a wash and had its first successes round about 1760. Finally, all these techniques were combined to imitate the drawings sought after by art lovers: "crayon manner" in 1759, "wash manner" in 1766, and even "pastel manner" in 1769, and "watercolour manner" in 1772.

Jacques-Fabien Gautier d'Agoty (1710–1785):
Lady in her Dressing-Room by Candlelight.
Colour engraving, varnished.
(455 × 370 mm.)

Théodore Géricault (1791–1824):
Horse Artillery Changing
Position, 1819.
Lithograph. (300 × 385 mm.)

An art for the Notables

It was the invention of lithography in 1798 that brought the long-awaited solution to the problem of reproducing drawing. It was not, however, the demands of art that fostered this development but the desire to introduce engraving into the emerging industrial sector. Lithography was considered initially for making up typographical shortcomings in the printing of musical scores and maps. When the patent was imported into France in 1802, it was seen as a useful process for reproducing Egyptian or other Oriental texts written in unusual scripts, and Quatremère de Quincy was commissioned to do research on "all the objects of industry for which lithography would be applicable." The example of artists like Pierre Mongin persuaded some others to make use of it, but, according to Engelmann, the leading French lithographic printer, it was not until 1818 that J. B. Isabey became "the first to produce carefully executed drawings in lithography." [108] In 1824 lithography was given a section to itself in the Salon, [109] and by 1830 the number of lithographs exhibited (120) was almost as great as the number of engravings (147). Among artists, the lithograph was appreciated for meeting the requirements of drawing in the Romantic style, as defined by Théophile Gautier in a discussion of Delacroix's work: "His drawing is developed in the middle as well as on the contours, by modelling as much as by lines. Colourists like him have a tendency to draw objects in relief." The use of lithography by the Romantic artists would have been no more than an amusing pastime, had it not constituted an important step forward in the cheap and rapid printing of pictures. The lithograph was the ancestor of the photocopy, as can be seen from a passage in Léon Gozlan's novel *Aristide Froissart* (1844): "Skirting the streets next to the boulevards, Mme de Neuvillette went up as far as the Place du Caire and into the alley, where the gas lamps were just being lit. Among the less obtrusive shops, she picked out that of a lithographer and entered: 'I wonder,' she said, 'if you could make one of your presses available immediately to lithograph a circular, whose contents I shall write down for you?' 'Certainly, Madam,' the shopkeeper replied. 'I'll prepare the stone while you are writing it down.'" Round about the same time, Lemercier, the leading printer in Paris, had glassed in the tennis court which joined Rue de Seine to Rue Mazarine, and installed some eighty presses there. Finally, and most important of all, lithography made illustrations in newspapers possible, as in the case of *La Caricature* (founded in 1830) and *Le Charivari* (founded in 1832), "the first daily paper to publish a lithograph every day." Though the repertoire was rather limited, it did include the topical drawing, and during the July Revolution of 1830 Eugène Lami made sketches while on the barricades, with a view to their publication, thus qualifying as the first "lithographic reporter." The lithographic repertoire, however, consisted mainly of portraits and landscapes. The important thing was rapid, long-distance distribution: to reach the public in the provinces. This was achieved without difficulty, ensuring the success of various regional publications, the most famous of which was Baron Taylor's *Voyages pittoresques et romantiques dans l'ancienne France* (1820-1878), illustrated with lithographs after the work of many artists. The active mixture constituted by the provincial bourgeoisie under the Restoration, the so-called "France of the Notables," was fully represented in this venture. The subscribers to *Voyage pittoresque en Touraine* (1824) included the Archbishop and his coadjutor, the Prefect, local officers, the headmaster of the college, some teachers, bankers, businessmen, and a few tradesmen, together with the owners of the castles, mills, and other buildings appearing in the illustrations. This public enjoyed a special advantage in that the price of one franc a plate charged in Paris was reduced to forty centimes in the provinces.[110] The print had become an art of the "notables."

Domenico Quaglio (1787–1837):
Prunn Castle
in the Altmühl Valley, Bavaria.
Two-colour lithograph.
(573 × 445 mm.)

INDUSTRIALIZED PICTURES AND THEIR EFFECT ON THE PRINT

Prise de la Ville de Moscou.

Le 14 Septembre à midi, l'Armée Française est entrée à Moscou, l'une des capitales de l'Empire Russe ; c'est une ville aussi grande que Paris, extrêmement riche et remplie de palais. Notre avant-garde arrivée au milieu de la ville, fut accueillie par une fusillade partie du Kremlin. Le Roi de Naples fit mettre en batterie quelques pièces de canon, dissipa cette canaille et s'empara du Kremlin.

Le Gouverneur de Moscou, Rostopchin, avait fait enlever les pompiers et les pompes et fait mettre le feu en 500 endroits à la fois. Les cinq sixièmes des maisons sont en bois : le feu a pris avec une prodigieuse rapidité. Des églises, il y en avait 1600, des palais plus de 1000, d'immenses magasins ; presque tout a été consumé.

Moscou, une des plus belles et des plus riches villes du monde, située à 700 lieues de Paris, n'existe plus. On sauva le Kremlin, forteresse très - élevée ; ce fut là que se logea Sa Majesté l'Empereur, lors de son entrée en cette ville. Mais à son départ il ordonna qu'on le fit sauter.

De la Fabrique de PELLERIN, Imprimeur - Libraire, à ÉPINAL.

The Taking of Moscow.
Print from the Pellerin workshop at Epinal.
Hand-coloured woodcut, 1812.
Impression with lettering (307 × 344 mm.)

100

Gilles-Louis Chrétien (1754–1811):

Robespierre.
Physionotrace.
(Diameter 52 mm).

The Duchess of Osuna.
Physionotrace.
(Diameter 53 mm.)

During the eighteenth century there was a marked acceleration in the growth of print production: this may be regarded as an early indication of the spread of education, of advancing democratization in politics, of the industrial revolution. There was no difficulty in the way of applying industrialization to print production. As has been emphasized, the print was conceived with this very end in view. Clearly, the three explanations are related and mutually complementary.

Since the seventeenth century, pictures had been used to learn how to read, in France by means of the famous "roast pig" method inspired by the *Tablettes puériles et morales pour instruire les enfants* (1658). Even better known was Abbé Berthaud's *Quadrille des enfants*, which went through twenty-three editions between 1743 and 1860. This methodical exploitation of the printed image was part of the growth of industrialization and contributed to it. Many experiments were being made at this time for the manufacture of paper from vegetable fibres. In 1772 Jacob Christian Schaeffer published his *Sämtliche Papierversuche*, comprising eighty-one pulp specimens, many of which were wood-based. In 1786 Léorier de Lisle presented a further twelve specimens. Finally, a patent for machine-made paper was taken out by Nicolas-Louis Robert in 1797.

This is just one example. Much could also be said about the progress of the steam press, which first went into operation in 1814, and about the manufacture of industrial ink, begun by Lorilleux in 1818. But the main problem throughout the second half of the eighteenth century was how to mechanize the work of the engraver himself, and even of the original draughtsman. This was achieved by the use of the camera lucida and the pantograph. A completely new phase was opening in the history of the printed image.

One of the most remarkable inventions was the "physionotrace." This was a genuine mechanical portrait. Starting from a life-size silhouette, a jointed arm drew a small etching. A six-minute sitting, four days to print a dozen impressions two inches wide, and these could be delivered, hand-coloured if desired, with the copper plate, for fifteen francs. There was a great demand for them from the inventor, Gilles-Louis Chrétien, among the nobility at Versailles; an even greater demand during the Revolution, when they could be had in the shops of the Palais-Royal. A hundred of them were shown at the Salon of 1793, six hundred at the Salon of 1796.[111]

But mass production, on its own, could not meet the demands of a growing, widely scattered public: it was accordingly followed by new channels of distribution. Engravings inserted in magazines and the lithographs of *Le Charivari* were aimed at a further public of well-to-do subscribers, people of some taste and discernment.[112] The production of "folk" imagery reached its peak in France at Epinal, in the early nineteenth century. Designed for a public that was still illiterate, but with an awakening sense of political issues, these picture sheets emanated from centralized workshops; they illustrated civic, moral and religious themes. At first they were distributed through a wide network of hawkers, but more and more, after 1835, by commercial travellers and, above all, by the railway parcel service. For from the start of the Second Empire

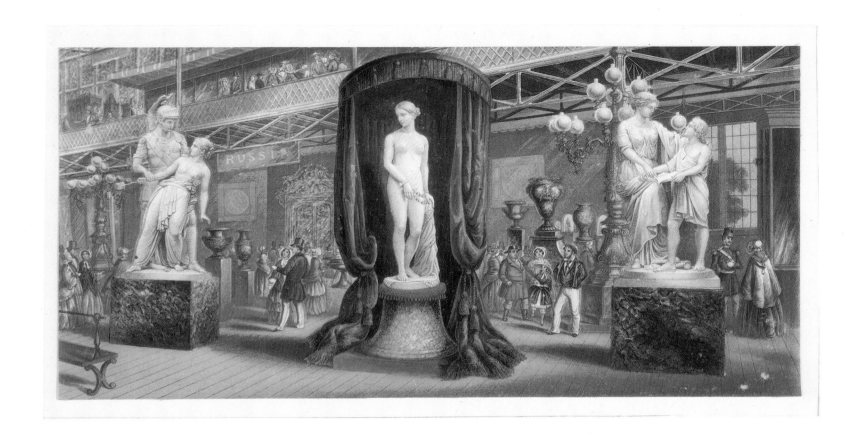

The new processes

George Baxter (1804–1867):
Interior of the Crystal Palace, London, in 1851–1852.
Wood engraving printed in colours.
(120 × 242 mm.)

The New York Crystal Palace
for the Exhibition of Industrial Products.
Illustration from "The Scientific American,"
No. 6, 1852. Wood engraving. (162 × 232 mm.)

NEW YORK CRYSTAL PALACE FOR THE EXHIBITION OF INDUSTRIAL PRODUCTS.

(1852) the police viewed these hawkers of *images d'Epinal* as political agitators; under harrassment their numbers dropped from 30,000 in 1849 to 500 in 1874.[113] The demand for such "folk" imagery was met in the United States by the firm of Currier and Ives, which followed the westward expansion of the country.

Photography was simply the laboured outcome of this long period of gestation and experiment. To be sure, lithography had achieved a decisive step forward by freeing the print from the engraving process. Even so, as a printer wrote in 1835: "Though widespread for some years now, lithography is still not in such general use as a branch of industry that a publisher could maintain an output which would profitably satisfy even the most modest ambition."[114] Lithography had still to be adapted for use under a mechanical press. Wood engraving was a preferred method, as the woodblock printed in the same way as the text. Its disadvantage was that the design had to be laboriously gouged in the block. As it could not be mechanized, this work was at first parcelled out in large workshops among dozens of engravers, each one bent over a few square inches of a picture and toiling in day and night shifts under the watchful eye of an overseer. The finished pieces were fitted together to form large blocks serving to illustrate cheap books and the first educational magazines. These latter were launched in England by Charles Knight, beginning with the *Penny Magazine* in 1832, promptly imitated in France by *Le Magasin Pittoresque,* a weekly selling for ten centimes. Then came the news magazines: the *Illustrated London News* in 1842, followed in France by *L'Illustration.* In 1838 the Paris publisher Charpentier launched his "pocket" editions, selling for three francs fifty. These new publications designed for a wider public met with occasional setbacks, but the movement thus launched was irreversible.

Especially for illustrations, steel engraving was used as a back-up for the more fragile etching. In the United States it had been used for printing bank notes since 1810. In England George Baxter launched his "Baxter prints," wood or steel cuts, and in colour. Apart from the fact that it could stand up to long and rapid print runs, steel was considered more refined than lithography.

THE CHAMPIONS OF THE MISSISSIPPI.
"A Race for the Buckhorns."

Currier and Ives:
The Champions of the Mississippi,
"A Race for the Buckhorns."
Hand-coloured lithograph, 1866.
(467 × 705 mm.)

L'épicier qui n'était pas bête leur envoyait de la réglisse qui n'était pas sucré du tout!

Publishers argued in favour of its resemblance to the copper etching and its fineness of line.[115] But the most important invention in printmaking, prior to photography, was electroplating (1836). By means of electrolysis, soft metals were made more durable by coating them with a microscopic layer of steel. Since the eighteenth century, use had been made of "polytypages," hard metal castings of engraved blocks or plates; they were followed by Firmin-Didot's "stereotypes" in the early nineteenth century. Electroplating became a standard process. A further advantage was that it reinforced the slopes of cuts in a printing surface, or the whole surface, at will, converting an intaglio engraving or a lithograph into a relief engraving, and so solving the problems created by mechanical printing. Printmaking techniques multiplied: "Tissierography" (1841) and "Paniconography" (1850), invented by the printer Gillot.[116] In 1845 appeared the first *Manuel Roret,* a handbook devoted to the connected processes of daguerreotypy and electroplating. The drawback was that a lithograph could not be converted into a line block without loss to the drawing, which lost its grey tones. Though these processes did yeoman service between 1850 and 1880, electroplating was chiefly used in printmaking to steel-face copper plates, so giving them extended wear and avoiding the business of re-engraving by hand for long print runs.

These facilities raised some ethical problems: a fresh prospect was opened up for the use of popular imagery as a medium of mass education. In 1835 Benjamin Delessert, director of the Caisse d'Epargne, founded a "Competition for Useful Prints." In 1841 it was noted in *L'Artiste*: "Lithographs and engravings are meeting with an ever wider response... They popularize the works of artists... and give pleasure to more and more people at low cost. Collections of paintings are the privilege of the envied few: engravings and lithographs may be collected by all: they find their way into the finest galleries as they do into the most modest of drawing-rooms." [117]

But this argument did not go unopposed. In 1833 the conservative *Journal des Artistes* published a sarcastic article on the penny illustrated papers: "Where will good taste find refuge, if the wretched public is to be saturated in this way? The scheme is a clever one, admittedly. These coarse illustrations cut in wood, the product of a false revival, with their shapeless figures and mangled limbs, are bound to spread far and wide." [118] Controversy was not only a matter of taste, of aesthetics, but also of economics. Spokesmen of industrial interests, like the Marquis de Laborde, pleaded the cause of the reproductive arts. In a report on the Great Exhibition of 1851 in

Honoré Daumier (1808–1879):

◁ "The grocer who was no fool was plying them
with liquorice which did not taste sweet at all." 1830.
Lithograph printed directly from the stone. (205 × 171 mm.)

"The Republic calls us, it is up to us ▽
to win or die," illustration for "Le Charivari,"
20 September 1870. Lithograph printed by
the "gillotage" process. (245 × 223 mm.)

La République nous appelle,
Sachons vaincre ou sachons mourir!

The shock of photography

Camille Corot (1796–1875):
Recollection of the Fortifications
of Arras, 1854.
Glass print.
(183 × 142 mm.)

London, he put the question: "Does popularization spell the ruin of art?"[119] Misgivings had been compounded by the invention of photography in 1839. In announcing it, François Arago wrote: "The fine prints hitherto found only in the drawing-rooms of the wealthy art lover will soon adorn even the humble home of the worker and the peasant." So began a period of uncertainty for the print.

Because they were unsuitable for printing purposes, the daguerreotype and calotype posed no direct threat to engravers. But it was realized that what Niepce had been after, and would soon be worked out, was the photogravure process, and this would mark the end of manual engraving. Historians of printmaking generally pass quickly over the years 1840–1860. This was in fact the most important period in its whole history, the period which saw the final transformation of the print into an art form under the impact of the printed photograph.[120]

Up to 1860 the photographic model still had to be recopied onto wood blocks or copperplates by the manual engraver; only the original drawing had been replaced by the photograph. Yet in 1843 the album *Excursions Daguerriennes* had been published, containing the first daguerreotype converted into an engraved plate "by purely chemical means and with no artist's retouching." The method used was the Fizeau process. But the repeated experiments had proved capricious and costly. In the same album an engraver, Daubigny, had been entrusted with re-engraving a daguerreotype by hand, still a simpler method. In 1851 a "photographic printing press" was opened at Lille by Blanquart-Evrard; but the "printing" actually consisted in gumming the photographs into place, as Talbot had already done in his *Pencil of Nature* (1844). Even had it proved possible to print a photograph, it would have had to be retouched by hand. Some engravers specialized in this work, if only to enliven the image with figures and give it the movement which the photograph could not yet achieve. Others, more confident in the photographic process, tried their hand at drawing on a glass plate, which was then printed on light-sensitive paper. The resulting "glass print" stood somewhere between a drawing, an etching and a photograph.

To cope with the difficulties, an art patron, the Duc de Luynes, sponsored a competition to encourage practical application of photo-mechanical processes. In 1862 the prize was won by Poitevin; then, in 1867, medals were awarded to Nègre, Pretsch, Placet and Lemercier. It looked as if the fate of the engraver was sealed. At this point some French artists, including Calametta, Henriquel-Dupont and Célestin Nanteuil, the most famous engravers of the day, signed their famous protest: "Photography consists of a series of entirely manual operations... the resulting prints can in no wise be likened to works born of intellectual effort and artistic study." The occasion was that of the Meyer-Pierson lawsuit demanding the recognition of copyright for photographers. But this corporate defence by the artists was an act of despair. The death-knell of reproductive engraving was sounded by the invention of the half-tone screen, facilitating the economic reproduction of pictures. Berchtold had taken out a patent for the process in 1857, though it was not applied to book illustration until 1884. It first appeared on the front page of *Le Journal Illustré* on 5 September 1886.

Adolphe-Pierre Riffaut (1821–1859):
The Louvre, Pavillon de l'Horloge, 1855.
Photogravure on steel, retouched by hand.

Charles-François Daubigny (1817–1878):
Riverscape at Bas-Meudon, 1843.
Aquatint and etching on steel,
after a daguerreotype. (143 × 203 mm.)

From reproduction to interpretation

△ ◁ Attributed to Théodore
Géricault (1791–1824):
The Hon. Sylvester Douglas,
after Ingres. Lithograph.
(185 × 140 mm.)

◁ Jean-Auguste-Dominique Ingres
(1780–1867):
The Hon. Sylvester Douglas,
1815. Pencil.
(210 × 162 mm.)

Since the eighteenth century, and especially after the rise of the middle class from 1830 on, painting had aroused the interest of an ever wider public in France, and reproductive engraving gained in importance accordingly. Its role became similar to that of a criticism or review, particularly with prospective buyers. It became a thermometer of the picture's reputation, a boost to its promotion. Ingres was quoted as saying: "There are people who visit the Louvre, flitting past a host of interesting pictures, until they stop in front of one that has been popularized in prints. Then they emerge with a satisfied smile, saying: I know my museum." Illustrated journals like *L'Artiste* and dealers' catalogues offered more and more outlets to the engraver. Painters found they could make more money from reproductions of a picture than from the picture itself. Thus Ingres earned more from lithographs of his *Odalisque* than Pourtalès had paid him for the original painting. According to Lamartine, the engraver Mercuri "made millions" from his reproductions of Léopold Robert's famous picture, *Return of the Harvesters*. Charles Blanc wrote in the *Gazette des Beaux-Arts*: "What really made the fortune of Paul Delaroche's mural in the hemicycle of the Palais des Beaux-Arts was the splendid etching of it made by Henriquel-Dupont." It came to the point where dealers only bought a given picture with a view to having it engraved and selling the reproductions. This gave rise to the controversy over proprietary rights and copyrights which led to a major debate in the French National Assembly in 1841.[121]

As early as 1834, with his small publication *Le Musée,* Alexandre Decamps had conceived the idea of asking artists themselves to provide a reproduction of their works, thus raising the problem of "original" reproductions. To be sure, photography was bound to invade this field. But for a long time preference was given to ill-defined methods of cheap facsimile reproduction which maintained a certain aura of "authenticity" (according to the publisher's prospectus at least). The 1845 Durand-Ruel catalogue is hand-engraved; that of 1860, illustrated by photographs; in 1873 it reverts to etchings. "Authentic" reproductions of artists' sketches were made possible by "gillotage" and they were published systematically in *L'Autographe au Salon* from 1863 to 1865, and in *Le Salon, dessin autographe des artistes* in 1868. After 1879 "paniconography" was used to illustrate the official catalogue of the Paris Salon. The magazines invited artists to re-copy their own works for reproduction: *L'Artiste* after 1830, *L'Art au XIXe siècle* after 1860, the *Gazette des Beaux Arts* in 1859. Publishers embarked on encyclopaedic works of reproductions. A "national" spirit had already been introduced into these major sets of prints by the English publisher John Boydell, with undertakings like *A Collection of Prints engraved after the most Capital Paintings in England* (1769-1785). Later French counterparts were Victor Frond's *Panthéon des illustrations françaises du XIXe siècle,* Claude Sauvageot's *L'Art pour tous* (1860-1871) and Edouard Lièvre's *Le Musée Universel* (1861). The first major history of art to be published with a wealth of

◁ Charles-Albert Waltner
(1846–1925):
Portrait of a Girl,
called *Study* or *Singing,*
after Fragonard.
Etching (317 × 263 mm.)

Louis-Pierre Henriquel-Dupont
(1797–1892):
Part of "The Hemicycle of the
Palais des Beaux-Arts," after
Paul Delaroche, 1847.
Etching. (405 × 580 mm.)

L'HEMICYCLE DU PALAIS DES BEAUX-ARTS

illustrations was Charles Blanc's *Histoire des peintres de toutes les écoles* (1861-1876). With publications of this nature in full spate, manual engraving was gradually ousted by mechanical processes. But at the same time a new trend began to assert itself: the need for originality in the print, which always has the effect of emphasizing the close tie with the artist, while glossing over the gap between the reproduction and the original.

Threatened on one side by original work and on the other by mechanical processes, reproductive engravers were led to make a show of their virtuosity and special skills, by turning their reproductions, ever more daringly, into "interpretations" of the original. Increasing use was made of etchings, to give the touch of originality that would justify the liberties taken by the printmaker. The academic line-engravers were scandalised by Henriquel-Dupont's etchings. In 1863 Bracquemond's etching of Holbein's *Erasmus* was relegated to the Salon des Refusés, and it was 1908 before Waltner became the first etcher to be admitted to the Académie des Beaux-Arts. By then photography had won the battle which was still in the balance in 1855 when A.E. Disdéri wrote: "Appointed photographer at the Palais des Beaux-Arts, I reproduced many of the finest paintings on exhibition. Interesting though this publication was, from the importance of the works reproduced, it did not achieve the purpose I had in mind. Because of its high price, the format chosen was beyond the reach of the public at large." [122]

Edouard Manet (1832–1883):

△◁ Woman with a Parasol.
Pen and brush in black ink
on albumin photographic paper. (313 × 212 mm.)

◁ Spring (Mademoiselle Jeanne de Marsy), 1881.
Oil. (73 × 51 cm.)

Jeanne: Spring, 1882.
Etching and aquatint. (154 × 107 mm.) △

Jeanne, 1882.
Drawing by the artist after his painting.
Illustration for Antonin Proust's review
of the 1882 Salon, *Gazette des Beaux-Arts*,
June 1882. (120 × 90 mm.)   ▷

In the Prints section of the Paris Salons during the first half of the nineteenth century, etchers could be counted on the fingers of one hand: Paul Huet or the Lyonese artist Stéphane Baron with a few landscapes in the Romantic or eighteenth-century tradition. But at the same time the growing demand for illustrations had drawn many to the steel engraver's art, conscientious craftsmen who, as industrialization gained ground, either lost their jobs or emerged as original artists. The first engravers to move on from reproductive manual engraving to "art for art's sake" were trained in the school of industrial production. Daubigny started as a woodcut illustrator, Whistler and Meryon as map engravers. Their change-over to original work began in the 1850s with the Second Empire. In 1851 Daubigny brought out his first set of "original" etchings. In 1852 his friends Charles Jacque, a fellow-engraver in the same situation, published some articles in *Le Magasin Pittoresque* on manual techniques of engraving; these were already regarded as something of a curiosity, if not an archaism.[123] Meryon issued some etchings in 1852; Whistler followed in 1856.

Other painters, not normally tempted by printmaking, were drawn by the opportunity for the painter-etcher to reproduce his own pictures at low cost. Manet did so late in life but was dissatisfied with his etching of *Jeanne*: "This etching business is definitely not for me."

Nevertheless, the etchings he made after his own paintings met with considerable success. *Jeanne* (or *Spring*) was etched after the painting he exhibited at the 1882 Salon. He also made a drawing of it; reproduced from a line block, it was published in the *Gazette des Beaux-Arts*. Then the collector Ernest Hoschedé used it to illustrate the cover of his pamphlet *Promenade au Salon de 1882*, written as a tribute to Manet; here it was reproduced in colour by a photo-engraving process devised by Charles Cros. So for the same work we have a painting, a drawing, an etching, a photo-engraving and a line block. There was no clear-cut hierarchy at that time between these different processes. And nobody, including Manet, could have said which one was most "modern," at a time when the great problem was to establish a working partnership between art and industry. The case of Millet is even more significant. When in 1856 his friend and supporter Alfred Sensier urged him to do some etchings, in order to make his paintings better known, Millet had no idea of the issues involved. Nevertheless, he did as suggested, entrusting the publisher Alfred Cadart with the sale of the prints, though Millet – as his correspondence shows – was unaware of the role

What work of art
for the modern age?

Edouard Manet (1832–1883):
Jeanne.
Cover for Ernest Hoschedé's pamphlet
Promenade au Salon de 1882.
Photo-engraving in colour by
the Charles Cros process. (160 × 102 mm.) ▷

JEANNE, PAR M. ÉDOUARD MANET
(Dessin de l'artiste d'après son tableau. — Salon de 1882.)

that a publisher could play; he left it to Cadart to fix the prices, feeling lost in such a business venture. In May 1863 Sensier wrote to Millet: "I've seen some more people. Two young enthusiasts, begging for your etchings. As I told you, your name is going up and up." In October he wrote again: "An old lady wants to buy two prints for 100 francs apiece." (No mean price for a print, seeing that Cadart was selling them at one franc each!)

Sensier then conceived the idea of founding a print society of patrons and business partners, the "Societé des Dix," for which Millet etched a plate in 1863. One of the ten, the critic Philippe Burty, put forward a new idea: that the number of prints should be limited and the original plate destroyed. Cadart himself had never thought of this, simply pulling impressions as long as there were purchasers for them; hence the low prices he charged, comparable to those of reproductive prints, calculated on production costs. Sensier indignantly refused Burty's proposal. But when in 1869 Burty himself commissioned an etching from Millet to illustrate the book *Sonnets et Eaux-fortes* which he was editing, he insisted on the destruction of the plate after printing 350 copies, the edition of his book being limited to that number. Millet was shocked: "I find this destruction of the plate a most brutal and barbarous matter. I don't know enough about business schemes to tell what all this will come to, but I am sure that if this had been done to Rembrandt and Ostade, their work would have come to nothing" (24 January 1869).

The claims of originality

Johan Barthold Jongkind (1819–1891):
View of the Town of Maassluis, South Holland, 1862.
From the set of six Jongkind etchings
published by Alfred Cadart, Paris, 1862.
Etching. (223 × 312 mm.)

Although the idea of applying industrial methods to art was disparaged, the contrary idea of producing unique works of art, or differential works limited in number, from printmaking techniques, gained ground in the latter half of the Second Empire. The years 1859–1862 mark the period of change when definite positions were taken up. In 1859 photography was admitted to the Salon as a specific section. One critic commented as follows: "If in our century we have not had the quarrel between the Ancients and the Moderns, we have at least had the quarrel between engravers and photographers." In 1859, too, the dealer Cadart began marketing photographs in addition to prints. During this phase, when the issues were still undecided, he published the Chifflart album, a curious medley in which a single artist, the painter Chifflart, put his signature to photographs of his own paintings, a reproductive lithograph, some etchings and an original lithograph. But in 1862 Cadart gave up photographs: he decided in favour of the artist's print, with a view to reviving the idea of the "painter-engraver."[124] It is clear that he opted for prints as against photographs, daunted perhaps by the prejudice against them expressed by Théophile Gautier in the preface to one of his albums of painter's etchings, when he wrote: "We must take a stand against this mirror-copy device." In 1859 a new art journal appeared, the *Gazette des Beaux-Arts*. From its very first issues it carried a column on print sales, written by the critic Philippe Burty. In the first leading article of the new periodical, the editor Charles Blanc wrote: "How has this change come about, and what has been happening in the world? How is it that in so short a period such a vast public has emerged, with such a ready interest in the arts? It would be too much to say that our organs of perception have acquired an unexpected delicacy, that our minds have suddenly been more finely attuned… France has witnessed the emergence on every side of overnight fortunes, as in the days of John Law… Hence this extraordinary upward revision of the value of all works of art."

So the print in turn became an object of speculation. In 1861 Burty attempted to include the lithograph among fine prints, writing in his preface to the sales catalogue of the famous Parguez collection: "There can be no doubt that in the near future fine lithographs will fetch exceptional prices. They are the most spontaneous reproduction of the painter's ideas and should always render those ideas with the force and freshness of an original drawing. The number of copies printed has always been relatively few. The stones wear quickly, so that they soon produce only a blurred image; unlike copper plates or even wood blocks, they cannot be reworked, and their weight and size (in storage) mean that the publisher has to erase the design after a few years." All the arguments—including specious ones—have been brought together here. Yet Cadart failed in 1862 when he tried to commercialize the lithographs of modern painters like Manet, Ribot, Bonvin, Legros and Fantin-Latour. The lithograph was still regarded with suspicion; not until the 1890s was it accepted as a pure art form.

Etchings however, though equally "spontaneous," sold well. The most striking example of their success was provided by a South American, Arozarena. Coming to France in 1859, he systematically overbidded in the sales rooms and in less than two years he brought together a fabulous collection of etchings. He then sold them all off in March 1861. In his preface to the catalogue, the young critic Emile Galichon extolled "these masters of spontaneity, who are alone of significance in the history of art, and who epitomize it." He pointed out "the gap which separates these etchings, transcribed directly by the artist himself putting his soul into the work, and those of the 'translators,' who, though perhaps working with a more scrupulous attention, only execute cold reproductions of others' masterpieces."

Galichon had issued the challenge. It was taken up by the dealer Rochoux, who wrote two pamphlets deploring this "insult to the engraver's art." He sprang to the defence of those who "admire Schelte Bolswert's *Crowning with Thorns*... and Lucas Vorsterman's *Angels weeping at the sight of the body of Jesus Christ,* and Edelinck's *Holy Family*... What chagrin they would feel in reading your brilliant preface!" To him it seemed wrongheaded that this taste for "spontaneity" should prevail over what most art lovers regarded as "true" engraving. But his protests went for nothing. A change in aesthetic values was taking place and nothing could stop it.

Henri Fantin-Latour (1836–1904):
Two Women Embroidering by a Window, 1862.
Lithograph. (270 × 407 mm.)

In 1862 Cadart founded the Société des Aquafortistes, photography was recognized as an art form in the Meyer-Pierson lawsuit, and Poitevin won the competition for photomechanical reproduction sponsored by the Duc de Luynes. All this helped to put the print on a new and surer footing. Cadart was followed by others. In 1869 an etching society, best known for the work of Giovanni Fattori and the Macchiaioli, was founded in Turin. In England Seymour Haden revived the old Etching Club of 1838, and similar groups began springing up in Europe and the United States. Cadart made a business trip to the United States in 1865; and Haden went too in 1882, five years after the foundation of the New York Etching Club.

Some artists, among them Whistler and Degas, saw that the print had a future of its own, independent of reproductive engraving. From about 1856 they threw off the constraints imposed by a uniform print run. Treating each print as an individual work, varying the paper used, the inking, and the heightening, they turned the whole technique of printmaking into a sophisticated manner

The etching treated as painting

of drawing. Each impression was unique, and it was in this sense that Degas spoke of "original" prints and Jongkind called his etchings "drawings." States were multiplied to as many as twenty, ink was used like paint, and pastel added to the ink. Variations and improvisations were indulged in, each signed individually (since each was unique) and sometimes numbered (since they formed sets). When the economic slump of 1879-1880 left the Impressionists with no further hope of selling their pictures to a wider public, Degas and Pissarro turned to printmaking – improvising in this way, making shift with the means at their disposal.[125] At the fifth Impressionist exhibition in 1880, Pissarro displayed the different states of the same print. At the same period Degas was producing "drawings printed from greasy ink" (monotypes). At the time, this differentiation between impressions, each one being signed and numbered, simply amounted to a new style of printmaking, on a par with drawing and painting. But the day was not far off when these marks of originality would be turned to commercial account in uniform print runs, just to indicate to the new-found public that these were individual works of art and not objects of mass production.

delicate and elusive inflexions of the mind." Redon had also had another teacher, Rodolphe Bresdin, who had encouraged him to undertake "these haphazard experiments, alien to the methods usually adopted in working on the stone." Bresdin had been known since 1861 for his pen-drawn lithograph of *The Good Samaritan*. Before leaving for Canada in 1873, he asked the printer Lemercier to transfer eight of his etchings onto stones, to facilitate their printing. For Bresdin in the 1870s, as perhaps also for his pupil Redon in 1879, lithography – whatever the personal use they made of it – was first and foremost the cheapest available method of mass dissemination in the graphic arts. But this very characteristic prejudiced many collectors against it.

Added to this was the prejudice against coloured prints, always under suspicion as being aimed at an undiscriminating public. In 1898 the chairman of the print and lithography section of the Paris Salon wrote: "By its very nature, its origins and its traditions, the art of printmaking is without question the art of black and white." In this opinion he was supported by the critic Thiébault-Sisson, who saw in prints "the pursuit of effects which have no place in lithography." From Roger Marx and Charles Maurin came a riposte in which they spoke of the "revival of the print." To satisfy the demand for lithographs, use was also made of "stone copyists," skilled craftsmen who recopied an artist's design onto the stone. This practice became a further subject of dispute. André Mellério, the apostle of this "revival", defended the role of the "assayer": "the trained craftsman who attends to all the trials and adjustments required to make the plate ready for printing, the actual print run, if extensive, then being left to the ordinary workmen or the machine." In refusing the help of these intermediaries, what some artists were really refusing was a certain conception of the print, as a wall decoration, to be framed and displayed as an object of ostentation, or fashion, or semi-luxury – a conception diametrically opposed to that of older collectors, who kept their prints in portfolios, only taking them out on special occasions.

Rodolphe Bresdin
(1825–1885):
Rest on the Flight
into Egypt with
Loaded Donkey, 1871.
Etching. (229 × 197 mm.)

119

Cézanne, one of the painters solicited by Vollard
for his editions of colour lithographs

Paul Cézanne (1839– 1906):

Large Bathers, 1896–1897.

△ Lithograph in black heightened with watercolour, maquette for the colour lithograph, 1896–1898. (410 × 500 mm.)

◁ Lithograph in black. (410 × 500 mm.)

Paul Cézanne (1839–1906):
Large Bathers.
Colour lithograph.
1st state, c. 1898.
(410 × 500 mm.)

But these disputes did nothing to check the growing popularity of prints in general and colour lithographs in particular. In March 1893 André Marty launched *L'Estampe originale,* a print quarterly offering impressions from all the graphic media; *L'Epreuve* began publication in 1894, and *L'Estampe moderne* followed in 1897, the same year as *L'Estampe et l'Affiche,* whose editor André Mellério pleaded for "the democratization of art." In 1896 Vollard bought a lithographic press and appealed to well-known artists to make prints for him.[128] This was one of the first publishing houses for prints of the modern type. To assert its artistic character, it had to depend on artists with an established reputation, even if, like Sisley, they contributed only a canvas or watercolour to be transferred to the stone by others. So it was that Puvis de Chavannes made a name as a lithographer, even becoming chairman of the French committee for the centenary celebration of lithography in 1895, though he had never actually worked in the medium![129] Roger Milès' book *Art et Nature* (1897) and the Germinal Album (1899) disingenuously fail to make any distinction between prints "by" and prints "after" a given artist. In 1910 the publisher Bernheim issued an album of pastel facsimiles "signed by" Degas.

Imagery
and
avant-garde

Jacques Villon (1875–1963):

△ Lili with Black Boa, 1906.
Drypoint, definitive state.
(360 × 235 mm.)

◁ Nude Doing her Hair, 1933.
Drypoint. (295 × 206 mm.)

By 1900 the growing number of printmakers' or print collectors' societies, and of "systematic" catalogues of artists' works, annotated inventories designed for those who owned works or wished to buy them, showed that the print market had won an established place in the art world. This market covered a wide range of graphic media. On the one hand, it still included the hand-made reproductive engravings which catered for lovers of "fine workmanship." A whole generation of conscientious engravers were still reproducing the paintings appreciated in conventional circles; the last of them was still engraving paintings by Meissonier in 1950 for dealers in London and New York. At the other end of the scale were the innovations of the so-called avant-garde who, for the sake of their reputation, could not limit themselves to painting but had to venture on parallel experiments in graphic art, whatever the cost to their publishers. When D. H. Kahnweiler proposed to Braque in 1911 to publish two of his prints in a run of a hundred copies each, he was taking a bold step. Braque had pulled only two or three impressions of his first prints. But Kahnweiler had not forgotten that it was by reselling prints bought cheaply from the dealer Le Véel that he himself, as a student, had been able to buy his first pictures by Lautrec, Cézanne and Signac.[130] Like Vollard, Kahnweiler realized that print publishing was a useful factor in the redeployment of the art market.

Despite all the efforts in this direction, however, the distinction between "prints" and "picture sheets" had no real foundation. Technically, print production remained very much an open field with a popular appeal. It afforded artists a direct channel of communication with the public at large, indeed with the man in the street. In 1900, for example, it was very difficult to distinguish between the popularity of colour lithographs and the popularity of the illustrated satirical magazines selling all over Europe. To divide the lithographs of Toulouse-Lautrec or Félix Vallotton into "prints," "posters" and "press illustrations" is simply the arbitrary action of catalogue compilers. Periodicals like *Simplicissimus* in Germany and *L'Assiette au Beurre* in France broke down these frontiers by offering artists both a platform for their opinions and a paid outlet for work.[131] Some artists, like Jacques Villon, Frank Kupka and Kees van Dongen, regarded such work as a stop-gap, a temporary livelihood, pending the day when they could sell their pictures. Others, like Hermann-Paul and Steinlen, committed themselves wholeheartedly to printmaking and used it to militate for a social art. Neither side had clearly defined positions. For those on both sides considered themselves to be artists in the full sense of the term, and the individual and indefeasible nature of their work frequently led them to sympathize with anarchist views.

Georges Braque (1882–1963):
Nude Study, 1908.
Etching, printed in
55 copies in 1953. (280 × 195 mm.)

So we must note the appearance of a new attitude of artists towards the print. It was true that the art market had taken possession of it. But just as industry posed a threat to elitist production, so artists could make use of this medium to boycott commercialized production, because this widely diffused artefact, the print, nevertheless remained a product of craftsmanship, based on pre-industrial techniques, which the printmaker controlled personally so long as he refused the mechanized techniques which the art market justifiably abhorred. Just at this time, for example, there was a revival of the woodcut. This manifested itself, not only as a new style expressive of revolt, but also as an object symbolizing production by primitive methods. The woodcuts made by Gauguin in Tahiti were the prototype. The craft techniques of printmaking, together with the popular demand for illustrated magazines, explain why the German Expressionists took to prints and especially to woodcuts, published by periodicals like *Die Aktion* or *Der Sturm*. The print gave the artist a medium of expression which was cheap and easily diffused, like a tract. "For both Munch and the Brücke," writes Jean-Michel Palmier, "graphic work afforded a means of appealing to a much wider public than could be reached by a mere canvas. Marginal, unconnected with any particular art group or movement, and not fitting easily into the established circuit of dealers and galleries, the woodcut in their hands, given their subject matter and freedom of handling, was at once a means of challenging and appealing to a wide audience which would not fail to react to the violence of their style."[132]

VERLAG · DIE AKTION · BERLIN-WILMERSDORF

A primitive work of art

Albert Gleizes (1881–1953): ▷
Cover for the periodical
Action, No. 1, Paris, February 1920.
Stencil. (225 × 185 mm.)

◁ Franz Maria Jansen (1885–1958):
Revolt, woodcut illustration for the
periodical *Die Aktion*, No. 12,
Berlin, 1923.
(162 × 155 mm.)

El Lissitzky (1890–1941):
Composition for the periodical
De Stijl, No. 9, Leyden, 1922.

Printmaking allowed the artist to control not only the production but also the wider diffusion of his work, without at the same time falling into the clutches of big business. The result was not necessarily marginal or anarchistic workshops. Some saw them as advanced laboratories of art, kept under the artist's control but ready at the same time for industrial exploitation should the need arise. It is significant that, at the Weimar Bauhaus, the graphic arts atelier which functioned from 1919 to 1924 maintained its status as a place of "pure" creativity, linked at first to Expressionism, but "relatively independent of the Bauhaus masters and of outside influences thanks to the spontaneous side of this free activity carried on outside the framework of general studies"; and that, after the transfer to Dessau in 1925, "the graphic arts atelier was replaced by a printing shop devoted to experiment in typographical and publicity design. In the last years of the Bauhaus, in Berlin, typography and printing techniques became part of the programme of the publicity workshop."[133]

A "hackneyed" work of art

John Sloan (1871–1951):
The Woman's Page, 1905.
From the *New York City Life* set.
Etching. (129 × 175 mm.)

Käthe Kollwitz (1867–1945): ▷
Poverty, 1893–1894.
From *The Weavers* set.
Etching. (189 × 162 mm.)

So between the wars the printmaking workshop became a centre of conflict. The artists won out on the question of the printed image, and victory was conceded to them, temporarily at least, by political forces anxious for popularity. Thus in the United States, following the crash of 1929 and the depression, the federal government opened printmaking ateliers which became in effect national workshops for artists. The W.P.A. (Works Progress Administration) sponsored the making of thousands of prints, mostly eclectic in style but also including bold and experimental work; some went to decorate public places, others to gather dust in the archives. Here again the point was to give a stimulus to creative work, outside the commercial circuit, which was then languishing. One result was to develop an interest in silk-screen printing as an art form; till then it had been restricted to packaging and labels. The W.P.A. capitalized on the growing taste of middle-class Americans for prints reflecting "everyday life," a taste which had been catered for by the artists of the Ashcan School; commonplace objects were abundantly featured in etchings and lithographs.[134] The initiatives of the W.P.A. led on logically to the founding of Associated American Artists, in New York in 1935 – an emporium of artists' prints, in highly eclectic styles, but sold at low prices and so helping to reinsert the print into the circuit of "consumer goods."

The social movements of the 1930s thus gave new life to the idea of the "popular print," introducing it into petit bourgeois and intellectual circles. Following in the footsteps of the U.S.S.R., revolutionary China rediscovered its own woodcut traditions. Inspired by politically committed European engravers, such as Käthe Kollwitz and Frans Masereel, the Chinese founded schools whose output was in line with the political ambitions of socialism, while maintaining the character of genuine works of art. For these prints to play such a role − inevitably an equivocal and conciliatory role − they had to have a certain "aura," a transcendence lending credibility to their message. So, between the wars, we find an increasing number of art lovers prepared to accept the print as an art form no different in its essence from painting or music. Even when there was no market for it, official or otherwise, such as to ensure the livelihood of graphic artists or printers, interest in the print as an independent, self-sufficing medium never quite disappeared, even though in pre-war Paris the Leblanc printing shop only survived thanks to the commissions given by Bernheim to Jacques Villon, and the workshop of Lacourière was only saved in extremis (1939) by Vollard's commissions from Picasso. As we have seen, the print had its own vocabulary (sets) and its own syntax (transfers), the specific nature of which could always be pointed to by the artists. And, when works so different in spirit and so similar in appearance are placed side by side, we can see that the relations between the art for art's sake of some and the social art of others may be much closer and more complex than supposed.

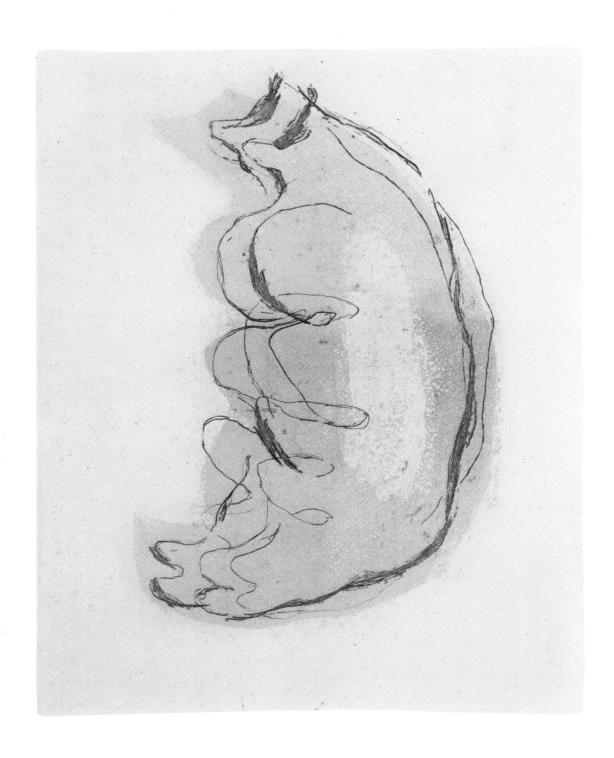

Jean Fautrier (1898–1964):
Small Female Torso, 1947.
Coloured etching.
(Plate 315 × 250 mm.)
(Design c. 265 × 170 mm.)

Raoul Ubac (1910): ▷
Illustration for Yves Bonnefoy's
book of verse *Pierre écrite*,
Paris, 1958.
Engraved slate, transferred
to and pulled from the
lithographic stone.
(Page 380 × 280 mm.)

One place in which these contradictions were richly exemplified was Atelier 17, founded by the English printmaker S. W. Hayter. Here, perhaps for the first time, was a print workshop which was no more and no less than an artists' workshop, with no commercial views and no division of labour. Here, the more the specific idiom of the print was emphasized by the artists concerned, the nearer its application came to that of any other of the graphic arts. The workshops run by Hayter, Friedlaender and Goetz operated on the same principle as painters' studios, the sole difference being that the end product was the print. Free play was given to any technical innovations devised by the artists and giving added force to the language of the print, inasmuch as these works were self-justifying and accountable to no one. Atelier 17, opened in Paris in 1927, transferred to New York in 1940, then re-established in Paris in 1950, made an extraordinary reputation for itself.[135] In the same way as the political print formed part of an international movement under way in post-revolutionary Russia and the United States, in Germany and in China, so Atelier 17 attracted artists from all over in the world.

In the depression years of the 1930s and again during the war, printmakers were short of paper and reduced to using makeshift workshops. Yet some produced unusual, often unique prints and carried out experiments akin to sculpture or drawing. A very significant group, in this respect, was the one that exhibited in Paris in 1949 under the name of "Graphies" and published *A la Gloire de la Main*. It included the engraver and theorist Albert Flocon; the sculptor Raoul Ubac, the maker of "fossil photographs" and later of slate engravings; Anton Prinner, who pasted strips of cardboard together to make printing plates; and Jean Fautrier, who coloured individually each proof he pulled.[136]

The economic prosperity of the 1950s caused the prints deriving from the social movement of the 1930s to fall into oblivion, if not into contempt, as viewed retrospectively; it had the further effect now of making the experimental, marginal workshops of the day look like academies of freedom and turned them into models destined to have a great success.

Ernest Pignon-Ernest (1942):
Apartheid, 1974.
Silkscreen print.
(1 m. × 2.80 m.)

So what we are now facing is no longer a new territory, but a number of streams converging on one place which, for various and often contradictory reasons, offers advantages to all of them. These advantages lie in the potential nature of the "print," as defined in these pages, and take material form in the printmaker's workshop. Contrasting figures still meet there – the aesthete and the militant, the worker and the prophet, the upstart and the déclassé – but one thing they have in common: the desire to produce not just art, but art nurtured on speech and embodying parallel practices. The public to which it appeals has been more or less extended, but its appreciation does not go beyond that circle. Some artists have tried to go beyond it: Picasso, with his *Dove of Peace* lithograph printed as a poster; Hundertwasser and Tom Phillips, selling their unnumbered prints cheaply, printed like a mass-produced image in thousands of copies. But their name and their very desire to make a "print" work against them. It is as if they were isolated by a magic circle from the world of mass-produced pictures which flood in from all sides. Reading the few students of the print, such as William Ivins, one comes to feel that there is a strong connection between this relentless glut of pictures overloaded with messages and the "guarded world" of the print. After all, the print, in the restricted sense that the word has taken on, has its due place in the overall history of picture-making. Would it be too paradoxical to state that the print, as a work of art, exists only in terms of an industry whose role is to diffuse ideas and which therefore needs to be idealized? Printmakers at one extreme would proclaim that the print has nothing to do with reproduction and diffusion; at the opposite extreme, that the print should be demystified and brought back into the humble ranks of the printed picture sheet. The former forget that, whatever they do, the print is by its nature a reproduction. The latter forget that, whatever they do, the print has become a reproduction with a difference.

Geneviève Asse (1923):
Wire, 1973.
Drypoint and burin.
(495 × 348 mm.)

131

II

THE ART
AND HAND
OF THE
PRINTMAKER

Antony Griffiths

Hendrick Goudt (1585-1630):
The Mocking of Ceres, after
Adam Elsheimer, 1610.
Entire and detail.
Engraving. (321 x 245 mm.)

The following pages contain a series of short essays, each of which is designed to occupy two facing pages, with illustrations and text lending each other mutual support. The choice of the topics has not been simple, and it would be far from difficult to suggest a completely different set. The intention, however, was not to be in any sense comprehensive, but to use the topics as specimens to elucidate some of the problems and possibilities that have faced artists through the centuries and how they have reacted to them. The arrangement is in approximately chronological order, both to provide some continuous narrative thread and to allow the demonstration of how artists have built on the achievements of their predecessors or have reacted against them.

Each essay has been written as an independent unit, whose length varies according to the exigencies of space and the point being made. Nor is there any correlation between the length and an artist's stature: Rembrandt, for example, is certainly the towering figure in the history of printmaking, but space only allows discussion of one of the numerous contributions that he made to the art.

We hope that the essays, when read together, will give some insights into printmaking as an art form, and will convince the reader that it possesses an autonomy and self-sufficiency which entitle it to be judged alongside the better-known and better-understood arts of painting and drawing.

Painting and drawing are also activities that are pursued in a variety of media (fresco, tempera, oils; or silverpoint, chalk, pen, watercolour) and these parallel the available range of printmaking techniques. This variety can be called on by the artist at will to provide whatever effect he requires. It is the stimulus of all these possibilities that has provided much of the dynamic force behind European art; and this in itself is enough to justify a close examination of them.

The earliest woodcuts

The invention of printing images on to sheets of paper was a momentous innovation in the history of human culture, and as important in many ways as Gutenberg's later invention of printing texts from movable type. Yet we know virtually nothing about it. There are no written documents, no names of artists, not even any late traditions which might preserve some element of truth. There are only large numbers of the woodcuts themselves, mostly undated and unprovenanced, and all anonymous. The labours of scholars over many years have imposed some order on the chaos. A convincing stylistic sequence has been established, and carefully drawn parallels with painting and sculpture have enabled an approximate chronology to be drawn up.

South German master (early 15th century): St Dorothy, c. 1410–1420. Woodcut heightened with hand-colouring. (380 × 195 mm.)

South German master ▷ (early 15th century): Rest on the Flight into Egypt. Woodcut heightened with hand-colouring. (284 × 212 mm.)

Two of the earliest prints thus identified are reproduced here; it is thought that they were made in southern Germany in the first decades of the fifteenth century. What is so striking about them is their ambition, sophistication and quality. They are large both absolutely and in scale. St Dorothy fills the ground with absolute assurance, and the subtlety of the design is evident in the pattern of folds on her left sleeve which fall away below the basket of flowers, and the oval hooks which define the pattern of drapery. The care taken in applying colour can be seen in the *Rest on the Flight into Egypt*. It is used both naturalistically, in the shades of blue on the Virgin's dress, and non-naturalistically, in the same shade of blue on St Joseph's beard. The subjects chosen are remarkable for their iconographic originality, and this originality is used in the service of a greater emotional expressiveness. It would be difficult to find a parallel for the scene of Joseph boiling eggs, but the contrast between his humdrum occupation and the stately crowned Virgin beside him is both humorous and poignant.

How should we explain these remarkable achievements? It is apparent that these earliest prints on paper were preceded by a long tradition of block-printing on to textiles, but nothing among the few surviving printed textiles could lead us to expect works of this sophistication. Nor can we find drawings of the same period that show the same delight in the possibilities of the arabesque of a thick curling line. We are thus forced to the conclusion that the creation of the new work of art, the print, went hand-in-hand with the development of a new drawing style, and that the birth of the medium was attended, if not directly caused, by some of the finest artistic sensibilities of the period.

The graver, or burin, is a tool which had been used for centuries by smiths to embellish the surfaces of the metal that they were working. Yet the first prints taken from metal plates cannot be dated before the 1430s, several decades after the beginnings of printing from woodblocks. By then the great conceptual leap had been taken and the idea of portable printed images established. Thus the first engravings show none of the boldness or ambition that mark the earliest woodcuts. The engraver was a metalsmith by training and still conceptually tied to the appearance of the highly worked metal plate; the printed image itself took second place. Surfaces were closely worked with a mass of flicks of the graver and only a strongly defined contour could save the image from collapsing into confusion.

The artist who freed the printed engraving from the tyranny of the metal plate and the jeweller's approach to surface ornamentation was Martin Schongauer. His father was, by chance, a gold-smith working in Colmar, but Schongauer himself, having matriculated at the University of Leipzig in 1465, was trained as a painter, and as such passed his short career. Few of his paintings survive, but we do possess considerable numbers of his drawings and these reveal his painterly approach to draughtsmanship. Given this background it is easy to understand why, when he turned to making engravings, he was in no way shackled by the traditions of the craft. Even in an early work like the *Temptation of St Anthony* a new mastery is evident. By devising systems of close cross-hatching, he has been able to mark off shadows from highlights, and thus introduce a sense of volume by tonal modelling. The figures are established as standing in a defined space by setting a rock in the lower right-hand corner, and the way that the light intensifies in the upper sky is marked by a series of heavier and more closely spaced parallel flecks. A curious tension is maintained between the stately and graceful spiral of the devils and the ferocity of their assault. It must have been this aspect of the print that appealed to Michelangelo, for Vasari relates that as a young man he made a copy of it.

From this starting point, Schongauer went on to develop an art of increasing subtlety and assurance. A later print of the *Martyrdom of St Sebastian* is outstanding for the boldness with which the spiral of the tree and of the saint's body are set in counterpoint. Even more mannered is the twist of crumpled drapery that hangs motionless in mid-fall as if carved out of limewood; and these prints were indeed often used as models by later sculptors. Yet the spareness of the design and the simplicity of the concept save the print from a charge of sentimentality. Schongauer's development, which can be followed to his last prints, is towards a greater emptiness and simplification, which has led writers to invoke the concept of "classicism" in discussion of his late style. For the historian of prints, however, Schongauer's importance lies in his demonstration that the engraved plate could produce a work of art in terms independent of the arts of the goldsmith or even the painter.

Martin Schongauer

Martin Schongauer (c. 1430 or c. 1450–1491):

◁ The Temptation of St Anthony.
Engraving. (314 × 231 mm.)

The Martyrdom of St Sebastian.
Engraving. (156 × 111 mm.)

Mantegna

The seven engravings made by Andrea Mantegna between about 1470 and 1490 are very surprising and original works. The first surprise is that he made them at all. There seems to have been no tradition of engraving in the area of north-east Italy where he was trained. The surviving early Italian engravings come for the most part from Florence, with a few from Ferrara, and seem to have been made by goldsmiths and niellists. The one major exception, the *Battle of the Nude Men*, the sole print made by Antonio Pollaiuolo and a work of great size and ambition, seems to be later than Mantegna's earliest print. The clearest link between Mantegna and the Florentine tradition is in his manner of engraving. The *Virgin and Child* demonstrates how he first incised the contours of the figure and then laid in the modelling with a succession of short parallel lines. The direction from lower left to upper right is uniform, while extra density of shading is supplied by slightly angled re-entrant lines which connect the parallels. The pose with the Virgin's face against the Child's is an old Byzantine formula, but is invested with a new poignancy, particularly in the tender way in which the Child is enveloped and protected from harm by the huge linked hands of the Virgin. But the pose is frozen and formalized by the recession-defying penumbra of closely-worked shadow that robs the pair of any particular location in space and time. What lies behind such a remarkable achievement?

We know of Mantegna's obsession with antiquity, his humanist friendships and the months that he spent in the study of antique remains; and I feel that it is his attraction to the sculptural ideal of classical art which helps to explain his manner of engraving, as it also explains his extraordinary paintings in grisaille. In the two *Bacchanals* and the pair which join to form a frieze of a *Battle of Sea-Monsters*, style and content merge in a remarkable way. The subject of the *Bacchanal with a Wine-Vat* is set in a timeless classical Arcadia in which humans and satyrs mingle in an easy familiarity as votaries of Dionysus, the god of wine and inspiration. There does not seem to be any precise literary source either classical or humanist for the scene, nor can any of the poses be directly related to any surviving piece of antique sculpture. Nevertheless the heroic nude at the left is obviously inspired by the Apollo Belvedere, as the frieze conception of the whole is based on a sarcophagus relief—but in a similarly indirect way. The space of the scene is much deeper than that of a sarcophagus, and the spatial logic much clearer, but the dense shading at the back implies the presence of the containing marble into which the background details of the tree and reeds have been incised in the lightest of relief. The strong light throws the figures into the sharpest definition and their shadows on to the background. Thus they live in a half-world, their liveliness testified by their energetic gestures and expressive faces, but yet held fast by the background from which they never more than three-quarters emerge. One is tempted to see this as a symbol of the Renaissance's inability ever to bring the lost world of antiquity fully to life.

Andrea Mantegna (1431–1506):

◁ The Virgin and Child, c. 1470–1490.
Engraving. (345 × 268 mm.)

Bacchanal with a Wine Vat, c. 1470–1490.
Engraving. (335 × 454 mm.)

Dürer
and the woodcut

Albrecht Dürer (1471–1528):

The Great Whore of Babylon,
plate 15 of the *Apocalypse* series, 1498.
Woodcut. (392 × 282 mm.)

The Mass of St Gregory, 1511.
Woodcut. (295 × 205 mm.) ▷

As engraver, Dürer was Schongauer's most distinguished heir. As designer of woodcuts, he had no such precursor, and his greatest achievement as a printmaker was single-handedly to have resuscitated the woodcut and reinstated it as a major artistic medium. The quality of the intelligence and thought that he applied to his designs can be judged by the evolution between the two prints reproduced here. *The Great Whore of Babylon* is typical of the complexity of design found in the *Apocalypse* series of 1498. The subject is a vision and it would perhaps be wrong to expect much logical coherence in the design. Instead Dürer has achieved visual coherence by an astonishing use of transitional devices; at the centre left, for example, both sea and land transform themselves into a swirl of cloud. Lighting is uniform and distance is conveyed merely by a variation of scale. By about 1510 such visual sleight of hand no longer satisfied Dürer. He had by now trained his cutters to a degree of skill that has never again been equalled, and this allowed him to give his designs a logical as well as visual coherence. The *Mass of St Gregory* of 1511 shows the new style, which was to be of such importance to his successors. A carefully constructed perspective grid underlies the composition but is matched and restated by a change in light. The figures in the middle distance behind the altar are shown in half-tone, defined by a uniform horizontal striation across hats, faces and clothes, completely regardless of texture or form, while a consistent light falls across the scene from left to right. With this new structure, Dürer enabled the woodcut to meet the challenge of the pictorial advances of the Renaissance.

143

The first decades of the sixteenth century saw a remarkable increase in the production of printed images both north of the Alps and in Italy; they were both product and cause of the new art-historical consciousness that marks the High Renaissance. Dürer's prints had carried his fame to Italy and given him an international reputation that no painting could ever have achieved. This lesson was not lost on Raphael. Possibly his provincial origins, or his rivalry at the papal court of Julius II with Michelangelo, made him determined to secure his prestige as firmly as possible. By following Dürer's example and publishing prints, he won in his short life of only thirty-seven years the widest renown and influence of any Italian artist.

His chosen vehicle was the engraving and his chosen engraver a certain Marcantonio Raimondi of Bologna, who had begun as a rather pedestrian engraver of religious and mythological subjects of his own design. After a period in Venice spent in pirating Dürer's woodcuts, Marcantonio moved to seek his fortune in Rome. He there joined forces with Raphael, who set him up with an assistant Il Baviera to act as publisher. Their close personal connection is proven by a document of 1515 in which Marcantonio witnessed the joint purchase of a house by Raphael and Il Baviera. One of the first fruits of their collaboration was the engraving of the *Massacre of the Innocents*. A series of surviving drawings by Raphael enables us to follow the genesis of this print. It began as an idea for the *Judgment of Solomon* on the ceiling of the Stanza della Segnatura. A drawing in the Albertina shows a kneeling woman with a soldier about to divide the disputed child into

Marcantonio and Raphael

Raphael (1483–1520):

The Massacre of the Innocents.
Red chalk over a tracing in pencil and stylus outline. (248 × 411 mm.)

Raphael (1483–1520): ▷△
The Massacre of the Innocents.
Drawing in pen and brown ink over red chalk underdrawing, pricked for transfer. (232 × 377 mm.)

halves. Unfortunately the small area available meant that the striding soldier had to be abandoned in favour of a more compact figure, but the invention was too good to waste. Raphael accordingly began to devise a new composition around the lunging soldier for Marcantonio to engrave. Two preparatory drawings are reproduced here together with Marcantonio's final engraving. In the earlier drawing in the British Museum the contours of all the figures are pricked with the exception of the group in the right background. The transferred dots can be seen in the Windsor drawing, joined up in outline in lead point. Then certain areas only were worked up and finished in red chalk. There must have been a third (lost) drawing which was actually used by Marcantonio for the print, in which some foreground and background figures were added. The landscape was however supplied by Marcantonio himself from the design of another artist. The fascination of these drawings is as examples not merely of Raphael's creativity, but also of how deliberately he was working with the engraver in mind. The British Museum drawing is drawn in pen and ink in an untypically careful manner, so untypical in fact that doubts have often been cast on its authenticity. But the explanation is certainly that Raphael was deliberately creating a style in line which could be capable of translating the volume-creating properties of his more habitual medium of red chalk. This invention gave engraving the possibility of capturing the tonal properties of paintings or drawings, and this ensured its future as the reproductive medium *par excellence*.

Marcantonio Raimondi (c. 1480–c. 1534): ▽
The Massacre of the Innocents,
after Raphael, c. 1510.
Engraving. (284 × 435 mm.)

145

Antonio da Trento (c. 1508–after 1550):
The Martyrdom of SS. Peter and Paul,
after Parmigianino. Chiaroscuro
woodcut. (296 × 481 mm.)

Colour printing of woodcuts was invented in Germany in the early years of the sixteenth century. We know enough about the invention to be sure that it was not a natural development out of handcolouring popular images. The evidence is in fact quite unambiguous and proves that it began as a princely game carried on between two rival German courts; Lucas Cranach represented the court of Saxony, Hans Burgkmair the Imperial court at Augsburg. For a few years after 1507 astonishingly elaborate prints using a wide range of printed and hand-applied colours as well as gold and silver dust, were despatched through the posts north and south. But, like all games, it staled after a time and the colour woodcut in general was abandoned in northern Europe. There was no further use for it.

In Italy things were different. Examples from one phase of the development in Germany reached Venice, where they were enthusiastically greeted by Ugo da Carpi (who falsely claimed the invention as his own); from him derived the entire Italian tradition. This phase was the chiaroscuro woodcut, so called because it is built up from two or three blocks printed in varying tones of the same colour, with highlights cut out of both blocks and reserved as white paper. The problem here is to explain why Italian artists found chiaroscuro woodcuts so satisfactory as to exclude all other types of colour woodcut. The Germans had made fully polychrome cuts, and

The chiaroscuro woodcut

Domenico Beccafumi (c. 1486–1551):

◁ Reclining Male Nude.
Pen and brown ink, heightened with
white on yellowish paper. (250 × 392 mm.)

An Apostle.
Chiaroscuro woodcut.
(414 × 208 mm.)

the Japanese were later to obtain wonderful effects in this way. It would be convenient to be able to argue that they were intended as facsimiles of chiaroscuro drawings, but the evidence tends to disprove this. Chiaroscuro drawing was not fashionable before the introduction of chiaroscuro woodcut, and many of the drawings in the style that survive seem to have been intended as models for the printmaker. The most plausible answer seems to be that chiaroscuro painting at that time was highly fashionable in Italy for grisaille panels and for decorating house façades, and this tradition conditioned the acceptability of chiaroscuro woodcuts. Thus these woodcuts were never really intended as reproductions. Painters such as Raphael and Parmigianino made designs for the woodcutter (Parmigianino's *Martyrdom of SS. Peter and Paul* cut by Antonio da Trento is reproduced here) in the same way as they might supply drawings for a house façade decoration.

Beccafumi's designs have a unique sensitivity to the nature of the wooden block, and he may have cut them himself. In the print illustrated here he has gone so far as to cut an imitation grain of wood into the background block. The delight that Beccafumi took in tricks like this went even further: with a characteristic mannerist reversal he made a drawing of a *Reclining Nude* which is a deliberate imitation of a chiaroscuro woodcut.

Some artists of the 16th century

The first thirty years of the sixteenth century was a period of outstanding technical and stylistic advance in printmaking. The breakthroughs made by Dürer and Marcantonio were closely followed by the extension of etching from a method of decorating metal to a means of printmaking; it was not until the mid eighteenth century that the technical range of printmaking was again significantly extended. An open-minded mentality towards the possibilities of the print, characteristic of the sixteenth century, is the factor that links the three artists grouped on this page, whose work is otherwise so dissimilar. Giulio Campagnola was a Venetian painter who was strongly influenced by the work of Giorgione. The remarkable dotted manner of

◁ Urs Graf (1485–1529):
Standard Bearer of Bern, 1527.
White-line woodcut. (193 × 108 mm.)

Giulio Campagnola (1482–after 1514):
Christ and the Woman of Samaria.
Engraving. (130 × 185 mm.)

LE CONSEIL mis en effect, sur la prinse de la Licorne.

Jean Duvet (1485–after 1561):
The Capture of the Unicorn,
plate 4 of the *Unicorn* series, c. 1560.
Engraving. (230 × 355 mm.)

engraving with flicks of the burin which he invented
is a successful graphic equivalent to the *sfumato* of
Giorgionesque paintings. Urs Graf of Basle, who practised as mercenary and artist with equal success,
turned the tradition of woodcut inside out by designing
in white lines cut into a black field. In this he had as
few successors as Campagnola had in his stipple technique. The third of our artists, Jean Duvet, who
worked mainly in Langres and Dijon, was the exact
contemporary of the other two. He was, however,
trained not as a painter or draughtsman, but as a
goldsmith. His most famous engravings are a set of
the *Apocalypse,* which shows an extreme mystic agi-
tation quite unlike Dürer's clarity, and a set of six on
the theme of the unicorn. A superficially crude technique of short jabs of the burin is used to build up an
all-over density of surface in a design that evokes the
chivalric world of late mediaeval tapestries.

Goltzius and mannerist engraving

Hendrick Goltzius (1558–1617):
Judith with the Head of Holofernes,
after Bartholomeus Spranger, c. 1585.
Engraving. (Diameter without inscription 147 mm.)

With Hendrick Goltzius and the school of mannerist engraving which he founded in Haarlem, we see the triumph of the line-engraving and an example whose importance for the future course of reproductive printmaking can hardly be exaggerated. As a child he was apprenticed to the engraver Dirck Volkertsz Coornhert, much of whose output was after specially prepared drawings by his friend and fellow humanist Maerten van Heemskerck. In this studio Goltzius would have become accustomed to the knotted flesh and awkward forms of contemporary Netherlandish art. It is not therefore surprising that he was enormously impressed by the drawings of Bartholomeus Spranger which Carel van Mander showed him in the early 1580s. Spranger was an Antwerp artist, who had travelled over much of Europe before becoming court painter to Rudolf II in Prague in 1581. His wide visual culture had led him to develop an extreme form of mannerism, which imposes an overall elegance on bizarre distortions of form and scale. *Judith with the Head of Holofernes* is among the first of Goltzius' engravings after Spranger, and we can see the delight with which he rose to meet the challenge of translating a wash drawing into a network of lines. Examine, for example, Judith's neck: it is composed of two series of intersecting curved parallel lines, each of which thickens towards the centre and tapers away at the ends. But the wonder of these lines is that neither series by itself defines anything; the lines that in fact model the contour of the neck and the cheek are an optical effect formed by the moiré of the intersecting curves. The very technical brilliance became part of the meaning of prints such as these, and the logical development was to publish unfinished prints so that the working should be even more obvious.

The *Adoration of the Shepherds* forces us to admire rather than to take for granted the artist's skill at summoning form out of a void. However, by this stage Goltzius was growing tired with engraving and had moved on to demonstrate his virtuosity in other fields. The *Young Man* of 1614 is entirely drawn with the pen, but deliberately denies the resources of drawing by confining all the work to the manner of an engraving. How should we explain this unremitting insistence on technical skill, a bravura found equally in his pastiches of the manner of other engravers and his revival of the chiaroscuro woodcut? Certainly it was part of contemporary mannerist aesthetics, but we might also interpret it as Goltzius' refusal to accept the severe burns which he received on his right hand in childhood and which left him a cripple for life.

Hendrick Goltzius (1558–1617):

The Adoration of the Shepherds. ▷
Engraving, 1st state. (203 × 151 mm.)

A Young Man Holding a Skull and a Tulip, 1614.
Pen and brown ink. (460 × 354 mm.)

Quid Simon huic tentas onerj succedere, solus
Ille potest tantæ pondera ferre crúcis

Callot

Jacques Callot (1592–1635):

Christ Carrying the Cross,   △
from *The Great Passion*, c. 1618–1625.
Etching. (116 × 215 mm.)

The Two Pantaloons, c. 1616.
Etching. (94 × 142 mm.)

Jacques Callot is a figure of great significance in any history of printmaking. He practised solely as a printmaker; he never made any paintings, while his drawings, magnificent though they are, are usually preparatory to his prints and certainly were never widely known. In most artists such a specialization in a minor genre has been an insuperable bar to recognition, but Callot has always been accepted as one of the outstanding artists of his time. He worked for four different courts in three different countries, yet remained tied to none of them; his biography was included among the lives written by two of the leading contemporary art-historians, Baldinucci and Félibien; and after his death he retained a fanatical band of admirers. The collector of Callot already figures in La Bruyère's book, *Les Caractères,* published in 1688.

How did Callot achieve such fame? He was born in Nancy, and his father was a herald-at-arms to the Dukes of Lorraine, who in 1608 played an important part in the elaborate arrangements for the funeral of Charles III. This early introduction to the ritual world of the court, in which events have their significance heightened by ceremonial, left its mark on all Callot's subsequent work. Around 1608 he left for Italy to become an artist, and soon gravitated to Florence where the Medici held the most spectacular court of the time. *The Parade in the Amphitheatre,* or more precisely *The Entry of the Carriages of Africa and Asia,* is one of four etchings by him made to illustrate a book by Andrea Salvadori, *Guerra d'Amore,* which describes a ballet entitled "The War of Love," performed in Florence, in the Piazza Santa Croce, before the Grand Duke Cosimo II at carnival time in February 1616 (1615 by the Florentine calendar, the new year beginning on 25 March). The print purports to be an accurate description of the event: the façade of Santa Croce and the houses on the south side of the square are quite recognizable, and there is no reason to doubt the depiction of the temporary wooden structure erected to hold the spectators. But can we say the same of the scarecrow performers in the ring, or the masked pantaloons, dwarfs and jesters that improbably occupy the foreground? The theatre is set within another theatre into which the darkly shaded bystanders at the right and left foreground, like us, are looking.

The device of turning the whole world into a stage was Callot's great invention. It enabled him to be unexpected, amusing and profound. In the centre foreground of the *Parade* are two figures in contrapposto, a motif too good to waste and which reappears in reverse in the *Two Pantaloons*. Their crazy dance takes place on a high stage in the foreground, while behind them, in a reversal of the usual position, are the spectators, a group of fashionably dressed gallants with their ladies. But maybe the spectators are the true subject of the print, and, as we look, we notice the deliberate parallel that Callot has established between the contortions of the clowns and the scarcely less mannered poses of the courtiers. Callot's use of his device was wonderfully fertile. *Christ Carrying the Cross*, one of a set of Passion subjects, appears to be a tableau frozen on a stage. The artificiality of the setting, the toylike figures and the graceful elegance of the poses produce a detached aesthetic pleasure. But with a sudden shock, we realize the real import and horror of the scene that we are witnessing. Callot has startled us from our complacency, and produced a true dramatic *frisson*.

Jacques Callot (1592–1635):
The Parade in the Amphitheatre:
The Entry of the Carriages of Africa and Asia,
plate 2 of the *Guerra d'Amore* series, 1616.
Etching. (227 × 303 mm.)

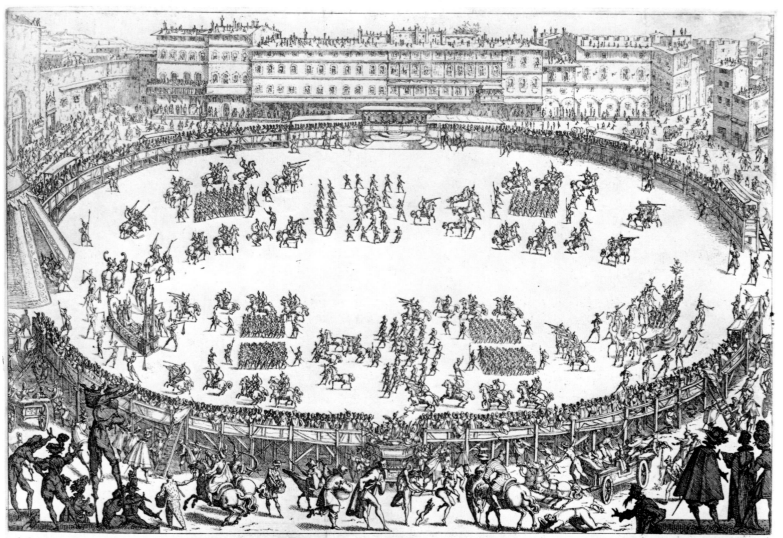

MOSTRA DELLA GVERRA D'AMORE FESTA DEL SER.ᴹᴼ GRAN DVCA DI TOSCANA FATTA L'ANNO 1615

Giovanni Benedetto Castiglione of Genoa is a minor, although distinguished, figure in the history of Italian art. Students of his paintings have rapidly tired of his limited range of subject matter, which to the jaded eye can appear to consist solely of endless lines of animals introduced into every manner of improbable context. The redeeming feature of the paintings is their brilliance in the handling of paint, and the delight that Castiglione took in this may have encouraged him to try out other effects in works on paper. His achievements in this field were of a much higher order, combining extreme technical originality with iconographic novelties of a most interesting kind.

Most seventeenth-century Italian artists, subscribing to the traditional primacy attributed to *disegno,* regarded drawing as a preparation and aid to painting. Castiglione was more interested in using drawings as works of art in themselves, and the Windsor *Christ on the Cross* is an excellent example of this type. The weeping women and the angels are to be expected, but a strange and disturbing element is added by the group of old men making anguished gestures. It has been suggested that they represented the penitence of the Jews for the death of Christ, but no one really knows, and it is quite possible that Castiglione did not either. The drawing is executed in coloured thinned oil-paints, an unusual medium that Castiglione made very much his own.

It was probably his liking for it that led to his most remarkable feat, the invention of the monotype; in this technique he had no successors for over two hundred years. The design is drawn on a flat surface before being printed on to paper, thus allowing pigment or printing ink to be handled in the most fluid way possible. It encourages negative drawing—scraping highlights out of a black background—and Castiglione at once sought suitably tenebrist subjects.

*The Finding of the Remains of SS. Peter and Paul in
a Catacomb* is one of these, a weird theme, hardly ever
portrayed before. In Castiglione's imagination it becomes haunted, with spectral figures shuffling through
deep caverns, their forms shining out from the black
in scribbled lines. But what is most impressive is that
he did not stop here. His realization of how the medium
affected the meaning led him to recreate the scene in
a different medium, etching, and he was rewarded
with a quite different result. The rapid hatchings of
the etching needle define a warm grotto with rich
foliage in which the saints are revealed to a crowd of
startled onlookers. The feeling of oppression is replaced by one of comfort and optimism.

Giovanni Benedetto Castiglione (c. 1610–c. 1665):

◁ Christ on the Cross.
Oil sketch on paper. (264 × 396 mm.)

The Finding of the Remains of SS. Peter ▷
and Paul in a Catacomb, late 1640s.
Etching. (288 × 203 mm.)

The Finding of the Remains of SS. Peter ▽
and Paul in a Catacomb, late 1640s.
Monotype. (297 × 205 mm.)

Hercules Segers

Hercules Segers may not be the greatest of all printmakers, but he was unquestionably the most consistently inventive artist to handle the medium before the twentieth century. In 1678 the historian Samuel van Hoogstraten wrote that Segers had "printed painting," and this awkward expression captures the essence of his originality rather well. He did not see printmaking as a means to multiply an identical image; the etched plate was rather a theme from which to wring as many variations as possible. Of the 183 impressions now known from fifty-four plates, hardly any two are identical. Most striking is their use of colour, of coloured inks, coloured papers and a liberal application of hand-colouring to complete the image. He printed on unusual surfaces, he trimmed impressions, he devised new ways of etching. And what astonishing images emerged! Segers' world is of unparalleled bleakness, a landscape which belongs to the moon more than the earth. Huge piles of rock plunge into vast abysses; the barren reticulations hold no vegetation while trees are reduced to broken stumps. Occasionally a plateau discloses a hamlet and a few fields, but they lie abandoned in their total solitude. The colours add their own unnatural hues. *The Mossy Tree* is perhaps the culminating image of Segers' art, an extraordinary apparition, unlike anything since Altdorfer, looming out of a ground mist. The clinging tentacles fall everywhere, completely obliterating the identity of the tree. In fact there is no tree at all; the tentacles hang but there are no branches or trunk to support them.

Rembrandt

Rembrandt (1606–1669):
The Entombment, c. 1654.
Etching, with drypoint and engraving. (211 × 161 mm.)

◁ 1st state (clean-wiped).

2nd state (with heavy plate tone). ▷

4th state (clean-wiped but heightened △
with white body colour).

The quality of Rembrandt's greatness as a printmaker cannot be described precisely; his talent is too multifarious, individual and surprising. But if we were forced to specify one central virtue, it must be the imaginative depth with which he nurtured his images. Segers had transformed and re-imagined each impression he printed; Rembrandt nursed his creations and in each successive state and impression explored a further aspect of what lay dormant within a plate. *The Entombment of Christ* allows us to follow the process as well as any other example. The first state defines the image in etched lines bitten to a single depth, applied sometimes to define contour, more often grouped in tight masses of parallel or hatched shading that at once create light, depth and a wonderfully dramatic energy. The flickering light and shadow must have suggested the transformation that occurs in the second state; the whole plate was reworked in etching and drypoint and so darkened that only a few forms emerged from the blackness. So intent was Rembrandt on deepening the shadow that he printed impressions on a yellow Japanese paper and left thick films of ink on the surface in the wiping, effects which are seen clearly in the colour reproduction. These extremes of darkness exhausted, Rembrandt reworked the plate further to create a looming arch in the background by burnishing an arc above the two skulls. Clean-wiped impressions of the fourth state show a glaring intensity of light; others are printed with surface tone to mellow the contrasts. The impression reproduced here resolves the two polarities in an extraordinary way: it is printed with a heavy surface tone, but highlights are touched in with white body colour.

AMELIA ELISABETHA, D.G. HASSIÆ LANDGRAVIA etc.
COMITISSA HANOVIÆ MVNTZENB:

Illustrissimo ac Cel. Pr ac Dño Dño WILHELMO VI. D.G. HASSIÆ LANDGR. etc. filius Serenissimæ Matris et Incomparabilis Heroinæ effigiem ad vivum a se genuinè depictam novoq. jam sculpturæ modo expressam dedicat conse crat. S. 18 Ao Dni cIↃIↃcXLIII.

The inventor of mezzotint was not an artist, but a soldier, a certain Ludwig von Siegen. The court of Hesse to which he was attached had little, if any, concern for the visual arts, but there was a strong interest in the sciences, and it is in this context that Siegen's invention must be placed. The letter in which he dedicated to the Landgrave of Hesse the portrait of his mother, Amelia Elizabeth, insists purely on the technical novelty of the process, and does not mention any particular qualities that can be associated with it. The aura of the arcane and scientific long clung to mezzotint. Many of Siegen's successors, who further developed the technique, were leading figures in seventeeth-century intellectual life: Prince Rupert of the Rhine, and members of the Royal Society like John Evelyn, who wrote a treatise on the medium, or Sir Christopher Wren, who made a few experimental prints himself.

◁ Ludwig von Siegen (1609–after 1676):
Amelia Elizabeth, Landgravine of Hesse, 1643.
Mezzotint. (440 × 327 mm.)

Wallerant Vaillant (1623–1677):
Self-Portrait.
Mezzotint. (231 × 169 mm.)

The uses
of mezzotint

Jacques Vaillant (1631–1691):
Fête Champêtre, after Giorgione.
Mezzotint. (276 × 370 mm.)

But as the century wore on, a certain embarrassment became evident. All agreed that a wonderful new process had been invented, but no one had really worked out what it could be used for. Siegen had no interest in this matter; his prints occupy a very low position from an artistic point of view, and his choice of a portrait as the subject for his first print was a simple response to the demands of patronage. His successors tried to apply mezzotint to a wide range of subjects, but with very mixed results. The problem can be followed in the two prints reproduced here by Wallerant Vaillant, the best of Prince Rupert's pupils, and his brother Jacques. Mezzotint is a process that reveals form by scraping down highlights on a plate prepared to print a uniform black. Accordingly it is an entirely tonal process which does not allow defined lines. The limited range of scraped black cannot convey a wide variety of colour and texture, such as engravers had learnt to produce from their networks of lines. Jacques' print is an attempt at one of the most important categories of printmaking, the reproductive print, and the result is a failure: the complexity of the sky, trees and foliage of the background was too much and he was reduced to a wild impressionism. But with a simpler subject like the *Self-Portrait* such despair was unnecessary. The rich burr of the plate gives the rich black for the tunic; considerable scraping reveals the highlights and contours of the face, while the background is neutral but enlivened by streaks. Since in this way the beauties of the mezzotint are emphasized and the limitations avoided, it is not surprising that the tradition was deflected into the paths of the portrait print, with remarkably few exceptions.

Hogarth the moralist

William Hogarth (1697–1764):

She is ensnared by a procuress,
plate 1 from *A Harlot's Progress*, 1732.
Etching and engraving. (284 × 364 mm.) △

She expires while the doctors are disputing,
plate 5 from *A Harlot's Progress*, 1732.
Etching and engraving. (300 × 364 mm.)

Hogarth was essentially a moralist; the central impulse behind his art was the desire to improve and reform people. He also wished to be recognized as a serious painter, and was very concerned that he himself should reap the entire financial rewards of his success. This possibly typical combination of eighteenth-century English qualities led Hogarth to some remarkable innovations in print making and print publishing. His training as an engraver and his early success as a painter of small conversation pieces, as he said, turned his thoughts "to a still more new way of proceeding, viz painting and engraving modern moral subject a field unbroke up in any country or any age." Hogarth's claim to originality here is quite justified. The first such series, *A Harlot's Progress*, was published in 1732. The six prints tell the story of Mary Hackabout, from her first arrival in London (plate 1) to her death (plate 5) and funeral. Interpretation of the events does not depend on a written key, but on the clues provided in the prints themselves, and this forces the viewer to analyse intently all the tiny details that elucidate the meaning of the scene.

It is not our intention here to narrate how Hogarth's fury at his designs being pirated led to the first artistic copyright act in 1735, an event of enormous consequence, not just for the history of printmaking but also for painting. Rather we wish to insist on the sophistication and flexibility of Hogarth's attitude towards engraving. He did not feel that anything would do. He engraved *A Harlot's Progress* himself because he was dissatisfied with the work of assistants he had intended to use. Standards were deliberately lowered to keep down the price of the *Four Stages of Cruelty*, and he tried the experiment of issuing two of the plates as woodcuts: as he explained, "neither great correctness of drawing or fine engraving were at all necessary but on the contrary would set the price of them out of the reach of those for whom they were chiefly intended." The opposite procedure was adopted in *Marriage à la Mode*. which was intended as a satire on foreign manners. Plate 4, of the wife's levée, is an obvious parody of a French painting, from the Frenchified characters and interior to the circular compositional format beloved of French painters. As a series too *Marriage à la Mode* was intended as a parody of one of the sets of magnificent engravings then coming out of France, such as the series of times of the day after artists like Lancret. So in order to make the satire fit, he employed some of the leading French engravers then working in England, Scotin, Baron and Ravenet, to give the prints the immaculate finish of the finest French engravings.

William Hogarth (1697–1764):
The Wife's Levée, plate 4 from
Marriage à la Mode, 1745.
Etching and engraving. (352 × 448 mm.)

The search
for the facsimile

François Boucher (1703–1770):

Two Nereids and a Triton,
study for *The Rising of the Sun*.
Red and black chalk heightened with
white on brownish paper. (291 × 469 mm.)

The Rising of the Sun (detail), 1753.
Oil on canvas.

The eighteenth century in France brings to the fore an aspect of printmaking that otherwise finds little place in this section, for it was in this century that the skills of reproducing works of all kinds as prints reached their highest pitch of perfection. The public of the period gave an unprejudiced acceptance to the works of the crafts, and the sureness of taste allied to the catholicity of interest led to one of the great ages of the decorative arts. Paintings, drawings and prints were drawn in to this movement, and in their turn became part of the art of interior decoration. Prints, perhaps for the first time, were intended to be framed, not stored in a portfolio, and a sumptuous perfection of finish and presentation became essential.

The illustrations give an insight into one aspect of the closely interdependent relationship between the various arts in the period. The two enormous paintings of *The Rising* and *The Setting of the Sun* (1753, both now in the Wallace Collection) were commissioned from Boucher in order to be turned into tapestries at the Gobelins; this was their primary function. But the

164

paintings were not considered dispensable once the tapestries had been finished, for Mme de Pompadour begged them from Louis XV for herself. The same is true of the drawings that Boucher had made as preparatory studies. The group in the lower right corner of *The Rising of the Sun* is developed in a drawing in the Louvre, although numerous changes were made when transferring it to the painting. Now there can be no doubt that Boucher regarded drawings such as this as works in their own right; in 1745 he had been the first to exhibit some of them at the Salon. This explains its tidy, finished appearance, and its immediate disappearance into a private collection. Clearly therefore there would also be a demand for prints of such drawings, but none of the traditional techniques could match the texture of chalk. This encouraged the experimenters, and in 1757 Jean-Charles François invented the solution, the so-called "crayon manner," which in turn was adapted for colour printing a few years later by Louis-Marin Bonnet. Unfortunately, Demarteau engraved our drawing too early to make use of this, and thus we find a final twist in the fortunes of the composition. Crayon manner could not match the colours or finish of the drawing as well as it could its underlying chalk structure. Demarteau therefore had to rethink it in terms of his medium. Accordingly he decided to introduce an element of the sketchiness of a more deliberately compositional drawing by adding the two incomplete heads to the background.

Gilles Demarteau (1729–1776):
Two Nereids and a Triton,
after Boucher, after 1761.
Engraving in the crayon manner.
(384 × 530 mm.)

Giambattista Tiepolo (1696–1770):

Magician and Figure Group Looking
at a Snake, from the *Scherzi di
Fantasia* series.
Etching. (225 × 175 mm.)

Two Magicians with Punchinello,
from the *Scherzi di Fantasia* series.
Etching. (223 × 184 mm.) ▷
Reproduction slightly enlarged.

For all their variety, the great Venetian prints of the eighteenth century share two formal characteristics, the use of a pure etched line and an avoidance of cross-hatching, and one material factor, a wonderfully thick and creamy paper against which etched lines stand out in a shimmering relief. Out of these ingredients Giambattista Tiepolo made something quite fresh in the two series entitled *Capricci* and *Scherzi* which were probably all made in the early 1740s. The simplicity of means is striking: he used only one width of needle and one depth of biting, which led Focillon to call him a "half-printmaker." But Tiepolo's self-restriction was quite deliberate. When expertly printed, the areas of closely paralleled lines hold solid masses of ink which sparkle with light against the warm paper. One almost feels that the simplicity of the technique suggests the subjects. Free play is given to the needle as it dances over the copper and the artist himself watches to see the world his fantasy uncovers of frozen, inconsequential tableaux of magicians, punchinelli, youths, maidens, snakes and owls, all posed out of doors in full light of day with lines of heads of enthralled onlookers. There is much evidence for the fascination of Tiepolo's contemporaries with witchcraft and suchlike, but here we have magic as seen by the age of the enlightenment, as something interesting and curious. It was left to Goya in the next great series of *Caprichos* to make it terrifying and threatening.

Venice and the 18th century: Canaletto and Piranesi

Canaletto (1697–1768):
The Tower of Malghera, from
the series *Vedute: altre prese
dai luoghi, altre ideate.*
Etching. (290 × 424 mm.)

All of Canaletto's etchings, with only three exceptions, were published in a single series with a dedication to his patron, Consul Joseph Smith. One is dated 1741 and they must all have been made around that year. The title, *Vedute: altre prese dai luoghi, altre ideate,* gives an idea of the wide variety of types that could be classified as "Vedute," from the strictly topographical to the entirely imaginary. The most appealing perhaps are those, like the *Torre di Malghera,* a fifteenth-century watch-tower in the lagoons, which turn real buildings into elements in imaginative compositions. As a whole the series gives the impression of being deliberately chosen to represent the range of Canaletto's repertoire. Their technique represents a development from Tiepolo's single line. Canaletto also avoids cross-hatching, but bites to different depths by stopping-out passages and rebiting through a second ground after printing a trial proof. In consequence his range of tone is much wider. Sudden strengthenings of line in the water and the massing of shading into blocks in the sky set the scene alive with a dancing vitality. Yet the strongest impression is of sunlit tranquillity; the scene is ordered and all elements of chance removed. This is no accident as the surviving preparatory drawings show how carefully each composition was thought out in advance.

With Piranesi, whose earliest prints were also made around 1743, we meet a genius of an entirely different order. The overflowing abundance of his imagination and his constant productivity led to an œuvre of over one thousand plates. Despite his ambition to be an architect, he was in effect a professional printmaker and made his living from his publications. This constant familiarity with the medium led him to treat the etched plate with a carefree recklessness in the certainty that whatever he did would work. He scarcely ever bothered to make drawings of more than the rudiments of a composition. So plates were reworked again and again, often over many years, and lines bitten so deeply that the plates became so ravaged and devastated that only extreme skill on the printer's part could make the image legible. On the other hand he could also use the most delicate touch in fine detail: in certain passages of the *Baths of Caracalla* each individual brick is drawn with a double contour. The excitement in Piranesi's prints reaches its greatest heights when his penchant for theatrical fantasy is put in the service of his love of antiquity. In his earliest prints the fantasy is given free reign. Works such as the four *Capricci* show a rather chaotic exuberance, a diapason of Piranesian motifs, while the *Carceri* explore the extremes of dramatic architecture. But all these can, I think, be seen as preparations for the antiquarian works and the *Vedute di Roma,* which do something even more remarkable. They convey in immediate visual form Piranesi's passionate love of ancient Rome by investing its ruins with such overwhelming grandeur that we too can only feel like the scarecrows that populate the views and wave our arms around in mute admiration.

Giovanni Battista Piranesi (1720–1778):
The Baths of Caracalla, Rome ("Rovine del
Sisto, o sia della gran sala delle Terme
Antoniniane"), from the *Vedute di Roma* series, c. 1765.
Etching. (425 × 655 mm.)

Francisco Goya (1746–1828):

Maid Combing a Young Lady's Hair,
preparatory drawing for plate 31
of *Los Caprichos*, 1796–1797.
Pen, brush and Indian ink wash.
(237 × 145 mm.) △

Ruega por ella (She prays for her),
plate 31 of *Los Caprichos*, 1796–1797.
Etching and burnished aquatint with
drypoint and engraving. (205 × 150 mm.)

Of all the great artists of Europe, Goya is perhaps the one whose greatness is most closely
bound up with his prints. Remove the *Caprichos*, the *Disasters of War* and *Los Disparates,* and
Goya's most distinctive and original achievements are lost. The stages by which he arrives at
these results are fascinating, and repay close attention : rarely can one approach so closely to
the springs of artistic creativity. Goya's early career before the age of nearly fifty was relatively
provincial and undistinguished. It took a curious juxtaposition of events in the 1790s to turn him
into an artist of European stature : the illness in 1792 which left him deaf, the political ferment
of the widening French revolution, and his encounter with the Duchess of Alba in the summer
of 1796. When staying with her, he began a small album of intimate drawings of women of the
household. So far as we know, this was the first time that he had seriously made any drawings,
and the excitement he found in the new medium and washes of ink is obvious.

Thus inspired, he began on his return to Madrid a second album (the " Madrid Album "). The
medium is the same, but the subjects have changed : no longer sketches from life, but imaginative
compositions with vignettes of everyday events, especially of the comedy of the sexes. It is a
moving experience to follow the pages in order, and watch as the subjects continually grow in
complexity and psychological profundity. Elements of satire creep in, then suddenly we have lost
contact with the everyday world and enter a grim parody of it, populated by witches,
monkeys and freaks. Simultaneously Goya begins to add titles to point the moral, and the
images assume a rich universality. Goya's previous experience of printmaking had been
restricted, but he realized that his newly invented images could readily be translated into prints
which could reach a wide public. The outcome was the set of eighty *Caprichos* published in 1799,
and intended (in Goya's words) " to banish harmful vulgar beliefs and to perpetuate the solid
testimony of truth."

Plate 31 of the *Caprichos* is a good example of the way in which Goya expanded the meaning of his images. The drawing is on one of the earlier pages of the Madrid album, and shows a maid combing the hair of a young woman ; a certain erotic tension is implied by her knowing look and exposed leg. In the print a new element is added in the old crone, immediately recognizable as a procuress. Underneath is an ambiguous comment : " Ruega por ella." If understood as an imperative, it is addressed to the viewer : " Pray for her." If, however, it is the present indicative, " she prays for her," the prayer comes from the procuress. Either prayer, of course, would be to precisely the opposite intent. The medium adds a sinister cast, for the girl is picked out in white against a dense black background, where aquatint provides an equivalent for the ink wash of the drawing. Goya's greatest images all have this rich and inexhaustible suggestiveness. The so-called *Colossus,* an aquatinted plate out of which the highlights have been scraped, needs no title at all. We are left to make what we like of it.

Goya

Francisco Goya (1746–1828):
The Colossus, c. 1810–1817.
Scraped aquatint. (285 × 210 mm.)

Blake

Blake is one of the very few artists who is equally famous as a poet, and these two aspects of his creativity are inextricably linked. His father was a London hosier, and at an early age Blake was apprenticed to a professional reproductive engraver. To someone of his bursting imagination, however, line-engraving meant slavery to the conceptions of another artist; and so, when he came to produce illustrated editions of his poems, he invented a new process of relief etching: design and letters were left in relief on a metal plate while the background was etched away. *Songs of Innocence* of 1789 was one of the first of his books, and the deceptively simple ditties mask a serious message of optimism about human potentialities which was linked to the revolutionary events in France. Blake's own account of his process shows the significance with which he invested his medium: "But first the notion that man has a body distinct from his soul is to be expunged; this I shall do by printing in

William Blake (1757–1827):

◁ △ Bearded Man Squatting in Fetters Lamenting, from *The First Book of Urizen*, 1794. Relief etching, colour-printed. (155 × 102 mm.)

The Little Boy Lost, and The Little Boy Found, from *Songs of Innocence*, 1789. Relief etchings, tinted with watercolour. (116 × 73 mm. and 115 × 73 mm.)

the infernal method by corrosives... melting apparent surfaces away and displaying the infinite which was hid."

The early copies of the *Songs of Innocence* are hand-coloured ; by the mid 1790s he had progressed to inking the plates in different colours before printing. The change from transparent watercolour washes to the rich opaque colours seen in the *Book of Urizen* matches Blake's increasing pessimism, and his retreat into a world created in his own imagination, for he seems to have associated colour printing, through its lack of clear definition, with Chaos and the world after the Fall. Symbolic figures and abstract ideas gain immediacy through a visual presentation, and the *Bearded Man Squatting in Fetters* reproduced here has an inarticulate potency that immediately recalls Goya's *Colossus*. It is extraordinary how these two artists, virtual contemporaries who can never have heard of each other, could arrive at such similar symbols of suppressed or potential power. Blake, however, never had the fundamental humanism that makes Goya such a universal artist, and his abstruse symbolism led him into arcane regions where few have cared to follow him. It was therefore a lucky chance that he was commissioned by a friend at the end of his life to illustrate Dante : the watercolours and seven engravings that survive can justifiably be called the greatest illustrations ever made. The stupendous visual images of Blake at last find a worthy and easily accessible parallel in the huge theme of Dante, and, in recognition, he abandoned his " infernal method " in favour of the classic simplicity of line engraving, but handled not as he had been trained but in the way that Dürer and his contemporaries had handled it.

William Blake (1757–1827):
The Circle of the Falsifiers: Dante and Virgil
Covering their Noses because of the Stench,
illustration for Dante's *Divine Comedy*,
Inferno, Canto XXIX, 1827.
Engraving. (240 × 338 mm.)

Delacroix inv.¹ et Lithog.   Lith. de Villain

Faust.__ Ma belle Demoiselle, oserai-je vous offrir mon bras et vous reconduire chez vous?..

Early lithography

The early history of lithography presents some interesting analogies with the history of mezzotint. As a process it made an even sharper break with existing traditions because it uses entirely different materials—stone rather than copper or wood—and a completely new manner of printing which depends on the chemical antipathy between grease and water. Its origins also lay outside the field of the fine arts. Senefelder, who invented it in 1798, was a minor playwright who wished to print his works more cheaply, while his backer, Johann André, was a music publisher. Both men, however, realized at once that the medium allowed artists' drawings to be reproduced indefinitely, and since they had devised ways of printing pen and ink as well as chalk drawings, they confidently invited artists to make use of their invention. Despite this, the early years of lithography ended in failure, and, after looking through the initial productions, it is easy to see why. The artists had drawn on stone in the same way as they would have drawn on paper, and the resulting prints looked precisely like reproductions of drawings—useful for conveying visual information, but of negligible artistic worth. The medium looked completely uninteresting and was promptly dropped by most creative artists.

This probably would have been the end of lithography were it not for its obvious usefulness in commercial printing, in fields such as cartography or music in which typesetting was impossible and engraving very expensive. So publishers kept the medium up, while brilliant technicians developed better materials and methods of drawing and printing. This was the essential technical prerequisite, but the sudden flowering of lithography in the 1820s would never have occurred had not a new generation of artists discovered that drawing on a stone was not the same as drawing on paper. The secret, they realized, was to draw on the stone in such a way that the resulting print brought out to the fullest extent the beauties of the lithographic medium itself. The three lithographs here show how rapidly this realization spread around Europe. It is perhaps predictable that the tireless Goya would turn to it, and the French Romantics, who liked the appearance of autographic spontaneity. More surprising is the marvellous series of the " Seven landscapes of the seven days of the week " by Ferdinand Olivier, who was closely associated with the Nazarenes. He made preparatory drawings intending to etch them, but turned to lithography instead. His use of a tint stone suffices to prove that he intended to create parallels and not facsimiles for his drawings : and the lithographs indeed stand as works of art in their own right.

◁ Eugène Delacroix (1798–1863):
Faust Seducing Margaret,
illustration for Goethe's *Faust*, 1828.
Lithograph. (262 × 208 mm.)

Ferdinand Olivier (1785–1841):
Monday: The Rosenecker Garden in Salzburg,
plate 1 of the series *Seven Landscapes
of the Seven Days of the Week*, 1823.
Lithograph. (196 × 273 mm.)

Montag.

Meryon

Charles Meryon (1821–1868):

◁ The Church of Saint-Etienne-du-Mont, Paris, 1852.
Etching. (247 × 127 mm.)

The Morgue, Paris, 1854. ▷
Etching. (232 × 207 mm.)

The nineteenth century challenged the art of the print in almost every respect. The competition from newly invented processes was not confined to lithography: photography and photo-mechanical technology set the very existence of the hand-crafted print in doubt. Social changes made traditional categories of production obsolete, and the far-reaching transformations in the function and iconography of painting raised the question of how printmaking should react. It was obvious that no single solution would meet the challenges, and indeed they have not been fully answered to the present day. The importance of Meryon was that he was the first to demonstrate that even in the circumstances of the mid-nineteenth century etching could offer something entirely new and distinctive. Admittedly he cannot be put in the first rank of printmakers for he had but a single voice, but his views of Paris do have an undeniable originality and exerted an enormous influence. Romantic painters and lithographers had long been fascinated by town views and buildings, but their eyes had been fixed solely on the picturesque and mediaeval. Meryon was not an antiquarian, and was not really interested in the individual monument; his concern was the urban mass and the menace that is inherent in huge accumulations of brick and stone. In his prints Paris is a brooding monster, the pitiless spectator of human misery and madness. Their reverberations have lasted into the present century. The American Edward Hopper generalized Meryon's insights in a series of what, in my opinion, are even greater prints. His subject was not the threat of the buildings themselves, but the desolation of the urban environment of which the buildings become the symbols.

Edward Hopper (1882–1967):
Night in the Park,
New York, 1921.
Etching. (173 × 210 mm.)

Gauguin

Paul Gauguin (1848–1903):

Three Tahitian Idols, after 1891.
Woodcut. (Motif 200 × 170 mm.)

The Universe is created, 1894–1895.
Woodcut printed in black on
coloured paper. (205 × 355 mm.)

"I would say that what Gauguin is attempting to do today will bring about nothing less than a revolution tomorrow in the arts of printmaking and water-colour." So wrote Charles Morice in a review of an exhibition in 1894, and subsequent developments have proved him right. So wide-ranging were Gauguin's innovations that it is still very difficult to grasp all their implications. The woodcut and monotype lay at the centre of his achievement in printmaking, and its essence was a deliberate impurity – a constant struggle to contaminate one procedure with another, and anni-hilate the conventional distinctions between them. Thus in the same way as he converted one of his disused woodblocks into a piece of low-relief sculp-ture, he cut beautifully detailed blocks and proceeded to deny all the fine points by a deliberately gauche printing. He had to start from conventional artistic

Paul Gauguin (1848–1903):
Two Marquesans, c. 1902.
Traced monotype, printed in
black, retouched slightly with
yellow-green, white, blue, grey,
and brown. (372 × 325 mm.)

practices, but his struggles to deny their traditional application and appearance and subvert them to express the pagan iconography of his Polynesian world were heroic. The three reproductions illustrate his assault on the print. The simplest is the scene with the three Tahitian idols, which shows how he cut the block in a manner half-way between that of a woodcut and a wood engraving. The impression of *The Universe is created* is printed far more dramatically. Gauguin must have laid the rose-coloured paper down on the inked block, and then rubbed the verso with some blunt instrument to transfer the ink in vigorous scribbled lines, thickly in the foreground and lightly in the background. The design, in effect, comes as much from the printing as from the block. This led to the traced monotype, such as the *Two Marquesans.* Here the inked surface on which the paper is laid bears no design at all; the image is created by drawing on the verso.

Munch

Edvard Munch (1863–1944):

◁ Madonna, 1895.
Hand-coloured lithograph,
1st state. (600 × 440 mm.)

The Kiss, fourth version, 1902.
Colour woodcut. (447 × 447 mm.)

Although both Gauguin and Munch are sometimes loosely classified as symbolists, the content of their art is very different. Gauguin's primitive mythology risks being inscrutable, whereas Munch's images of psychological torture are raw and immediate; on the other hand, Gauguin, even at his most mysterious, is always interesting, while Munch, when the emotional content has drained away, becomes bombastic and empty. This reflects itself in their prints: Gauguin is always searching for a new way to create a new image, while Munch's best prints restate the themes of his paintings. This might suggest that they are merely reproductions, but curiously the opposite is the case. Munch's paintings are often superficially unattractive and the impact is occasionally diluted by a muddy surface; the print, coming later, distils the essence of the image and presents it with a conclusive immediacy of effect. The *Madonna* is a clear example: the painting has an ill-defined image of the swooning woman; the lithograph is more elaborate and adds the frame containing spermatozoa and a malevolent embryo. The figure and colour are tauter—black on green paper—and each impression (of the first edition) is handcoloured in red and blue. *The Kiss* is even more impressive. We can trace its development through numerous painted and etched versions before it became a woodcut. But it is the woodcut that is the definitive statement. Two blocks only are used: one unworked plank of pine printed in grey to provide the background, and one sawn-out shape overprinted in black to define the figures. The means are possibly the simplest ever employed in a woodcut, but the effect is perhaps the most haunting.

Ernst Ludwig Kirchner (1880–1938):

Nude Girl on a Sofa, 1905. △
Woodcut. (84 × 100 mm.)

Women on Potsdamer Platz, Berlin, 1914.
Woodcut. (520 × 375 mm.)

The last decade of the nineteenth century and the first fourteen years of the present century saw the most astonishing transformation in the visual arts. In the field of the print the two great pioneers were Gauguin and Munch; the technical centre of their achievement, as we have seen, was the resuscitation of the woodcut after centuries of neglect, and its reinstatement as the most important vehicle of contemporary printed expression. The validity of this conclusion was most forcibly stated by the German Expressionists, whose woodcuts are often as significant as their paintings, and almost invariably more exciting than their drypoints or lithographs. But the curious feature of the Expressionist woodcut is how long it took to develop and how it started from a position diametrically opposed to that of Gauguin and Munch.

When Kirchner, Heckel and Schmidt-Rottluff came together to form *Die Brücke* in Dresden in 1905, their intention was avowedly revolutionary: "We want to wrest freedom for our gestures and for our lives from the older, comfortably established forces." But to start with they had no idea how to do this. The woodcut reproduced above by Kirchner of 1905 could easily be mistaken for a Vallotton—and Vallotton's woodcuts in their turn were decisively influenced by the black and white penwork of the illustrators and poster designers of the 1890s, led by Aubrey Beardsley, who had created the style not for the woodcut but for the photomechanically produced line-block. Artistically it belongs to a different world from one of his stunning prints of 1914 such as *Women on Potsdamer Platz*. Here the jagged crudeness of the woodcut block has been used to energize the composition and lend it an astonishing expressive intensity. For all its effortless authenticity this result depends on real compositional brilliance: the topsy-turvy perspective of plunging diagonals and inconsistencies of scale, together with the random blots of uncut-away wood, produce that emphasis on the surface plane that is the keynote of so much twentieth-century art.

How had the Expressionists made this spectacular breakthrough? The answer must lie in their discovery of Munch's woodcuts, either at first hand, or through the intermediary work of some lesser-known artist such as Wilhelm Laage, who had exhibited with *Die Brücke* in 1906. A woodcut by Heckel of 1907 shows their earliest adoption of the new ideals–albeit tentative, and with results that are faintly comic. This is still fundamentally a Jugendstil image; the contour is simply broken up in a random way. Heckel and his colleagues still had to discover how they could significantly incorporate into the designs the sense of the wooden block. Emil Nolde's *Dancers* shows the answer; the design is poised, while dynamism is supplied by the block. Although it is difficult to see in reproduction, the white sky and dresses of the dancers are deeply embossed by ridges of wood printed without any ink. Similar sophistications of inking have been used in the background: thickly spread ink reinforces the outlines of the figures, but careful wiping in the open areas has exposed the grain of the wood. So we are led to the paradoxical discovery that prints of such spontaneity of effect demanded the closest attention from the artist in the printing.

Emil Nolde (1867–1956):
Dancers, 1917.
Woodcut. (232 × 310 mm.)

Picasso's "Woman in an Armchair"

1

3

2

Pablo Picasso (1881–1973):
Woman in an Armchair, 1948–1949.
Lithograph on zinc.

1 1st state (10 December 1948).

2 5th state (20 December 1948).

3 2nd transfer state (13 January 1949).

4 Final state.

"He listened carefully, then he did the opposite of what he had been taught, and it worked. He always proceeded like this whatever he did; the way in which he worked the lithographic stone was not merely contrary to custom, but contrary to the most basic rules of the craft." The bewildered admiration of Fernand Mourlot, Picasso's favoured lithographic printer, is matched by that of his critics. Besides his countless paintings, drawings, sculptures and ceramics, Picasso made over 2,000 prints. Their number disguises a disturbing range of quality, but when, during various limited periods, he really concentrated on printmaking, the results were spectacular. The new techniques stimulated his creativity to astonishing feats. None is more interesting than the *Woman in an Armchair* made with Mourlot in 1949. Picasso had intended to make a colour lithograph of the subject

184

for which he drew five colour separations. But, not liking the result, he abandoned the idea and worked on each zinc plate in turn to transform it into a black and white lithograph in its own right. Our illustrations follow the eventful course of the plate originally intended for the red printing. There are ten states in all, but after five states the zinc was getting worn, so the printer simply transferred the image to a new plate on which the process could be continued. It is important to realize that Mourlot was quite correct to say that no one had handled a lithograph like this before. Such transformations had only been achieved in etching, but again there is an important difference. Etchers were used to building up or refining their images. Picasso, however, sought no such resolution; each state is as complete as the other, the order could readily be changed and the series indefinitely extended.

4

III

CONTEMPORARY TRENDS

Richard S. Field

Today's passionate interest in contemporary prints cannot be explained simply as the result of increased demands of the marketplace, a growth of technical facility and innovation, or an expansion of printing establishments.[1] It is my thesis that the extraordinary significance of modern prints during the past twenty years lies not in their size, beauty, or subject-matter, but in their meaning. Rather than merely repeating what had been accomplished in painting or drawing, the contemporary print has become deeply rooted in the examination of the various visual languages by which we represent reality to ourselves. True, art has always been fueled by man's implacable need to define his world, and art has always symbolized man's tentative and ambiguous relationship to that world. Yet, because art held a monopoly on the invention and practice of visual languages, it rarely, until recently, served as a commentator on those languages. But with the rise of other forms of visual imagery, including the photograph and photo-mechanical reproduction, modern painting became concerned with its own forms and choices. More importantly for this study, it slowly recognized the styles of the newer, technological media. As a result, the print—itself a forerunner of technological communications—was sprung loose from its role subordinate to painting or sculpture. By 1960, the printed image became central to artistic creativity because painting had turned to printed languages and had begun to explore their meanings. These symbolic languages embraced a gamut of styles from pure abstraction, through every type of reproduction of reality, to hybrids of the printed word. I am not merely alluding to an already well-documented idea—that art turned to commercial imagery and commercial processes of producing it—but to the fact that the modern print entered into a synergistic relationship with the entirety of its own class of objects: printed information. A great many of the most original and meaningful images of the past twenty years are those that involve the viewer in an active interpretation of what he sees. But unlike the complex symbolism of the Renaissance and Baroque print, the new interpretation is deliberately hinged to ambiguities that summon up conflicting modes of perception and usage. The new prints deliberately play off the formal and sensual against the symbolic and representational. In so doing, they call attention to the conventions, codes, and systems which we blithely accept or act upon as if they were indistinguishable from each other and even consonant with reality. Only recently have we understood that reality is not merely "nature seen through a temperament" but is embedded in our languages and perceptual systems. It is not by chance that Marshall McLuhan's dramatization, *Understanding Media*, made its appearance in 1964; and it is certainly significant that some of McLuhan's major ideas derived from William M. Ivins' pioneering study, *Prints and Visual Communication*, re-issued in 1953.[2] Nor should it be overlooked that in the late 1950s, just as Jasper Johns and Richard Hamilton were involving the spectator in subtle and sophisticated explorations of meaning and style, Ernst Gombrich's vastly influential *Art and Illusion* appeared.[3] All of these works sought to debunk expressionistic and mimetic theories of art in favor of structural, conceptional, and linguistic approaches. Gombrich, like Johns, insisted on the importance of the "beholder's share" in the utilization of visual languages.

The success of recent printmaking owes much to this anti-expressionistic element. The artist withdrew from an exclusive concern with the distillation of personal style through peculiarities of technique, by which I mean either emphatically personal gesture or mechanically achieved surface texture.[4] With the appearance of Andy Warhol's screenprinted paintings and prints of 1962, legions of self-satisfied printmakers were abandoned. Content was freed from technique *("cuisine"),* and style (personal gesture) was pried loose from drawing in the same way that the artist's hand was often replaced by the machine. The task of the artist was further and radically altered by a return to reality through incorporation of illusion-making systems. In other words, the content of prints shifted from personal views of the world to an in-depth examination of systems of representation of that world.

Significant prints of the sixties utilized or paraphrased systems of reproduction that were inextricably linked to specific kinds of objects, on the one hand, and to specific technological processes, on the other. Although many still think that Pop Art consists of flashy quotations from mass media and glorifications of the objects of mass consumption, the deeper meanings of Pop Art explore the substitution of representational symbols for objects. As Johns has often remarked, it is our ability to take one thing for another that is the unceasing source for wonderment. A twenty-five year history of Johns' art could be regarded as documenting a growing skepticism about the security of any rendering of reality; by the end of the sixties, the object and its representation were interchangeable.[5] In the last few years, however, a reaction to such extreme skepticism has set in; it seems clear that many artists have taken refuge in the tangible and physical means of making art, leaving aside all problems of representation. In printmaking, physical technique, in forms both more refined (Minimalism) and more blatant (paperworks), has become subject once more.

In the hands of the innovative painters of the sixties, printmaking became an ideal medium for experimentation because its images, codes, and technical systems were so closely knit. Just as readily available commercial processes became part of the content, so readily available popular imagery became part of the new subject-matter. Although ideas about mass media, about collage,[6] about common objects, had already been opposed to Expressionism and high-style art during the 1920s, the print was not then regarded as a technological tool with which to explore the meanings or emotional colorations of image-making systems. In the past twenty years, however, the flood of visual imagery has been so great that only an art form willing to appropriate the structure, methods, and styles of mass media could be called upon to reflect contemporary life. Thus the revolutionary prints of the sixties quite logically involved the viewer in situations novel for art: at once accessible, popular, recognizable, and commercial, as well as esoteric, discriminating, subtle, and allusive. After a hundred years of response to Baudelaire's insistence that the print reflect the artist's inspired hand (in opposition to the commercial lithograph or the naturalistic photograph), the idea of personal style was laid aside.[7] A wide gamut of technical strategies and experiments took over, but as we have already hinted, they maintained their charge for less than two decades. Recent printmaking has made a restrained return to the more conventional wisdom of personalized and autographic approaches.

From the standpoint of 1980, printmaking between 1900 and 1960 seems less intriguing than it did in 1960 when the School of Paris was regarded as the last word. There were indeed the handful of superbly inventive and intriguing cubist drypoints by Braque and Picasso, prints that utilized the spatial qualities of the velvety drypoint line to enhance the ambiguity of the cubist's shifting planes. And there were Matisse's Fauve-period relief prints as well as the brutal attacks on wood, stone, and copper launched by the German Expressionists in Dresden and by the Blaue Reiter group in Munich. After World War I came the biting Neue Sachlichkeit prints of Max Beckmann and the penetrating lithographic portraits by Oskar Kokoschka. But between 1920 and 1960 one struggles to find more than a handful of truly lasting and coherent *œuvres*. The prints of El Lissitzky, Kurt Schwitters and other Dada artists were only occasionally more than reproductions of graphic ideas in other media. Of course, one thinks of Picasso's work of the thirties and forties, a fountain of experiments in technique and style, of the work of Giorgio Morandi, of Paul Klee, of Matisse's lithographs of the 1920s and his *Jazz*, of Mauritius Escher, and perhaps of Edward Hopper. But what dominated the tastes of those who began to collect after World War II were the productions of the School of Paris—beautifully crafted color lithographs or intaglio prints produced by the ateliers of Lacourière, Desjobert, Mourlot, and others. Many of these works were so much the product of the craftsman that the print became little more than a transparent reproduction of a drawing, watercolor, or gouache.[8] Although the print was regarded as a precious object, it lacked intrinsic content, since the artists left the means of production virtually uninflected. Whereas Chagall, Miró, and Max Ernst, for example, had begun their printmaking activities with serious use of copper and stone, their post-1945 work was produced more often than not to satisfy the external demands of the marketplace rather than internal demands of artistic expression.

The vapid printmaking of many big-name artists in Europe was matched by the countless technological chefs on the other side of the Atlantic who restricted their endeavors to printmaking alone. Basically these more parochial printmakers were content to enhance mediocre draftsmanship by the complexities of the well-worked printmaking surface. Whereas a sketch or a finished drawing exists solely in the realm of art,[9] a print always conjoins art and technology. While a drawing must ultimately be judged for its aesthetic or informational characteristics, the print is valued in addition for its mechanical and technical aspects, for its structures and its textures. For this reason there have always been several foci for print collectors: the purely aesthetic (masterpieces of the history of prints), the historical (prints that mirror the history of style), the informational (prints as illustration of various subjects), *and* what I might call the technical (prints as technological *tours de force*). Prints of very little aesthetic worth have always been produced and collected because they possess some or all of these extra dimensions. But it is understandable that prints exert a technical fascination, because they are, after all, mechanical objects. In some deep and unrationalized manner, they tap one of the most fundamental substrates of technological culture: man's need for the mechanical replica or the repeatable image, that is, visual language. Yet man does not live by mechanical fascination alone; there must be significant meaning.

Although it may appear as an elitist view, I strongly believe that the significant prints of our times have come almost exclusively from the best painters and sculptors, for they are the most sensitive to the visual languages of our technological civilization. Accordingly, the rough divisions we have made among recent printmakers are determined by an amalgamation of stylistic and technical criteria rather than solely by medium, country, or individual artist.

Further, just as it ruffles no feathers to claim that it was in the Netherlands that prints bloomed most luxuriantly in the seventeenth century, it is reasonable to claim that the best in recent printmaking has been determined largely by events in England and America.

When Stanley William Hayter moved Atelier 17 from Paris to New York in 1940, European notions about the perfectibility of printmaking accompanied him. A host of Surrealists, such as Joan Miró, Matta, Yves Tanguy, Max Ernst, and André Masson, filled Hayter's etching studio, attracting increasing numbers of Americans.[10] Although he was known for his innovative printing techniques which had great appeal for technically deprived American artists,[11] Hayter's basic contribution was his insistence that painters learn the craft of printmaking from beginning to end. He also created an environment in which artists could share their ideas about matters both technical and stylistic. These flagrantly un-Parisian practices went counter to the long-established tradition of the collaborative dependence of artist upon craftsman.[12] In so doing, however, Hayter managed to subordinate ideas about art to the process of making it.

The test of Hayter's American sojourn, of course, may be found in the art and artists he inspired. Although Jackson Pollock and several other important American painters actively associated themselves with Hayter—and one could argue convincingly that Pollock's all-over style was formed by contact with the work of Masson and Hayter at Atelier 17—it is equally clear that the artists who persisted in printmaking were not the painters.[13] Karl Schrag, Gabor Peterdi, and Mauricio Lasansky went on during the late 1940s to establish a strong American school of printmaking, albeit one that functioned at some remove from the emerging Abstract Expressionist painters. The example of Hayter's own work fostered a surrealist-expressionist mode of drawing largely derived from Picasso's *Guernica* period.[14] Hayter's prints were bogged down in technical sophistication. By contrast, painters like Rothko, Newman, Pollock, de Kooning, Tomlin, and Gottlieb sought new images and techniques that would lead away from the fluent draftsmanly styles of the School of Paris (think of Picasso, Matisse, and Dali). Together the Americans created a new, frontal, explosive force in painting that would be regarded as quintessentially American. Fussing around with copper plates or massive limestones did not attract their attention, which was focussed on large-scale gesture and mural-like canvases. An upsurge in American printmaking had indeed come from Hayter, but it did not then attract the major painters as it would during the 1960s and 1970s.

American printmaking was revolutionized by two women, June Wayne and Tatyana Grosman. The stories of Tamarind Workshops and of Universal Limited Art Editions have often been told,[15] but it is important to distinguish their contributions, made in the later 1950s, from Hayter's of the middle 1940s. Both women championed color lithography and espoused the European separation of artist and craftsman to achieve the necessary technical sophistication; in his day, Hayter had pretty much discouraged both lithography and the division of labor. June Wayne founded Tamarind Workshops in Los Angeles in order to introduce painters to the medium of lithography and to train printers so that they could establish their own workshops throughout the United States. Tatyana Grosman, on the other hand, openly wished to publish significant prints by the best artists. There is no question that at ULAE (set up between 1957 and 1959 in West Islip, Long Island, New York) there was a need for skilled, devoted, and sensitive printers.

Jackson Pollock (1912–1956):
Untitled, 1951.
Screenprint. (584 × 737 mm.)

Yet, while Mrs. Grosman fully accepted the importance of collaboration between artist and printer, the needs and sensibilities of the artist always took precedence. At Tamarind, however, where proselytizing for the craft of printing ranked almost as high as the artistic goals, the stamp of the printer (and of Mrs. Wayne herself!) was evident on many of the lithographs produced by the invited artists. While Mrs. Grosman instinctively sought out the most avant-garde, Mrs. Wayne was more inclined to solicit the well-established.

Both workshops opened in 1957–1960 after the main waves of Abstract Expressionism had subsided. With remarkably few exceptions, prints in any medium had failed to capture the spontaneity, scale, color, and touch of the Abstract Expressionist painting. Hans Hartung and Pierre Soulages in Paris had managed to transfer their rather tame and measured brand of *Tachisme* to ink and paper. Jean Dubuffet's crude figures, experiments with abstract textures, and recombined fragments *(Les Phénomènes)* were the only serious French counterpart to the all-over style of Abstract Expressionism.[16] Although his prints set an example of how printing could be used for serial experimentation, they were too much surface texture (or drawing in the case of the figurative pieces) and consequently missed the dynamic tensions between surface tangibility and illusionistic energy that characterized the painted work of Pollock or de Kooning. In America, Abstract Expressionist printmaking had been confined to a marvelous book published in 1960, *21 Etchings and Poems*, to one de Kooning lithograph, and to six photo-screenprints produced by Jackson Pollock and his brother from a series of black Duco-enamel paintings of 1951.[17] Unfortunately Pollock's screenprints failed to capture either the tangibility of pigment or the new unity of the stained canvas; as a consequence, the prints lost the autographic energy and painterly subtleties so important to Pollock's work.

The most convincing new works of the late fifties were done by Kurt Sonderborg of Germany.[18] His flashing, lift-ground aquatints not only captured the excitement of the thickening, thinning, and stuttering brushstrokes of his paintings, but they did so with the palpable textures of aquatint. The immediacy and power of these prints derived from the pent-up energies of Sonderborg's tensile curves, from the strained but disciplined repetitions of his rapid strokes, and from a tendency towards barely controlled centripetality. Far from Sonderborg's sense of

Kurt Sonderborg (1923):
Composition, 1958.
Colour aquatint.
(587 × 327 mm.)

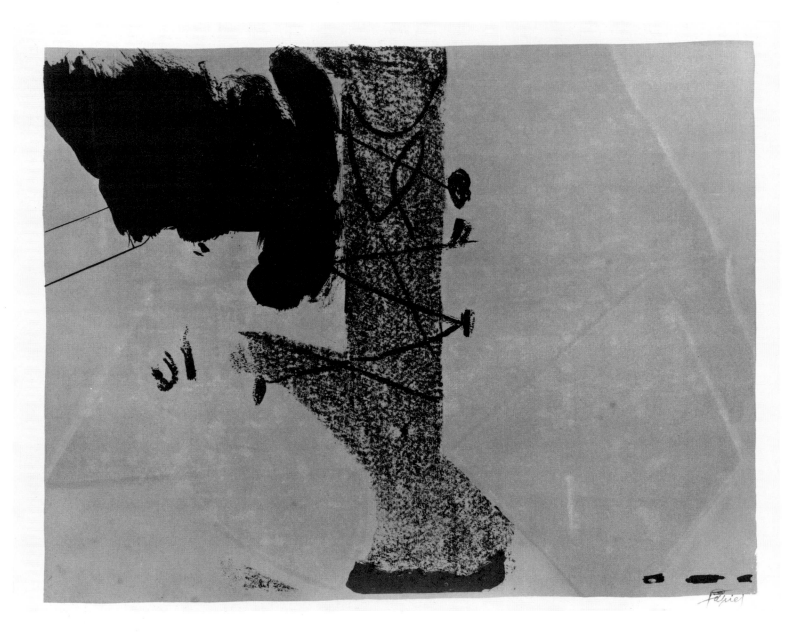

Antoni Tápies (1923):
Untitled, 1962.
Embossed colour lithograph.
(460 × 580 mm.)

containment are the colored frenzies of Asger Jorn and Karel Appel's lithographs which often overloaded the plane of the paper with barely figurative but nearly disorganized brushstrokes. Peaceful by comparison is the work of Sam Francis, whose first lithograph was actually begun at ULAE in 1959. While partaking of a more closed form of draftsmanship, Francis spread his forms to the edges of the paper. Whereas the European artists tended to centralize their imagery, Francis hollowed out the central space of the paper, dispersed his large, globule-like forms to the corners, and charged the intervening spaces with skeins and droplets of colored links. The prints Francis executed in Switzerland and more recently at Gemini in Los Angeles are particularly filled with a light-producing transparency, demonstrating the importance of sensitive printing. Exactly the opposite effect is often sought by the Spaniard, Antoni Tápies, one of the most important European, Abstract Expressionist painters.[19] His prints concentrate on accumulating textures, sometimes alluded to in ink, and sometimes tangible as folds or as sand worked into the surface itself. Although their tactile qualities link them with the relief prints of the fifties and the process-materials prints of the late seventies, Tápies' best work maintains a tension between the tangible and the optical; they possess an indefinable scale, a result of the painter's vision, which separates his work from countless numbers of textured etchings by his exclusively printmaking contemporaries.

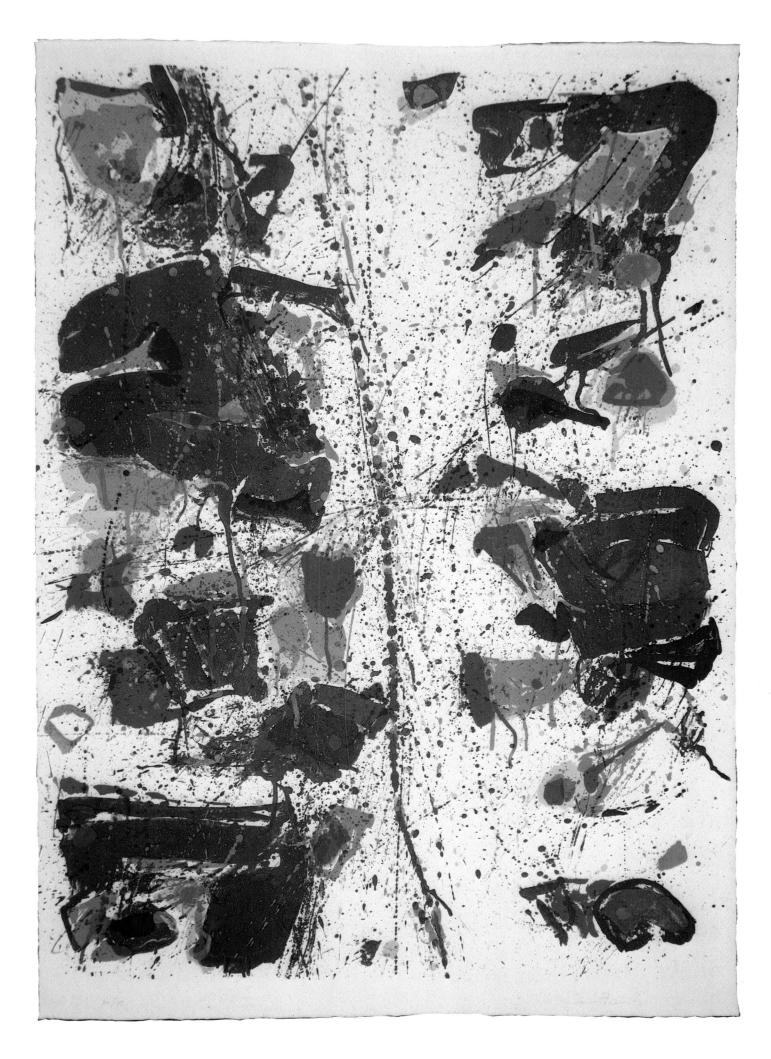

Sam Francis (1923):
The White Line, 1960.
Colour lithograph.
(908 × 631 mm.)

Tamarind and ULAE artists reacted differently to the dominance of Abstract Expressionism. The West Coast painters continued in a largely emotional and expressionistic vein, abstract or figurative as in the few early prints by Richard Diebenkorn, while the East Coast artists sought ways of dampening the excesses of gesture, illusion, or pathos. Larry Rivers, Fritz Glarner, Grace Hartigan, and Robert Motherwell made strikingly sparse lithographs for Mrs. Grosman.[20] They did not attempt to match the rich impastos of the painted surface, nor were they content to record the passions of a moment's activity on the stone. Rather they strove instinctively— perhaps under the influence of Tatyana Grosman's incredibly delicate patience—to develop the subtle transparencies and spaces of stone lithography. Into this space came an inevitable return to drawing. Rivers' early use of two-dimensional, mundane imagery (George Washington or Lucky Strike) to anchor a mock-gestural style of drawing was eminently suited to lithographic rendition. It bore something of the same irony as Glarner's flawed Neoplastic formalism, with its curious mixture of gestural and geometric shapes.

Mrs. Grosman's proclivity for books, for words and images, for irony and mixture, or what Johns would constantly refer to as an "impure" situation, tended to exclude from printmaking at ULAE the new formalists who were regarded as the inheritors of the Abstract Expressionistic ethic. Of Morris Louis, Kenneth Noland, Jules Olitski, Helen Frankenthaler, Ellsworth Kelly, and Frank Stella, who were just coming to maturity in the years around 1960, only Frankenthaler would make a substantial contribution to printmaking at ULAE before the end of the decade.[21] Consequently, it was to Jasper Johns that Mrs. Grosman gave some stones in 1960, with the hope that he would translate into lithography the incredibly rich surfaces of his flat subjects.[22] In his early *Targets, Coathangers, Flags,* and *0-9,* Johns drew on the stone with such an extraordinary variety of line, such subtlety of space and sculptural nuance, and such a sure command of tonality and texture, that in one blow he surpassed the finesse of all prior lithography. Johns wedded his already two-dimensional organizing motifs and the given flatness of the printed image to the transparent and opaque painterliness of lithographic drawing. Suddenly and unexpectedly these prints compressed categories of art that one had thought to be distinct and definable: drawing (the act of the artist) and image (the thing drawn). Since Johns' images were obviously printed, they logically suggested the reproduction of something that could be named (a drawing *of* an object or *of* a concept). Yet they did not provide the habitual mental or cognitive distinction between figure and ground.[23] The entire vocabulary of expressionistic, lithographic drawing was employed to create what seemed to be illusions of *flat* objects. The trouble was that these objects could not really be separated from the marks on the surface of the paper; the viewer was frustrated when he sought to use this printed information either as a diagram of, or as an illusion of, reality.

By beguiling us with a sensuosity and subtlety of handling that dissembled the attributes of great drawings, Johns distracted the viewer from the utterly mundane character of his organizing motifs. The fluency of touch inherent in lithography acted simultaneously as illusion, texture, and idea; each use served to control the other.[24] No better example could be found than *Two Maps I* of 1965–1966. Typically, Johns begins with a subject that is only a diagram and is found not in nature but only on the page. Yet he makes something palpable of it, something of art as

7/30

Jasper Johns (1930):
Two Maps I, 1965–1966.
Lithograph.
(838 × 673 mm.)

well as of information. The maps are heightened in their tactility and painterliness. They seduce the eye, and appeal to our sense of touch by summoning up prior haptic knowledge about the shapes of the "states." They provide an armature for a muted series of abstract brushstrokes, but their known diagrammatic flatness acts to control the indefinite spatial illusions that the same freedom of touch would have had in an Abstract Expressionist work. Although we realize that these maps cannot be used (they are not accurate and the two images differ), they remain inescapably maps that siphon off many of our feelings and memories about real maps. Yet each one remains a drawing—not *of* a map, not *as* a map, nor as abstract gesture, but as another, new and bewildering category to which we are unable to give a name.

Conflict, therefore, and not unity is the touchstone of Johns' and perhaps of most "impure" works of the 1960s. The best prints seem to play various levels of information and cultural reference against more visually defined stylistic ideas. In *Two Maps I* this sense of uncertainty is increased through the very process of printing. Not only does the artist give us two maps (the same territory) which are visually if not conceptually different, but in the second version he varies the printing inks and papers so that the very notions of positive and negative image, of figure and ground, of drawing and information are subverted yet again. These early lithographs

Michael Ponce de Leon (1922):
Entrapment, 1966.
Metal collage intaglio.
(672 × 620 × 20 mm.)

Robert Rauschenberg (1925): ▷
Breakthrough II, 1965.
Colour lithograph.
(1101 × 787 mm.)

served notice on the entire artistic world that printmaking was about to chart new courses whose originality lay not in technical innovation but the examination of the nature of art and visual communication. Johns was not alone in the quest.

In 1962 Robert Rauschenberg came to Tatyana Grosman's. His combine paintings had been more shocking and innovative than Johns' easel productions, since they forced real objects— often discarded memorabilia, useless junk, or appropriated studio paraphernalia—out into the inviolate space between the sacred picture plane and the viewer.[25] The impulse to collage objects to the canvas was not new, but the power and nature of these intrusions were. Although Rauschenberg made no prints during the 1950s, other artists experimented with a kind of precursor in the form of relief prints. These included the very formal works of Rolf Nesch, Paolo Boni, Angelo Savelli, Pierre Courtin, and Lucio Fontana in Europe, and the more object-like prints such as those of Antonio Berni, Norio Azuma, and Michael Ponce de Leon in the Americas.[26] Most of these works, popular in their day, were concerned with relief as texture rather than meaning, and they may best be regarded as parallels to the infinitely varied and technically captivating prints that derived from the Abstract Expressionist vogue of the same period.

1/34 RAUSCHENBERG 65

Rauschenberg, however, was concerned with positing alternatives to Abstract Expressionism while retaining many of its elements, especially its scale and painterliness. A jarring arbitrariness informed both his choice of objects and the wild painterly matrix into which they were set. When Rauschenberg finally did turn to printmaking in 1962, his objects had been tamed to two-dimensional surrogates. His photographic images were transferred to the lithographic stone by rubbing, printing, silkscreening, and finally by photo-sensitive resists.[27] These flat illusions of the real world, of public events, of places, and of people, were embedded in brushstrokes of opaque and transparent tusche (lithographic wash) which reinforced the dissonances of the images. The Dada-Surrealist "found object" was not the issue, for Rauschenberg's printed illusions of objects had little to do with discovered aesthetic quality, hidden associations, or jarring inappropriateness. Rather, these new "objects" were prized because they were dematerialized forms of reproduction, in short, because they were surrogates for everyday experience. Rauschenberg's shift to reproductive imagery was directly inspired by a double recognition: first, the infinitude and arbitrariness of the images that daily confront the modern observer; and second, the formal wish to juxtapose these types of structured pictorial spaces to the indefinite spaces of expressionistic brushstrokes. The printed image, therefore, permitted the painter to demonstrate the falseness of all kinds of illusionism and to control illusionistic potential by the inescapable flatness of the printed surface. One can no more construct a consistent pictorial space in a Rauschenberg than one can thread together a coherent reading of the disparate pieces of imagery. What one does experience is a dual expression, both personal and objective, of modern urban flux. But the visual frenzy is always mediated by the flatness of paper and reproduction.

What was significant about the fragments of reality appropriated by Johns and Rauschenberg was their utter familiarity and their de-emotionalized presentations. Rarely does Johns' restrained but virtuosic drawing or Rauschenberg's bravura handling of tusche alter the emotional detachment of their images. In Rauschenberg's work, these images are further neutralized by a variety of smudging, turning, reducing/enlarging, coloring, repeating, and inking procedures, as may be observed in works like *License, Breakthrough,* or *Front Roll* (1962-1964). The print (or printed painting) acquired new complexities of meaning that were coextensive with the fact of being printed. The cognitive difficulties presented by many of the best recent prints are due to the uncommonly close correlation between the nature of the subjects and the procedures used to render that subject. Although these prints possess a large capacity to allude to other systems, including the art of the past, their content resides in their own structures, in the facts of how each kind of mark was printed.

The discovery that photo-screenprinting could transpose reality onto canvas was Andy Warhol's. Late in the spring of 1962—the very same year when, in America, the National Serigraph Society, with its strictures against using photography and collaborative printing, ceased to exist—Warhol and then Rauschenberg threw open the doors of painting and printmaking to photography, commercial printing, and modern, urban imagery.[28] With simple, uneducated sweeps of the squeegee, the very antithesis of the personalized and emotion-laden gestures of the art of the fifties, they covered square yards of paintings with printed, photo-

Andy Warhol (1930):
Marilyn Monroe, from
portfolio *10 Marilyns*, 1967.
Colour screenprint.
(Each portrait 915 × 915 mm.)

Andy Warhol (1930):
Self-Portrait, 1966.
Silkscreen ink on silvered
paper. (584 × 584 mm.)

graphic illusions. How sweet to find stylistic solutions in ready-made processes, especially when one desperately needed non-personal ways for making art.

The new urban imagery was so varied, well known, and casually rendered that the screen-printed paintings and prints leveled their subjects in much the same manner as did the mass media. The charge of the Statue of Liberty, or of Marilyn Monroe, is hardly more than that of a glass of water or a map of the United States. And this single squeegeed stroke of genius, this American willingness to risk commitment to one overpowering idea, was like a frontal assault on all sacred ideas about originality in prints. Commercial imagery was sucked up into the mainstream of art, and along with it came the commercial printers, their processes, their shortcuts, their conventions, their finesse and banality, and their economics. Cheapness itself was a virtue to the early Warhol; it opposed (and later co-opted) chic, and it suppressed personality. Warhol's Marilyns, printed by untutored assistants at the Factory with one crude photographic screen and several flat color-screens, set up unforeseen tensions between the intensely private and the blandly public meanings of Marilyn Monroe. There she was, over-life size and crudely photographic, unmoving, waiting for the viewer's interpretation. Borrowing from the languages of mass-produced imagery, Warhol manipulated scale, degree of coarseness, color, context, and repetition patterns–directing the machines of commercial process. His own forms of repetitive imaging outrageously mimicked the saturation achieved by the mass media and questioned our reactions to media representations of grisly automobile accidents, suicides, brutalities, and celebrities (were these all a form of public death?). Were there not parallels among the deterioration of Warhol's images, the denigration of the individuality of a public idol, and our own postures of indifference to these printed surrogates for reality?

Warhol's famous pronouncement that he would prefer to work like a machine betrayed a completely empathic response to the anonymous quality of media. But it was also a pose. Not only did Warhol carefully select his subjects and the means by which they were manipulated, but in the sixties he would often instruct his printers to allow for chance events in order to encourage variation.[29] But, by the end of the decade, he had settled on a rigid, unvarying technique.[30] During the early seventies, however, he once more reversed his position by infiltrating various kinds of hand-manipulated textures into his prints, a choice that also predicted the general turning away from the impersonality of Pop Art.

Those who visited the Warhol retrospective at the Whitney Museum of American Art in New York in 1970 could have been shocked by the absolute sameness of the cow wallpaper. It was there, however, to act as a foil for—to make apparent—the subtle variations existing among the repeated images of the canvases. There were real differences between Warhol's more or less machine-made images, and these were quite like the differences between hand and machine so often pointed to in the work of Rauschenberg, Johns, and Hamilton. Implicitly, Warhol questioned the viewer about the value of responding to these subtle differences even as he was forced to scan the images to detect them. Although Warhol is indelibly associated with the

Arnulf Rainer (1929):
Self-Portrait, c. 1975.
Photogravure, etching, and
crayon. (536 × 383 mm.)

203

advent of the great Pop image, he was in fact exploring the viewer's reactions to the recent flood of all visual stimulae. Warhol's deadpan *Self-Portrait*, taken alone or in combinations, was no different from a *Brando* or a *Liz*. The artist had assumed the same passive role as his idols, and his image existed to be used or even consumed by the spectator like a Diane Arbus photograph. Less contrived than Johns, Warhol de-intellectualized the process by which the viewer became aware of his own perceiving, the "beholder's share" as Gombrich so aptly put it. If lithography was the medium of the late fifties and early sixties because it admirably accommodated the stylistic heritage of Abstract Expressionism (even as practiced by those committed to reforming it), screenprinting was the medium of the middle sixties.[31] As I have demonstrated elsewhere, silkscreen's advanced technology permitted the widest range of styles.[32] Josef Albers, Richard Anuszkiewicz, Eugenio Carmi, and all those concerned with Op and hard-edge formal styles welcomed the impersonal, machine-like precision of screenprinted color planes. Albers' optically transparent but physically opaque color planes, Victor Vasarely's warping

spatial patterns, and later, Bridget Riley's migrating colors could be translated by the tactile layers of opaque color deposited through the screenprinting stencil. It is worth noting that the interest in Op Art was contemporaneous with the arrival of Pop subjects and media commentary; it was marked in 1965 by the Museum of Modern Art's exhibition, *The Responsive Eye*. The concern for anti-expressionist structures and the search for illusion-denying flatness in the realm of abstract art were shared to some extent by color-field painting, Op Art, and even some aspects of Pop. These included the use of screenprinting for its commercial, impersonal, and optical qualities. Yet the post-painterly abstractionists, Noland, Olitski, Stella, Kelly, and Louis were not attracted by the medium; in no way did they wish to partake of an art form that seemed to embody a dialogue or to paraphrase popular media. Their color fields and structures were regarded as totally given and self-determined.

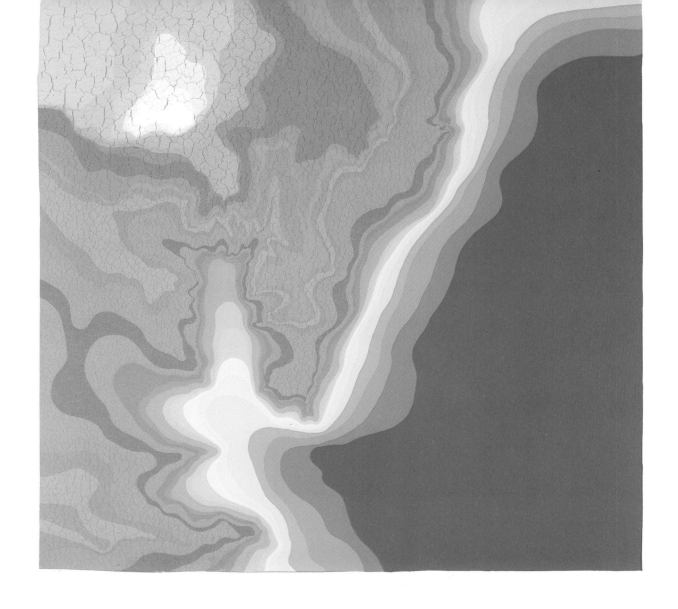

Dieter Roth (1930): △
Iceland from the Air, 1970.
Colour screenprint on
masonite. (620 × 620 mm.)

◁ Josef Albers (1888–1976):
Homage to the Square, 1962.
Colour screenprint.
(430 × 430 mm.)

◁◁ Bridget Riley (1931):
Untitled (Blue), 1978.
Colour screenprint.
(673 × 945 mm.)

The screenprint was particularly adaptable to contrasting styles. Impersonal, flat layers of pigment might be juxtaposed with autographic, painterly marks on the one hand, or with photographic materials on the other. One could "program" the fine mesh to carry any kind of data, and it was this versatility, this ability to paraphrase the look and feel of different media or styles that was invaluable for the Pop artist. For Pop was, ultimately, about communication styles. For example, Dieter Roth's images of *Piccadilly* were about photographic and pictorial space (in the guise of a postcard), while his *Iceland from the Air* makes a striking parallel between abstract, hard-edge painting and impressive visual experience (in the guise of a diagram).

In 1964-1966 there appeared five major Pop portfolios, mostly screenprinted.[33] They contained some of Roy Lichtenstein's first prints, including *POW!*. Much has been written about Lichtenstein's adaptation of comic book styles, about the roles of the printed words whose implied sounds and emotions contrast with the deadpan emotions of the "cleaned-up" and classicized drawing.[34] But less has been written about the subtle, optical languages of the dots and planes of color. Lichtenstein outraged the public not only because he paraphrased unworthy subject-matter, but because he included the mechanical system that reproduced it. As the decade progressed, he gradually refined and purified his images, drawing progressively closer to the underlying stylistic and intellectual values of formalist painting of the time.[35] Since Lichten-

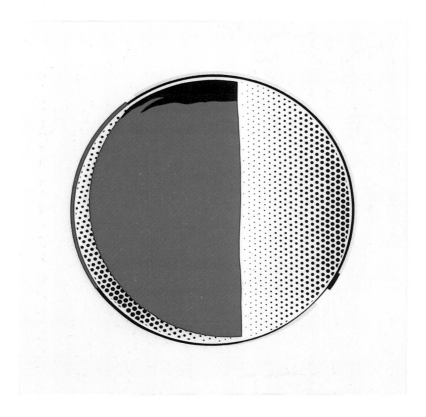

Roy Lichtenstein (1923):
Mirror No. 3, 1972.
Five-colour line cut, silkscreen,
embossing. (711 × 711 mm.)

stein's art was rooted in the paraphrase, it was inevitable that high art styles themselves would become his subject. His *Haystacks* and *Cathedrals* are not only siftings of Monet's formal and optical ideas, but are desensualized translations of these natural ideas into the artificial languages of reproductive printing. Lichtenstein shows that the very idea of serial imagery, of processed variation, is indigenous to the idea of repeated, printed imagery.[36]

But Lichtenstein's lithographic and screenprinted series are also discreetly modernistic. The information seems to float among the matrices of dots, and in such a way that we cannot adequately perceive or specify the locus of the image. The elusive opticality of these prints does not match Monet's exploration of the times of day or subtle variations of light, but it parallels in abstract and technological terms the same levels of perception. In his subsequent *Mirror* series, Lichtenstein suppresses observational data even further, so that reality is perceived simultaneously as pure mechanical process (the dots) and pure visual sensation (light, space, etc.). The illusion of depth, reflectivity, and surface (the mirrored image, the mirror, and the frame of the mirror) is almost inseparable from our perception of the surface of the paper (Monet's *Water Lilies* must have had much the same effect in the 1900s). As close as Lichtenstein comes to formal abstraction, his work is neither painterly nor abstract; the ironic seepage of reality into such systemized, unpainterly abstraction is the mirror image, so to speak, of the denial of illusion so carefully achieved in Johns' brushy *Flags* of 1960 or in his hatched prints of the 1970s.

Roy Lichtenstein (1923):
POW! Sweet Dreams, Baby!, 1965,
from portfolio *11 Pop Artists III*, 1966.
Colour screenprint. (941 × 691 mm.)

James Rosenquist (1933):
Spaghetti and Grass, 1965.
Colour lithograph.
(708 × 440 mm.)

As we have noted, Rauschenberg and Johns both experimented with actual objects in the years prior to 1960. Johns' *Ale Cans* became, almost overnight, a symbol for all that was good and bad, rightly apprehended and totally misunderstood, about Pop Art. That it concealed a growing distrust of the object hardly dawned on anyone in those days.[37] But the history of both artists, and of the sixties in general, slowly revealed what Lucy Lippard has called "the dematerialization of the object."[38] But what might have been thought of as a post-Pop phenomenon is clearly a part of it. Lichtenstein's *Mirrors* hover among abstraction, optical information, and likenesses of objects. A similar description could apply to James Rosenquist's *Spaghetti and Grass* of 1965. This lithograph compares optically disparate surfaces through means that are paradoxically but patently similar, i.e. the very simple means of drawing on stone with crayon. The two types of illusion are another instance of Pop Art's fondness for comparisons between media languages, especially among blatant advertising conventions with their attendant subliminal associations.

A good many of the artists of the sixties, including Rosenquist and Edward Ruscha, came to the fine arts from commercial backgrounds. Ruscha's seductive screenprints and lithographs offered a series of comments on the influence of design styles on public feelings. In his *Standard Stations* of 1965 and later, sleekness of plane and perspective were embedded in the flat but modulated surfaces of screenprinting. In his word prints, such as *Lisp*, the emotional impact was "isolated" by treating the word as if it were an object, occupying and making its own space, surface, form, atmosphere, and style. If the later sixties were often concerned with the dematerialization of the object, Ruscha's prints represent an ironic materialization of the word. Deceived by our willingness to believe in commercial conventions of printed illusionism,[39] we become convinced that just as the symbol is being given concrete form, so is its aura of meaning. To claim that the foregoing descriptions give an adequate overview of printmaking in the 1960s might be an exaggeration, yet one could seek the source for much of this period in the work of Jasper Johns alone. His *Flags, Ale Cans, Devices,* and *Numerals* all introduced many of the elements of the 1960s: the discharging of Abstract Expressionism, the introduction of everyday objects, the conflicts between the object and its representation, the record or memory implications of process, and the exploitation of seriality and technical vocabularies. In his *Device* prints, Johns alludes to acts and movements tangibly recorded in the surfaces of his paintings. Whereas a painting may contain a physical record of a past act, a print embodies only a symbolic representation of it. What was tangible in oil, encaustic, and moveable pieces is frozen and conceptualized by the printmaking process. Thus prints are not just repetitions of ideas discovered and first embodied in paintings; they are themselves symbols of thought and experience. Hostile indifference alone cannot explain our frequent inability to sense these subtle distinctions. Contemporary prints elude our understanding because we habitually mistake the languages that describe events for the events themselves.

Edward Ruscha (1937):
Lisp, 1970.
Colour lithograph.
(508 × 711 mm.)

Eduardo Paolozzi (1924):
Reality, from *As Is When*, 1965.
Colour screenprint.
(800 × 550 mm.)

If concern for media communications was the first of several reactions against the hegemony, the egotism, and the mystique of Abstract Expressionism, the first evidence of that reaction arose in England, not in America. Media collages and paraphrases of "modern" design and technology came to dominate the work of Eduardo Paolozzi and Richard Hamilton in the years after 1953.[40] These were not only regarded as a way out of the stylistic impasse of French *Tachisme* and *Art brut*, but also an active embrace of the products of mass culture, particularly American culture and imagery. Although the collages presented an alternative to the high styles of American and French art, the simultaneity of large scale and intimacy (the close-up view) of American action painting remained an important constituent of the new Pop Art. Constitutionally, the English were not disposed to isolate a single aspect of American hyperbolic culture, but were inclined to treat it comparatively. This was pioneered by Paolozzi's use of collage—introduced for reasons as much surrealist as the American experiments in assemblage were formalist.

Richard Hamilton (1922):
I'm Dreaming of a Black Christmas, 1971.
Colour collotype, screenprint,
and collage. (750 × 1000 mm.)

Yet it was not until the early 1960s that prints reflecting the new collage styles of Paolozzi and Hamilton could be executed. The impetus for their eventual appearance was the genius of Christopher Prater of Kelpra Studio, London.[41] Essentially a commercial printer, Prater had no reservations about combining diverse processes within one image so that his screenprints could be perfect analogues for media comparisons. No one had ever handled the stencil knife or had understood the inflections of photographic passages as did Chris Prater; his screenprints potentiated a new world of styles. The ingredients of Paolozzi's series of ten screenprints of 1965, *As Is When*, are astounding: found objects that were often not objects at all, but printed schemata. There were diagrams for needlepoint, advertisements for toys, magazine covers, textures for graphic artists, electronic schematics, comic strips, etc., all combined to suggest modern technologies, languages, and structures, as well as kitsch![42] With a keen sense of humor, these collages possessed the power to describe things that could not be said and to suggest things that lurked in the mysteries of the future. Hamilton, in ways more intellectual than other English painters (he was the most devoted of Duchamp's European disciples), consistently scrutinized the means of image-making, comparing various modernistic styles of both hand and machine.[43]

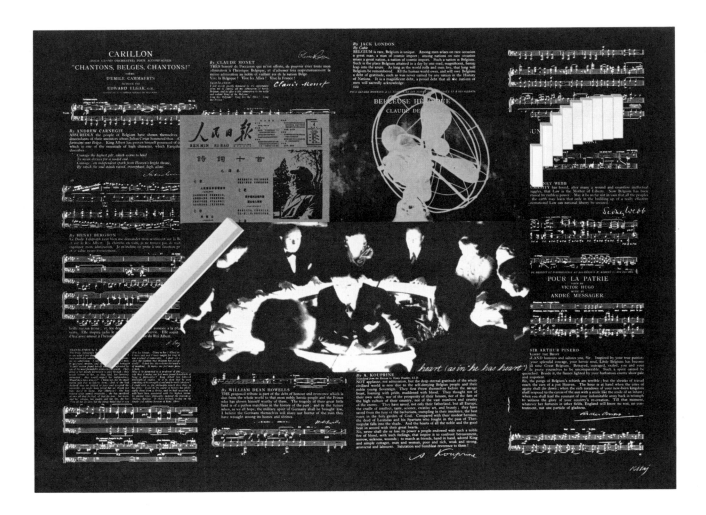

R.B. Kitaj (1932):
Heart, from *Mahler becomes
Politics, Beisbol*, 1964–1966.
Colour screenprint. (600 × 813 mm.)

He was able to isolate the emotional components, or what might be called conditioned associative responses, built up by years of exposure to mass media styles, and he was astute enough to point out repeatedly that style was not a phenomenon confined to the hand, to the expressive gesture, but a quality resident even in our apparently impersonal and mechanical means of image-making. His art goes further than any other artist's to reveal the humane beauty underlying all illusionistic systems, what Hamilton has often called "epiphanies." Nowhere is this more poignantly revealed than in the several versions of *I'm Dreaming of a White Christmas* and *I'm Dreaming of a Black Christmas* (1969-1971). They transform a meaningless Bing Crosby movie frame into a hauntingly mysterious event. Crosby hovers, self-absorbed, like a man spiritualized in an environment at once familiar and totally dream-like. Hamilton's transformations not only equivocate between positive and negative colors, but they suspend the image in an indeterminate world composed of photographic and hand-drawn realities. Fabricated by means of a most intimate understanding of photography and screenprinting, and composed of bits and pieces of offset, collotype, stencil, and collage, the prints, even more than the painting, are studies in the transmutation of the substance of reality. Passages that seem the most photographic are often drawn, while some of the most painterly were obtained from manipulated photographic emulsions.

Combining the influence of Hamilton, a wide knowledge of literature and art history, and the collaboration of Chris Prater, is the American, R.B. Kitaj, who has worked in England for almost three decades. No artist has used the collage method of printmaking more enigmatically than Kitaj who was introduced to Chris Prater in 1963 by Hamilton and Paolozzi. Kitaj's amalgams of imagery form moody ideograms that sport with the study of meaning, with Panofsky's insistence that the mind *sees* as well as reads visual meaning.[44] Compared to German iconographic printmakers like Paul Wunderlich, Friedrich Meckseper, or Ernst Fuchs,

Kitaj's imagery appears more rational and less exhaustible simply because it is based on events in the real world rather than on surrealist fantasies about the irrational. Curiously, all of these fantastic realists share a love of craft: their prints are marked by a precision and clarity descended directly from late Gothic art in which naturalism forced acceptance of the visionary. Kitaj's preoccupation with stylistic illusion, however, leads him away from the fantastic. The logic of each work is strengthened and unified by what might be called a stylistic mood lifted from some source in the art of the past one hundred-and-fifty years, a language he inflects as easily as the various photographic, drawn, and textured materials that compose his images. This tendency toward stylistic pluralism distinguishes many English prints from those created in the United States. Even Rauschenberg's free-wheeling incorporation of materials at hand is contained by the desire to achieve a high degree of oneness in the painted field, a unity that was clearly established by American painters, from Pollock to Kelly.

That the color-field painters of the 1960s failed to make substantial contributions to printmaking has already been remarked. We know of no prints by Morris Louis, and only occasional and not very convincing attempts by Kenneth Noland, Jules Olitski, and Ellsworth Kelly in the 1960s; obviously their ideas had no use for the realms of reproduced imagery and pictorial illusionism.[45] Only in 1967 did Frank Stella, working at Gemini in Los Angeles, initiate serious formalist printmaking. He began, as have so many artists, by recapitulating his early (1959–1960) paintings in a series of lithographs.[46] His assertive, but carefully drawn, black stripes established a compelling tension between the optical aspects of the design (i.e. the activity of the *white* stripes) and the object-like block of the whole design. Although the motifs were derived from the painted works, the formal problems were reworked in terms of printmaking. As was the case with the paintings, the structure of the motif was deduced from a few decisions; but the isolation created by the thickness and notching of the stretcher was supplanted, in the print, by

Frank Stella (1936):
Arbeit Macht Frei, 1967.
Two-colour lithograph.
(380 × 560 mm.)

Jack Beal (1931):
Self-Portrait, 1974.
Lithograph. (762 × 570 mm.)

Philip Pearlstein (1924): ▷
Girl on Empire Sofa, 1972.
Lithograph. (819 × 610 mm.)

the invasive whiteness of the paper. Placed carefully off-center on the paper, the inner movements of the motif seemed as much a part of the paper as of the drawn stripes. In some ways this
reciprocity of drawing was not unlike Jasper Johns' *Targets* and *Flags*.
Although Ellsworth Kelly early discovered the futility of attempts to compress the optical
experience of large shapes of color into the limited surface of the print, Stella's experiments
probably suggested ways in which color could be tensioned within the confines of a sheet of
paper. Furthermore, the purity of Kelly's colors was more and more transmuted into the purity
of shapes, so that the middle seventies witnessed some extraordinary works, including the very
refined, embossed screenprint, *Large Black Curve* of 1974. How are these prints different from
the hundreds of abstract, geometric works found in every country during the past two decades?
Perhaps it is again their "presence"—their singleness of purpose, their perfection of execution,
and their relatively large size. This object-like quality, informing many of the best American
prints of the 1970s, sought to move away from the concerns with illusionistic games of the 1960s.
By switching from color to form, Kelly joined forces with those minimalist etchers who
exploited the material givens of copperplate printmaking.
The need to subject Abstract Expressionism to various kinds of stylistic straitjackets took many
forms in the 1960s. Although it was barely noted at the time, the same urge toward limited
painterliness and systematic analysis impressed itself upon traditional American realist painting.
Philip Pearlstein emerged as a hero of older values. His painted works manifest a slow neutrali-
zation of the artist's hand, replacing emotional gesture with a rigidly disciplined, systematic
process of observation. While Pearlstein makes of himself a kind of anti-expressionist painting
machine, his figurative compositions are full of subtle skips and discontinuities that force the
viewer to scan rapidly his surfaces in a covert form of expressionist movement.[47] Now, the
energy is transferred to the viewer rather than residing in the surface.

Pearlstein only began making prints in the late 1960s (no major publisher was interested in a painter of nudes). True to the dictates of his process, every stone or plate was executed from the model; the artist was chained to his motif as was Cézanne. Most of the eroticism (the equivalent of personal emotion in the realm of subject-matter) was drained away: first, by the process of drawing without regard for content, the hand simply following the eye, the edge of the canvas, stone, or plate arbitrarily limiting the figures; second, by the absence of detailed information despite a directness and sense of scale that suggested intimate facts; third, because Pearlstein's drawing demanded eye movement; and last, because the seductive patterns and draftsmanly textures, like those of Jasper Johns, were repeatedly dampened by their insistent abstractness. Although such nudes could be found among European artists, none felt the urge to render the human body with so much sensuous realism only to discharge it with subtle, modernistic

Alex Katz (1927):
Portrait of a Poet: Kenneth Koch, 1970.
Five-colour lithograph.
(700 × 560 mm.)

devices. The same disciplined brushstroke inhabits the prints of Alex Katz, which are blatantly flatter and more subdued in color and drawing than Pearlstein's.[48] Katz, far more of a formalist than Pearlstein, endeavors to parody the large, moving, charged strokes of the expressionist fifties in the same manner that he freezes his sitters in the midst of thinking or feeling. Nowhere does he do this more convincingly than in his prints which are as formally reductive as they are psychologically restrictive. Each of his color planes is a separate drawing element, rarely meant to overlap or combine with the neighboring form. Space is evoked to the same degree as the laconic drawing of facial expression evokes character. Modernist flatness–achieved so naturally in printmaking through successive depositions of simple printing elements–becomes a systematic denial of physical, psychological, and abstract movement.

By 1972, the year of the impressive Documenta Superrealist Portfolio, realism was firmly a part of the post-Pop scene. The younger artists adopted styles far more photographic than had Pearlstein or Katz, each isolating specific aspects of photographic vision.[49] For many, the emphasis was on a totally grainless approach; their few prints were often unmanipulated, high quality photo-offset reproductions of their canvases. Others, from Robert Bechtle and Franz Gertsch to John Salt, attempted to use the full range of hand-drawn lithography. But certainly the most interesting painters and printmakers sought to conceptualize realism,[50] to reveal the conventions and techniques that underlie many of our pictures of the so-called real world. It is, however, a preoccupation prototypically American that has found few successful followers abroad.

Chuck Close, like Pearlstein, proceeds through his paintings and prints area by area; but, in his case, the image is transferred from a photograph and by means of a pre-established grid. His is one of the many strategies of the past twenty years that impose some form of external order and impersonal discipline on the way art is made, not unlike Frank Stella's *Black Series*, for example. The minute detail of Close's large paintings or of his outsized mezzotint, *Keith*, reveals how very generalized are the works of Pearlstein and Katz. Yet the viewer is forced to read the details of a Close image in such large scale that the illusion of verisimilitude is finally denied, very much as the carefully crafted "out-of-focus" passages also dissolve into pure paint or granular mezzotint.[51] Subtle discontinuities between adjacent areas in *Keith* further enforce the artificiality of the image. Ultimately, Close raises very disturbing questions about the nature of photography whose recent popularity has not particularly dampened the public's obliviousness to its elusive syntax, style, and symbolism. In his large, etched *Self-Portrait* of 1977, the illusion of photographic realism is broken down even further. The entire image is constructed on a smallscale grid, each partition of which is filled with varying numbers of slanted parallel strokes of the etching needle. In ways, the idea is not much different from the half-tone dots that compose a Warhol image (except that the "dots" are totally hand-drawn), but the process is turned inside out. Warhol degrades and denatures the machine-made image, while Close fashions by hand an encoded photograph. Ironies never cease.

Chuck Close (1940):
Self-Portrait, 1977.
Etching and aquatint.
(1372 × 1042 mm.)

217

Richard Estes (1936):
Grant's, from *Urban
Landscapes*, 1972.
Screenprint.
(503 × 650 mm.)

The notion of photographic reality is similarly challenged in the prints of Richard Estes. Both his paintings and his prints are filled with a magic, unpeopled urban clarity, and are informed by a bewildering complexity of optical reflections and surfaces.[52] However, where the paintings are continuous and smooth, the prints, composed of one- to two-hundred separate printing screens, are incredibly fragmented. Few prints of our time revel in the means of making art as much. The most complex optical events are rendered by the most sophisticated employment of distinct planes of color, yet Estes' technique is borrowed from commercial printing. So great is the ambiguity of certain passages, that at one moment a bit of color may be firmly seated on the supporting paper and the next it is part of the reflected environment behind the viewer.

The last of the realists I will discuss is less photographic, but more closely related to the serious formal overtones of Pop Art. Robert Cottingham, like Close and Estes, is not a prolific print-maker. His work draws from the urban scene, although his compositions are more restricted views and more simply constructed. On the other hand, they are more self-consciously arranged with particular sensitivity to relationships between color and shape. His lithographs have a sense of color that is shared by very few figurative artists of his generation. Printed by Jack Lemon at Landfall Press in Chicago, Cottingham's lithographs glow with a sensuosity that belies their seemingly simple construction. Although many recent printmakers seek out special palettes, and one thinks immediately of Alex Katz and Robert Mangold, Cottingham's flat motifs exude a pressure of color that one finds only in the photographs of a Joel Meyerowitz or a Stephen Shore. The interplay between contemporary photography and printmaking has many more facets than this chapter could intimate; for example, the parallels between Richard Estes and Lee Friedlander. For now, it must suffice to say that contemporary art, especially print-making, has served as a running commentary on the totally unchecked manner in which photography has invaded not only our daily existence but also our artistic sensibilities.

Robert Cottingham (1935):
Fox, 1973.
Lithograph in 24 colours.
(533 × 533 mm.)

As so often occurs in historical overviews, one is forced to backtrack in order to examine those somewhat contained developments that relate to broader movements but have an inner life of their own. Just as silkscreen printing offered so much to the Pop artist of the mid-sixties, so did etching suddenly flourish in the seventies, to serve the Minimalists.[53] It would be incorrect to believe that etching had lain fallow during the post-war years, since it has always been the most respected medium in Europe. We have already noted how Picasso and many of the School of Paris artists continued to visit the etching ateliers, how the *Tachistes* like Hartung, Sonderborg, and even such highly original, personal etchers like the great Anton Heyboer exploited the copperplate. But in the United States etching only returned to the fold of major painters in reaction to the flat and totally impersonal imagery of the sixties. The etched line was, first of all, autographic and nervous. It was also sculptural, affording a low relief in the shallow spatial field created by the platemark. Accordingly, etching was suddenly perceived as possessing a tangible

Robert Motherwell (1915):
Red 4-7, from *A la Pintura*,
poems by Rafael Alberti and
etchings by Motherwell, 1968–1972.
Aquatint with etching
and letterpress.
(642 × 965 mm.)

structure and surface that coincided with needs felt in painting and sculpture of the time. Secondly, the etched line was at once more symbolic and abstract, the aquatint plane at once more unitary and object-like than the more descriptive and highly illusionistic image of sixties' lithography. It was also more personal and intimate, and it embodied more elements of chance than the screenprint. Thus the etching combined refinement and restraint while preserving intimations of the subtly personal. In the hands of Barnett Newman, Jasper Johns, Robert Motherwell, Lee Bontecou, and Helen Frankenthaler (all working at ULAE), Richard Hamilton, David Hockney, Jim Dine, Henri Michaux, Philip Pearlstein, and Alex Katz, a sparse warmth replaced the excessive cool of the prints of the sixties.
Although the formalists have generally eschewed etching, the second generation artists, the post-Pop abstractionists like Brice Marden, Robert Ryman, Robert Mangold, Sol LeWitt, and Mel Bochner all exploited the Minimalist possibilities of the etching.[54] These variables consisted of the plane, texture, color, and edges of the paper, the platemark, the wire-like etched line, the plane of granular aquatint, the film of ink left on the surface, the imperfections that might be left in a tacky lift- or soft-ground, and the subtle textures possible in line and tone. By severely limiting their means and by consciously locating their meaning in the variables of the medium, they extended that typically American search for restrictiveness in a manner that paralleled the experiments by Donald Judd in woodcut or Ellsworth Kelly in lithography.

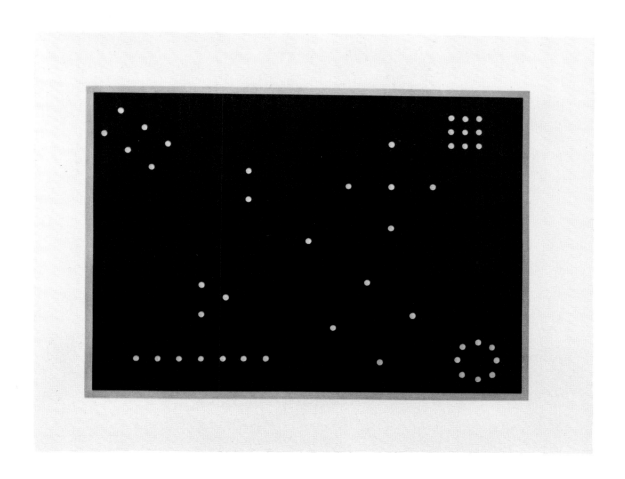

Mel Bochner (1940): △
Rules of Inference No. 8, 1974.
Aquatint. (761 × 1041 mm.)

Brice Marden (1938): ▽
Untitled (Grid with white
shading on black field),
from *Ten Days Portfolio*, 1971.
Etching and aquatint.
(304 × 383 mm.)

Just as Warhol demanded that the viewer respond to meaningless distinctions of execution, so Brice Marden or Robert Ryman were able to condense the experience of real and illusionistic abstract space into the relief established by the platemark. It would be futile to ask which of these Minimalist etchings demand more or less intellectual participation on the part of the viewer. What they have in common, and what they have inherited from the preceding generation, is the wish to involve the spectator in decisions, in self-awareness of a relative situation. Even Barnett Newman's two major etchings, which seem to be given totally to geometry, allow interpretation of the artist's choices: manifest irregularities of tone and texture, of black on black, of discontinuities and spatial innuendos where the black lines and bars abut on the limits of the embossed and polished surface at the platemark.[55] In fact, I would argue that these intimations of painterliness are precisely that which lends conviction and monumentality

Sol LeWitt (1928):
Lines to Specific Points, 1975.
Aquatint. (455 × 453 mm.)

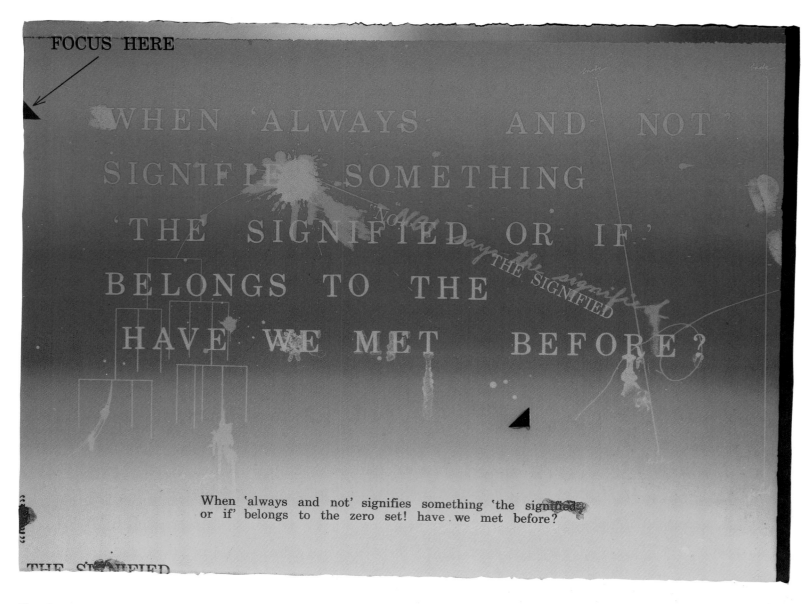

FOCUS HERE

WHEN 'ALWAYS AND NOT'
SIGNIFIES SOMETHING
'THE SIGNIFIED OR IF'
BELONGS TO THE
HAVE WE MET BEFORE?

When 'always and not' signifies something 'the signified
or if' belongs to the zero set! have we met before?

THE SIGNIFIED

Shusaku Arakawa (1936):
Untitled 4, from
No! Says the Signified Suite, 1973–1974.
Colour lithograph and collage with
hand-colouring. (559 × 762 mm.)

to the otherwise hard-edge compositions. The excruciatingly subtle infusion of the pictorial provides not only a hint of the artist's hand, but a hint of indeterminant space. By comparison Marden's etchings are more painterly and less mythic, while Bochner's are more intellectual.[56] But the experience of such works is a continuum and not an opposition, just as Arakawa's highly playful use of signs, words, and sensuous printing is a logical extension of Pop Art's inventions. The ultimate in purity, and reaction against painterliness in printmaking, might be located in some of the productions of Kathan Brown's Crown Point Press in Oakland, California, whose major productions have often been sponsored by Parasol Press. Aside from the fact that diagrammatic art is most naturally a printed art, one could wonder why such carefully crafted surfaces have been utilized by Sol LeWitt, Mel Bochner, and Robert Mangold, for example. The answer must relate not only to the tactile qualities of these prints, but the total control and lack of variation possible at Crown Point Press. Johns had shown, throughout the sixties, how the sensuosity of surface could be used as a foil for and in contrast to other kinds of acts, images, labels, and ideas. This is carried to an extreme in the descriptive orders that form an integral part of LeWitt's *Lines to Specific Points*. For the artists of the early seventies, the unmodulated aquatint surface could raise a diagram or a mental process to the level of a concrete demonstration. In ways, one could compare these prints and their ideas to the earthwork and its conceptual precursor, or even to the computer chip and its predetermined logic. The materialization of mental processes was as imaginative as the dematerialization of the object of the previous years.

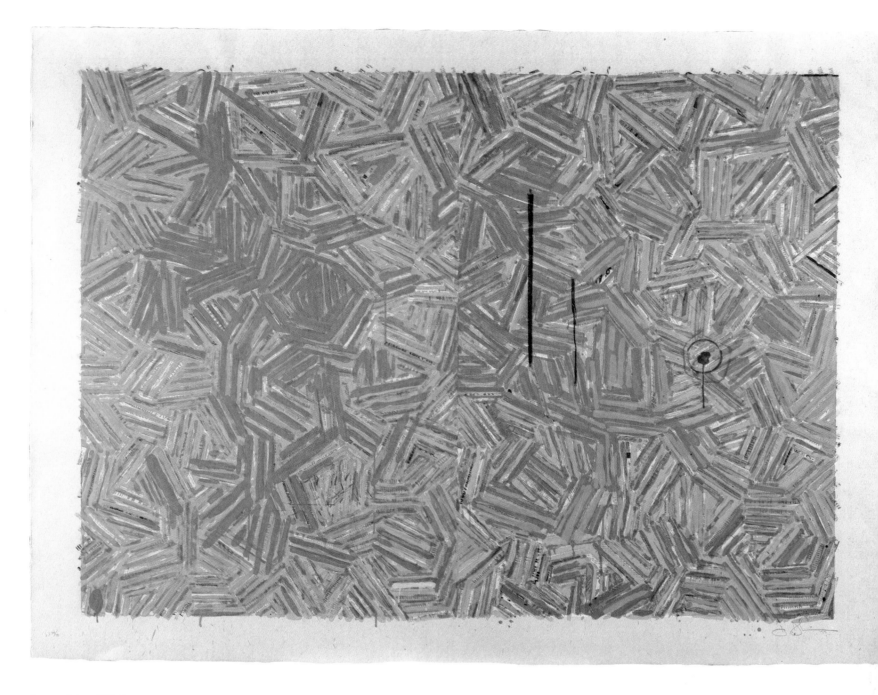

Jasper Johns (1930):
The Dutch Wives I, 1977.
Colour screenprint.
(1086 × 1422 mm.)

◁ Dorothea Rockburne (1934):
Untitled, from *The Locus Series*, 1975.
Relief etching and aquatint on
folded sheet. (1170 × 760 mm.)

Many of these American intellectual prints almost deny visual experience, but are nonetheless among the most significant prints of the decade. I am thinking in particular of the *Locus Suite* by Dorothea Rockburne. Etched lines and aquatinted planes (in white), printed on both sides of the sheet, combine with folded surfaces to document the process of making. The leaving of traces of former actions is an idea that stems directly from Jasper Johns, but it is no longer cluttered by the ambiguity that inhabited all of Johns' device motifs of the 1960s. As a matter of fact, during the seventies Johns himself has been increasingly concerned with the transfer of memory images by means of internal comparisons (as in the *Dutch Wives* or even in an etching from *Foirades/Fizzles*).[57]

Infiltration of systematic thinking occurs over and over again in his hatched paintings and prints, but Johns' work is clearly at the other end of the spectrum from that of Rockburne, Ryman, Richard Tuttle, and Fred Sandback whose sparseness contrasts directly with Johns' increasing use of texture and painterly processes.[58]

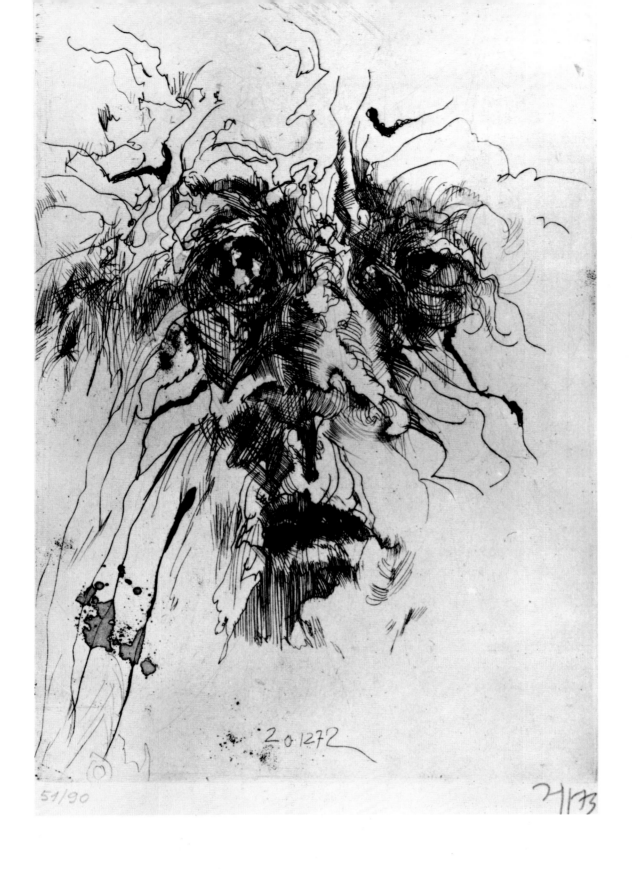

51/90   HJ/73

Horst Janssen (1929):
Self-Portrait, from
the set *Hanno's Tod*, 1972.
Etching. (228 × 150 mm.)

By 1975 it was apparent that the contemporary art scene was markedly pluralistic; prints, of course, were no exception. Along with the rise of Minimalist etching, there was a resurgence of narrative subject-matter; for example, in the prints of William Wiley, Peter Milton, Romare Bearden, Jiri Anderle, and Tetsuya Noda, and in the purveyors of "funk" like Red Grooms. Humor and nostalgia returned to prints, just as self-analysis showed up again in the etchings of Horst Janssen and Jim Dine. At the other end of the scale was the use of photo-offset lithography to record events and concepts that were not readily translated by paint or ink, for example the images of Christo's unrealized projects or Claes Oldenburg's drawings for monuments. Certainly the political works of Joseph Beuys–situations in which he himself is the central actor rather than the creating artist–or the documents of body art and earthworks could only be recorded and remembered through the medium of offset lithography.[59] Although all of these widespread narrative and autobiographical elements are worth mentioning, many appear as both perennial and momentary tendencies in the history of prints.[60] There were more important developments gathering force during the 1970s.

Surely it is too early to judge whether terms like "process art" and "anti-illusion" describe modes of art-making that opposed Pop, Minimal, Conceptual, and Abstract Illusionism. But it might be reasonable to relate these newer experiments with tangible materials to the rush towards painterliness and the exploitation of paper that rumbled through the print world in the past decade. Just when it seemed that the etchings of Newman, Johns, Ryman, and others had opened the road away from Pop iconography and abstract illusionism at the end of the sixties, Johns began to make screenprints. It was a typical Johnsian move against the grain. His adoption of the medium utilized neither its photographic nor its machine-made qualities, but was an exploration of its painterly potentials. He used the medium to make incredibly rich, almost painting-like prints, works which, like those of Rockburne, often enfolded into their layers of successive screened colors, traces of earlier ideas, of complementary colors, and of schematic drawing. But the richness of these prints echoed a growing sentiment, glimpsed in the revival of etching, to restore something of the hand of the artist to the "cool" manufactured art of the preceding decade. In 1970 Warhol told of his plans to "touch the screen again," and as predicted, the work of the seventies has embodied far more drawn elements by the master of machine-made art.

Joseph Beuys (1921):
We can't do it without roses, 1972.
Colour offset lithograph.
(860 × 610 mm.)

Richard Serra (1939):
183rd & Webster Avenue, 1972.
Three-colour lithograph.
(813 × 1124 mm.)

A return to Abstract Expressionist modes has been gathering force throughout the decade, perhaps beginning with Richard Serra's incredibly powerful lithographs of 1972, all of which contain elements of weight and space that the artist derived from a study of his own sculptures. The same trends operate in the work of Roman Opalka, Bryan Hunt, Arnulf Rainer, Rolf Iseli, and even Willem de Kooning who found the opportunity to create brilliantly transparent black and white lithographs in 1971. The return of Abstract Expressionist biases must, however, be regarded as an inevitable re-examination of the touchstone of modern art since 1950, just as a repeated consultation of Cubism has continued to inform much of the formalist and collage styles of the entire century. Nevertheless, the seventies' experiments show some of the effects of the intervening years, so that total abstraction and expressiveness is dampened or disciplined by a hint of system, by an infusion of logical space, or by an infiltration of some slight subject-matter.

Yet another hybrid style of the seventies should be noted, the resurgence of interest in woodcut. Those done by Georg Baselitz in Germany clearly betray the heritage of Cobra or the German *Informel*. Helen Frankenthaler, working at ULAE and the Tyler workshop in Bedford, New York, has produced woodcuts of unsurpassed sensual beauty.[61] They mediate Frankenthaler's Abstract Expressionist roots with her more recent interest in the nature of materials themselves. The indwelling beauty of the woodcut lies in its capacity for infinitely subtle gradations of color-as-space and in its natural, organizing surface texture. Many of these qualities have long been understood by the Japanese who, in the hands of artists like Tatsuo Ichien, keep their indigenous heritage alive.[62]

25/60   de Kooning '71

Willem de Kooning (1904):
Minnie Mouse, 1971.
Lithograph.
(698 × 532 mm.)

The urge to be part of the materials of the making of art, distinct from the habits of the Minima-lists and the Abstract Expressionists, accounts for the surge of paperworks in recent years. Why this should have occurred principally in the United States is somewhat of a mystery, since the manufacture of beautiful papers has always been a European and an Oriental stronghold. There is no doubt that, since the late sixties, Americans have reasserted their deep-rooted feelings about honest craftsmanship (perhaps in opposition to the deceptions of mass-produced, capitalist art). Although many paperworks should more properly be regarded as sculpture, and do bear a relationship to the work of Eva Hesse, Linda Benglis, Carl Andre, Robert Morris, and Richard Serra, there seem to be two factors that have led to their being grouped with prints.[63] One, of course, is the medium, paper; and the second is the fact that many of the artists who do print, weave, sew, layer, or dye the papers they employ, or who combine various sheets or mold pulp into structures, were trained in printmaking. Their mentors, Garner Tullis, Joe Wilfer, Laurence Barker, and others, came to paper some time ago, often under the influence of the relief print styles of the late fifties. This is not the place to attempt to characterize the varied approaches of William Weegee at the Fishy Whale Press in Madison, Wisconsin, of Caroline Greenwald, Martha Zelt, Winifred Lutz, Howardena Pindell, Michelle Stuart, Steven Sorman, or the Englishman, Richard Smith. Common to them all is an avoidance of illusion, a love of texture and relief, and very often the exploitation of physical process as a generator of visible structure.

◁ Ellsworth Kelly (1923):
Colored Paper Image XII, 1976.
Dyed pulp laminated to handmade paper. (1181 × 825 mm.)

Shoichi Ida (1941): ▽
Paper between Leaf and Road,
from the *Surface is the Between* series, 1977.
Lithograph and embossing on handmade Japanese paper. (940 × 597 mm.)

Helen Frankenthaler (1928):
Savage Breeze, 1974.
Colour woodcut.
(749 × 632 mm.)

A number of major painters have also worked with paper, most of them under the guidance of Kenneth Tyler. Chief among these is Robert Rauschenberg whose works chronicle a long history of utilizing materials found nearby, from studio and urban detritus in the fifties, newspaper images and photographs in the sixties, to cardboard cartons and clay casts in the early seventies. In 1974 Rauschenberg journeyed to France where at the paper mill of Richard De Bas he created the intensely object-like *Pages and Fuses*, often linking together sheets with strings, laminating to them thin pieces of paper with printed images and colors. In the same year, he produced one of the most ineffable series of prints of recent times, the *Hoarfrost* editions, in which veils of images were made by transfer, offset lithography, or screenprinting on suspended rails of cheese-cloth, silk, satin, paper, and chiffon. They float, move and transfer our attention as if they were memory images whose connections were determined by chance rather than logic. In 1975 Rauschenberg journeyed to India in order to fabricate his *Bones & Unions*, structures of paper stretched to dry around bamboo armatures, and heavy masses of mud and paper impregnated with spices and foreign ingredients such as glass, rope, and bamboo. At the same time Ellsworth Kelly, Frank Stella, and Kenneth Noland were working with Tyler and John Koller in Connecticut. Kelly, in particular, worked out some of his older ideas with masses of colored, wet pulp. Suddenly Kelly's severely delineated planes of pure color were materialized. What had been purely optical color in the form of ink atop a flat sheet of paper, now fused with the supporting pulp mass. What had been crisply defined areas were allowed to bleed ever so slightly into neighboring sections.

The pluralism within printmaking continues. An echo of this phenomenon may be found in the revival in both exhibition and practice of two painterly processes: the cliché-verre and the monotype.[64] Both media are pronouncedly autographic, and both allow for some elements of chance. Like the constructed and fabricated paperworks, they capitalize on structures provided by materials and physical events. But there is an inherent lack of conviction in many of these recent works, a slipping back into craft that ensures elegant, beautiful, crisp, complex, monumental, printed or fabricated works, but reflects a loss of drive and conviction. Perhaps this is a harsh indictment. The overbearing pressure of instant communication and the exploitation of the artist have certainly ensured shorter lives for artistic ideas. We have witnessed a remarkable twenty years in the print world, and we should expect continued experimentation and production, but perhaps not at so high a level of synthesis and significance. With the subsidence of elitism (i.e. concentrated meanings available only to the initiated) there is an increase in prints that appeal to a wider audience and to eclectic tastes. This would appear to be the way of the 1980s.

Robert Rauschenberg (1925):
Mule, from the *Hoarfrost Series*, 1974. ▷
Transfer of offset lithographed and
newspaper images; collage of paper
bags, fabric. (1651 × 914 mm.)

Steven Sorman (1948):
Spaces between Words a Deaf Man Sees, 1978.
Colour lithograph and collage.
(500 × 1004 mm.)

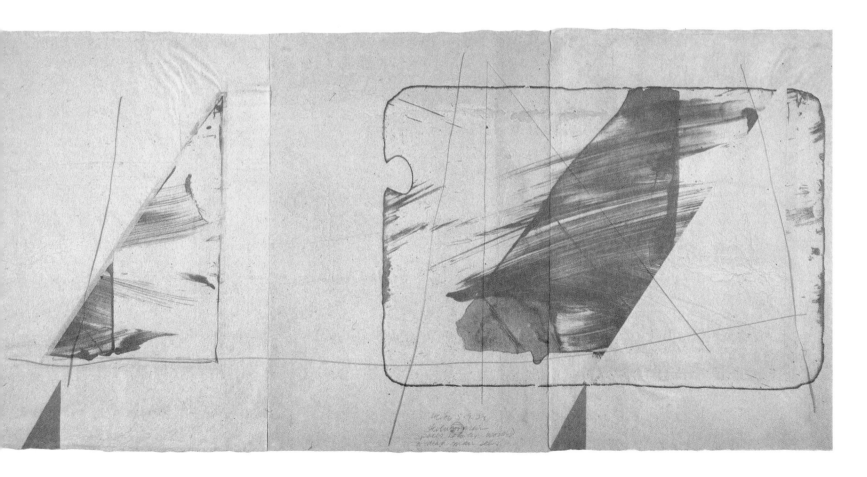

Notes

THE NATURE AND ROLE OF THE PRINT
Definition, Function and Language of the Print (page 8)

[1] Andrew W. Tuer, *Bartolozzi and his Works*, London, 1881, Vol. 2, p. 33.

[2] The early woodblock known as *le Bois Protat* was probably intended for printing on textile rather than paper; see Henri Bouchot, *Un ancêtre de la gravure sur bois: étude sur un xylographe taillé en Bourgogne vers 1370*, Paris, 1902, and also Arthur M. Hind, *An Introduction to a History of Woodcut*, London and New York, 1935 (reprinted New York, 1963), Vol. 1, pp. 70-71. So was the Strasbourg *Education of the Virgin*, reproduced in J.J. Delen, *Histoire de la gravure dans les anciens Pays-Bas*, Paris, 1924, plate II, 2. See also André Blum, *La Route du Papier*, Grenoble, 1946.

[3] Hervé Fischer, *Art et Communication marginale, Tampons d'artistes*, Paris, 1974.

[4] Jean Eugène Bersier, *Jean Duvet, le Maître à la Licorne, 1485-1570?*, Paris, 1977, p. 26.

[5] *Krasno, œuvre graphique, œuvre en papier*, exhibition in the Cabinet des Estampes, Bibliothèque Nationale, Paris 1971.

[6] For example, the experiments of Garner Tullis at the International Institute of Printmaking, Santa Cruz, California. See "The Spirit of Santa Cruz," *Art News*, January 1976.

[7] On the straight-stencil or *pochoir* process, now little used, see the report published in *Nouvelles de l'Estampe*, No. 21, May-June 1975.

[8] On monotypes see the excellent catalogue, amounting to a monograph on the subject, of the exhibition *The Painterly Print: Monotypes from the Seventeenth to the Twentieth Century*, Metropolitan Museum of Art, New York, October-December 1980.

[9] Eugenia Parry Janis, *Degas Monotypes. Essay, Catalogue & Checklist*, Fogg Art Museum, Harvard University, 1968. For Degas's *Dancer Taking her Bow*, see the exhibition catalogue *L'Estampe impressionniste*, Bibliothèque Nationale, Paris, 1974, No. 210, p. 94 (illustration).

[10] Françoise Cachin and Jean Adhémar, *Degas, gravures et monotypes*, Paris, 1973. See also Eugenia Parry Janis, "The role of the monotype in the working method of Degas," *Burlington Magazine*, 1967, pp. 20-27 and 71-81.

[11] See Charles Newton's essay in the exhibition catalogue *Photography in Printmaking*, Victoria and Albert Museum, London, 1979.

[12] Christine de Rendinger, *L'Affiche d'intérieur, le poster*, Paris, 1977.

[13] See the book by Marie-Odile Briot and Catherine Humblot, *La Peau des murs: Ernest Pignon-Ernest*, Paris, 1979.

[14] Erasmus of Rotterdam, *In Praise of Folly*, chapter XL.

[15] The finest collection of these prophylactic woodcuts, fourteen in number, is in the Département des Estampes of the Bibliothèque Nationale, Paris; they are of French origin, dating to the period 1490-1520.

[16] Paul Pelliot, *Les Débuts de l'imprimerie en Chine*, Paris, 1953.

[17] Jean Fribourg, "Gravure sur bois," in Werner Speiser, Roger Goepper and Jean Fribourg, *Arts de la Chine, peinture, calligraphie, estampages, estampes*, Fribourg (Switzerland), 1973.

[18] See the examples brought together by Allen Fern, "Prints as subject," in *Studies in Honor of Gertrude Rosenthal*, Part Two, Baltimore Museum of Art, 1972.
On the pilgrimage badges, see Emile H. van Heurck, *Les Drapelets de pèlerinage...*, Antwerp, 1922.

[19] Michel Melot, "Note sur une gravure encadrée du XVIᵉ siècle," *Nouvelles de l'Estampe*, No. 9, May-June 1973, pp. 9-11.

[20] Michèle Hébert, "Gravures d'illustration et peintures murales à la fin du moyen âge," *Bulletin de l'Association des Bibliothécaires français*, No. 20, June 1956, p. 66 ff.

[21] Jacques Thirion, "Panneaux sculptés d'après Philippe Galle aux Musées de Cluny et des Arts Décoratifs," *Revue du Louvre*, No. 3, 1965, pp. 103-110.

[22] Jacques Lethève, *La Vie quotidienne des artistes français au XIXᵉ siècle*, Paris, 1968, pp. 20 and 47.

[23] On emblems see Mario Praz, *Studies in Seventeenth Century Imagery*, Rome, 1964, and Robert Klein, "La Théorie de l'expression figurée dans les traités italiens sur les imprese, 1555-1612," in *La Forme et l'Intelligible*, Paris, 1970, pp. 125-150.

[24] Roberto Weiss, *The Renaissance Discovery of Classical Antiquity*, Oxford, 1969.

[25] Archives of the Kupferstichkabinett, Dresden.

[26] Marcel Proust, *Du Côté de chez Swann*, edited by Pierre Clarac and André Ferré, Collection Folio, Paris, pp. 52-53.

[27] Also the language of sexuality. Here is a characteristic statement of this kind by a "pure" engraver: "For me engraving is not a means of repro-
duction. The travail is difficult, the gestation slow. I never know what kind of a child it will give me... Every plate I take up is a fresh love affair... One embrace follows another, and the acid proves a wonderful helpmate, which I soon drop for the scraper, with its tenacious scratchings, or for the cutting tool which will open up some gaping wounds. The moment of birth is just ahead. The preparations have been made: the clean dry swaddling-clothes will be received by a press whose pressure will have been judiciously regulated... I would rather not, repeat rather not have twins" (Jean-Marie Signovert, in *Nouvelles de l'Estampe*, No. 40-41, July-October 1978, pp. 35-36.

[28] Henri Zerner, *Ecole de Fontainebleau, Gravures*, Paris, 1969.

[29] Jean Adhémar, "Les Concierges du château de Fontainebleau," *Gazette des Beaux-Arts*, 1956, pp. 119-120, and "Henri Zerner et les étapes de l'Ecole de Fontainebleau," *Gazette des Beaux-Arts*, August 1969, pp. 117-120.

[30] Michel Melot, "La Pratique d'un artiste: Pissarro graveur en 1880," in *Histoire et Critique des Arts*, No. 2, June 1977, pp. 14-31, and in particular p. 16: "L'Impressionnisme et le nouveau capitalisme: la réévaluation de l'idée du temps."

Product and Work of Art (page 40)

[31] Richard S. Field, introduction to the catalogue of the exhibition *Fifteenth-Century Woodcuts*, Metropolitan Museum of Art, New York, 1977.

[32] The most interesting documents are quoted in J.J. Delen, *Histoire de la gravure dans les anciens Pays-Bas*, Vol. 1, Paris, 1924. On Jan van den Berghe, see Vol. 1, pp. 24-25.

[33] Jacques Le Goff, *La Civilisation de l'Occident médiéval*, Paris, 1965, pp. 142-144. On late medieval spirituality, see the thesis of Jacques Toussaert, *Le Sentiment religieux en Flandre à la fin du Moyen Age*, Paris, 1963.

[34] Richard S. Field, *The Fable of the Sick Lion: A Fifteenth Century Blockbook*, Davison Art Center, Wesleyan University, Middletown, Connecticut, 1974, p. 91.

[35] Carel van Mander, *Het Schilder-boeck*, Haarlem, 1604. English translation by Constant van de Wall, *Dutch and Flemish Painters*, New York, 1936.

[36] Frederick Antal, *Florentine Painting and Its Social Background*, London, 1948, and New York, 1975 (Icon Editions, Harper and Row), p. 297. Grateful acknowledgment is made to Harper and Row, Publishers, New York, for permission to quote this passage.

[37] Jean-Pierre Seguin, *Le Jeu de Cartes*, Paris, 1968; Detlef Hoffmann, *Die Welt der Spielkarte, eine Kulturgeschichte*, Leipzig, 1972; R. Tilley, *A History of Playing Cards*, London and New York, 1973.

[38] See, for example, John Goldsmith Phillips, *Early Florentine Designers and Engravers*, Harvard University Press, 1955, and M.J. Schretlen, *Dutch and Flemish Woodcuts of the Fifteenth Century*, foreword by Max J. Friedländer, New York, 1925.

[39] Max Lehrs, "The Master F.V.B.," *The Print Collector's Quarterly*, Vol. 10, No. 1, February 1923, p. 18.

[40] Henri Zerner, "A propos de faux Marcantoine, notes sur les amateurs d'estampes à la Renaissance," *Bibliothèque d'Humanisme et Renaissance*, XXIII, 1961, pp. 477-481.

[41] Woldemar von Seidlitz, "La Propriété artistique et la contrefaçon d'après d'anciens exemples," *Gazette des Beaux-Arts*, XIV, October 1895, pp. 317-334.

[42] Peter Dreyer, "Tizianfälschungen des sechzehnten Jahrhunderts...," *Pantheon*, October-December 1979, pp. 365-375.

[43] On Titian and the Venetian woodcut, see the catalogue by Michelangelo Muraro and David Rosand for the exhibition *Tiziano e la silografia veneziana del cinquecento*, Fondazione Cini, Venice, 1976, in particular No. 7, p. 78.

[44] L.B. Voet, *Antwerp, The Golden Age*, Antwerp, 1973. See also L.B. Voet, *The Golden Compasses, A History and Evaluation of the Printing and Publishing Activities of the Officina Plantiniana at Antwerp*, 3 volumes, Amsterdam, London, New York, 1969.

[45] Quoted in Louis Lebeer, "Propos sur l'importance de l'étude des éditeurs d'estampes, particulièrement en ce qui concerne Jérôme Cock," *Revue belge d'Archéologie et d'Histoire de l'Art*, XXXVII, 1968, p. 122.

[46] On Frans Floris see Carel van Mander, *Het Schilder-boeck*, Haarlem, 1604; English translation by Constant van de Wall, *Dutch and Flemish Painters*, New York, 1936. For the accounts of the firm of Plantin, see L.B. Voet, *The Golden Compasses...*, Amsterdam, 1969; J.J. Delen, *Histoire de la gravure dans les anciens Pays-Bas*, Vol. 3, p. 149 ff., Paris, 1924; and Louis Lebeer in *Revue belge d'Archéologie et d'Histoire de l'Art*, XXXVII, 1968, p. 122.

[47] Bernard Palissy, "De l'Art de terre" in his *Discours admirables...*, Paris, 1580, reprinted Paris, 1930, p. 34.

[48] Letter from Plantin quoted in J.J. Delen, *Histoire de la gravure dans les anciens Pays-Bas*, Vol. 3, pp. 160-161, Paris, 1924.

[49] Yves Metman, "Pierre Milan et René Boyvin," appendix in the book by Jacques Levron, *René Boyvin, graveur angevin du XVIe siècle...*, Angers, 1941.

[50] Georges Wildenstein, "Les graveurs de Nicolas Poussin au XVIIe siècle," *Gazette des Beaux-Arts*, September-October 1955, pp. 77-371.

[51] Viktoria Schmidt-Linsenhoff, "Les estampes d'après Guido Reni, une introduction à la gravure de reproduction au XVIIe siècle," *Nouvelles de l'Estampe*, No. 40-41, July-October 1978, pp. 5-17.

[52] Egon Verheyen, "Marginalia to Vasari," *RACAR*, V, 1978, No. 1, pp. 37-40.

[53] Hans Vlieghe, "Erasmus Quellinus and Rubens's Studio Practice," *Burlington Magazine*, No. 894, September 1977, p. 639.

[54] José Lothe, *François de Poilly graveur et marchand d'estampes, 1623-1693*, doctoral dissertation, Ecole Pratique des Hautes Etudes, Paris, 1977.

[55] Arthur M. Hind, "Van Dyck, his original etchings and his Iconography," *The Print Collector's Quarterly*, V, 1915, pp. 3-37 and 221-253.

[56] Nikolaus Pevsner, *Academies, Past and Present*, Cambridge University Press, 1940.
On Leonardo as an engraver see André Blum, "Léonard de Vinci graveur," *Gazette des Beaux-Arts*, August-September 1932, pp. 89-104.

[57] Erwin Panofsky, *Galileo as Critic of the Arts*, The Hague, 1954.

[58] Francis Haskell, *Patrons and Painters, A Study in the Relations Between Italian Art and Society in the Age of the Baroque*, London, 1963, p. 124.

[59] On the print trade in Rome see Jacques Kuhnmünch, "Un marchand français d'estampes à Rome au XVIIe siècle, François Collignon," *Bulletin de la Société d'Histoire de l'Art français*, 1978, pp. 79-100, and "Le commerce de l'estampe à Rome et à Paris au XVIIe siècle," *Nouvelles de l'Estampe*, No. 55, January-February 1981.

[60] Marianne Grivel, *Le Commerce de l'estampe à Paris au XVIIe siècle*, thesis at the Ecole des Chartes, Paris, 1980. This thesis is well worth publishing in full, and so is that of Pierre Casselle, *Le Commerce des estampes à Paris dans la seconde moitié du XVIIIe siècle*, Ecole des Chartes, 1976.

[61] Roger de Piles, *Abrégé de la Vie des peintres avec réflexions sur leurs ouvrages... et de l'utilité des estampes*, Paris, 1699. See also Bernard Teyssèdre, *L'Histoire de l'art vue du Grand Siècle*, Paris, 1964.

[62] Robert Hecquet, *Catalogue des estampes gravées d'après Rubens...*, Paris, 1751; E.F. Gersaint, *Catalogue raisonné de toutes les pièces qui forment l'œuvre de Rembrandt...*, Paris, 1751; Robert Hecquet, *Catalogue de l'œuvre de François de Poilly*, Paris, 1752.

[63] Rembrandt's etchings have been catalogued by E.F. Gersaint (Paris, 1751), P. Yver (Amsterdam, 1756), D. Daulby (Liverpool, 1796), Adam Bartsch (Vienna, 1797), J.J. de Claussin (Paris, 1824), T. Wilson (London, 1836), Charles Blanc (Paris, 1873), C.H. Middleton-Wake (London, 1878), Eugène Dutuit (Paris, 1883), Dmitri Rovinski (St. Petersburg, 1890-1894), Woldemar von Seidlitz (Leipzig, 1895), Seymour Haden (London, 1896), Campbell Dodgson (London, 1904), H.W. Singer (Stuttgart, 1906-1910), A.M. Hind (London, 1912), A.C. Coppier (Paris, 1917), Ludwig Münz (London, 1952), K.G. Boon (Amsterdam, 1963), G. Biörklund and O.H. Barnard (Stockholm, 1968), K.G. Boon and Christopher White (Amsterdam, 1969), and Harry Salamon (Milan, 1972).

[64] Joachim von Sandrart, *Teutsche Academie*, Nuremberg, 1675, chapter XXII. Quoted by Cornelis Hofstede de Groot, *Die Urkunden über Rembrandt, 1575-1721*, The Hague, 1906 (No. 329, §4).

[65] A.M. Hind, *A Catalogue of Rembrandt's Etchings*, 2nd edition, London, 1923, reprinted New York, 1967, p. 67.

[66] André-Charles Coppier, *Les Eaux-fortes authentiques de Rembrandt...*, Paris, 1928.

[67] *Les Cuivres originaux de Rembrandt*, published by Michel Bernard and Alvin-Beaumont, Paris, 1906. Reimpressions of the 79 copperplates which are said to have come down from Mariette to Basan, then to the latter's successors, Jean, and then Bernard.

[68] Marie Mauquoy-Hendrickx, *L'Iconographie d'Antoine Van Dyck*, Brussels, 1956: chapter V, "Les Falsifications," pp. 85-94.

[69] For example the hand photogravures published by Amand-Durand; those of the Berlin Reichsdrückerei; those of Charreyre illustrating the catalogue of Eugène Dutuit; or the thousand collotypes illustrating Rovinski's catalogue.

[70] Osbert H. Barnard, "On the detection of forgeries," in G. Biörklund, *Rembrandt's Etchings, True and False*, Stockholm, 1968, pp. 185-187.

An Art of the Bourgeoisie (page 70)

[71] Richard Lane, *"Images from the Floating World": The Japanese Print*, Fribourg, Oxford, New York, 1978.

[72] On the similarity of subject matter between Japanese prints and Toulouse-Lautrec's set of lithographs *Elles*, see Michel Melot, "Questions au Japonisme," symposium on "Le Japonisme," Tokyo, December 1979 (forthcoming).

[73] Gabriel Naudé, quoted by Jean Adhémar, "Quelques images burlesques du Cabinet des Estampes," *Æsculape*, No. 3, March 1950.

[74] Daniel Ternois, *L'Art de Jacques Callot*, Paris, 1962, p. 43.

[75] Frederick Antal, *Hogarth and his Place in European Art*, London, 1962.

[76] [Berthold], *La Ville de Paris en vers burlesques*, Paris, 1652, reprinted Paris, 1856, p. 135.

[77] Georges Wildenstein, "Le Goût pour la peinture dans la bourgeoisie parisienne entre 1550 et 1610," *Gazette des Beaux-Arts*, Paris, 1962, and "Le Goût pour la peinture dans la bourgeoisie parisienne au début du règne de Louis XIII," *Gazette des Beaux-Arts*, October-December 1950, pp. 153-274.

[78] Michel de Marolles, *Le Livre des peintres et des graveurs*, edited by Georges Duplessis, Paris, 1855.

[79] *Menagiana, recueil de bons mots de M. Ménage...*, 2nd edition, Paris, 1693, Vol. 1, p. 30.

[80] Gérard de Lairesse, *Le Grand Livre des Peintres*, 2 volumes, Paris, 1787: Vol. 2, Book 7, p. 131, "Des Portraits."

[81] Jeanne Duportal, *La gravure en France au XVIIIe siècle: La gravure de portraits et de paysages*, Paris, 1926, p. 7.

[82] Louis-Sébastien Mercier, *Tableau de Paris*, new enlarged edition, Amsterdam, 1789, Vol. 10, p. 55 (chapter DCCLXXXV: Graveurs).

[83] F. Feuillet de Conches, "Les Apocryphes de la gravure de portraits," *Gazette des Beaux-Arts*, June 1859, pp. 337-348. See also Henri Bouchot, "Du suranné en iconographie," *Gazette des Beaux-Arts*, March 1904, pp. 211-214.

[84] Edmond Pognon, "Les portraits de Ronsard, essai d'épuration iconographique," *Gazette des Beaux-Arts*, September 1959, pp. 109-116.

[85] Eugène Bouvy, *Le portrait gravé et ses maîtres: Robert Nanteuil*, Paris, 1924, pp. 98-100.

[86] See the whole introduction of Gisèle Freund's book, *Photographie et Société*, Paris, 1974.

[87] José Lothe, "Images et Monarchie, les thèses gravées de François de Poilly," *Nouvelles de l'Estampe*, No. 29, September-October 1976, pp. 6-12.

[88] Georges Duplessis, "Le Cabinet du Roi, collection d'estampes commandées par Louis XIV," *Le Bibliophile français*, Paris, 1869, p. 3, note 2.

[89] Roger-Armand Weigert, "Les transformations d'une vignette, trois collaborateurs imprévus: Sébastien Leclerc, Eisen, Charles-Nicolas Cochin," *L'Amateur d'Estampes*, 11th year, October 1932, pp. 145-153. See also Maxime Préaud, *Sébastien Leclerc*, Inventaire du Fonds français du Cabinet des Estampes, Vol. XV, Paris, Bibliothèque Nationale, 1980, p. 42, No. 18 (with reproductions of the states of St Claude turned into Mary Magdalene, pp. 40-41).

[90] Michel de Marolles, *Discours en forme de préface à son Catalogue de livres d'estampes...*, Paris, 1666, p. 7.

[91] Germaine Guillaume, "La Collection d'Estampes du Duc de Mortemart (1681-1746)...," *Archives de la Société d'Histoire de l'Art français*, 1963, pp. 285-292.

[92] "Lettre de Monsieur Dezallier d'Argenville sur le choix et l'arrangement d'un cabinet curieux, à Monsieur de Fougeroux," *Le Mercure de France*, June 1727, p. 1295 ff.

[93] E.F. Gersaint, *Préface à un catalogue d'estampes de choix*, published by Jean Adhémar in *Nouvelles de l'Estampe*, No. 11, September-October 1973, p. 9.

[94] Philippe Burty, "La Belle Epreuve," preface to an album of etchings published by Alfred Cadart under the title *L'Eau-forte en 1875*. See also Roger Marx's preface to the catalogue of the third exhibition of the Société des Peintres-Graveurs français, Paris, 1891.

[95] Walter Koschatzky, "Adam von Bartsch, an introduction to his life and work," in *"Le Peintre-Graveur Illustré,"* illustrations to Adam Bartsch's *"Peintre-Graveur,"* vol. XII-XXI, Pennsylvania State University Press, 1971.

[96] Antony Griffiths, "Greuze et ses graveurs," *Nouvelles de l'Estampe*, No. 52-53, July-October 1980, pp. 9-12.

[97] Walter Koschatzky, *L'Albertina de Vienne, historique et fonction de la collection*, Vienna, n.d., p. 1.

[98] Laura Malvano, "Le sujet politique en peinture: événements et histoire pendant les années de la Révolution," *Histoire et Critique des Arts*, No. 13-14, 1980, p. 65, note 46.

[99] Léon Rosenthal, *Du romantisme au réalisme, essai sur l'évolution de la peinture en France de 1830 à 1848*, Paris, 1918, p. 72.

[100] Pierre-François Basan, *Projet de décret sur les graveurs et les propriétaires de planches gravées*, Paris, n.d. [1791], 8vo (Bibliothèque Nationale, Paris, Cabinet des Estampes Yc 94).

[101] Jean-Michel Papillon, *Traité historique et pratique de la gravure en bois*, Paris, 1766, Vol. 1, chapter 1, "De l'origine de la gravure en bois."

[102] The origins of engraving on metal have been studied by J.D. Passavant in *Archiv für die zeichnenden Künste*, Leipzig, 1858; Jules Renouvier, "Les Origines de la gravure en France," *Gazette des Beaux-Arts*, 1859; and Henri Delaborde, "Notice sur deux estampes de 1406 et les commencements de la gravure en criblé," *Gazette des Beaux-Arts*, 1869, p. 238.

[103] Polemics began in 1845 with Baron de Reiffenberg's paper "La plus ancienne gravure connue avec une date...," sitting of 7 May 1845, volume XIX of *Nouveaux Mémoires de l'Académie royale des Sciences et Belles Lettres de Bruxelles*, followed by articles by C. de Brou, Lutherau and others. A summing up was made much later by Henri Hymans in his *L'Estampe de 1418 et la validité de sa date*, Brussels, 1903.

[104] On the Protat woodblock see Henri Bouchot, *Un ancêtre de la gravure sur bois: étude sur un xylographe taillé en Bourgogne vers 1370*, Paris, 1902, and also Arthur M. Hind, *An Introduction to a History of Woodcut*, London and New York, 1935, reprinted New York, 1963, Vol. 1, pp. 70-71.

[105] On Goya's position as an etcher see Gwyn Williams, *Goya and the Impossible Revolution*, London, 1976.

[106] Françoise Arquié-Bruley, "Les graveurs amateurs français du XVIIIe siècle," *Nouvelles de l'Estampe*, No. 50, March-April 1980, pp. 5-13.

[107] See Michel Melot, "L'Histoire de l'art est-elle de l'histoire?", paper read at the symposium on the teaching of art, University of Quebec, Montreal, August 1980 (proceedings soon to be published).

[108] Léon Lang, *Godefroy Engelmann imprimeur-lithographe: les incunables, 1814-1817*, Colmar, 1977.

[109] William McAllister Johnson, *French Lithography: The Restauration Salons, 1817-1824*, Agnes Etherington Art Centre, Kingston, Ontario, 1977.

[110] Harrison C. White and Cynthia A. White, *Canvases and Careers, Institutional Change in the French Painting World*, New York, 1965, pp. 80-82.

Industrialized Pictures and their Effect on the Print (page 100)

[111] René Hennequin, *Avant les photographies: les portraits au physionotrace..., catalogue des 1800 premiers portraits...*, Troyes, 1932.

[112] See the proceedings of the colloquy "Daumier et les débuts du dessin de presse," Maison de la Culture, Grenoble, 1979, published in *Histoire et Critique des Arts*, No. 13-14, 1980.

[113] On the hawking of picture sheets in France under the Second Empire, see Jean-Jacques Darmon, *Le Colportage de librairie en France sous le Second Empire: grands colporteurs et culture populaire*, Paris, 1972.

[114] Auguste Bry, *L'Imprimeur lithographe, nouveau manuel à l'usage des élèves*, Paris, 1835.

[115] Basil Hunnisett, *Steel-Engraved Book Illustration in England*, London, 1980.

[116] On these early techniques of reproduction, see the book (a century old but reliable and well informed) by Jules Adeline, *Les Arts de reproduction vulgarisés*, Paris, n.d., and the well-researched essay by Eckhard Schaar in the exhibition catalogue *Von Delacroix bis Munch, Künstlergraphik im 19. Jahrhundert*, Kunsthalle, Hamburg, 1977.

[117] Unsigned Salon review, "Le Salon de 1841," in *L'Artiste*, VII, 1841, p. 381.

[118] Raoul de Croy, "Les Magasins pittoresques à deux sous," *Journal des Artistes et des Amateurs*, 7th year, No. XVIII, 3 November 1833, pp. 281-285.

[119] Léon de Laborde, *Exposition Universelle de 1851, travaux de la commission française sur l'industrie des nations... tome VIII, 30ᵉ jury: Application des arts à l'industrie... rapport de M. le Comte de Laborde*, Paris, Imprimerie impériale, 1856. See in particular pp. 445-503.

[120] This mid-nineteenth century transformation of the print into an art form is traced in detail in the catalogue introduction of Michel Melot, *Les Gravures de Boudin, Corot, Daubigny, Dupré, Jongkind, Millet, Rousseau*, Paris, 1978.

[121] This parliamentary debate on proprietary rights and copyrights was fully reported in *L'Artiste* of 1841, especially volume VII, p. 71 ff.

[122] Adolphe-Eugène Disdéri, *Application de la photographie...*, p. 7. Quoted by Ann MacCauley, "Adolphe-Eugène Disdéri," *Prestige de la Photographie*, No. 5, 1980.

[123] Series of articles by Charles Jacque in *Le Magasin Pittoresque*, XX, 1852, pp. 188, 236, 292, 331 and 372.

[124] Janine Bailly-Herzberg, *L'Eau-forte de peintre au dix-neuvième siècle, La Société des aquafortistes, 1862-1867*, 2 volumes, Paris, 1972.

[125] Michel Melot, "La Pratique d'un artiste: Pissarro graveur en 1880," *Histoire et Critique des Arts*, No. 2, 1977, in particular p. 21: "La crise économique et l'échec impressionniste."

[126] *George A. Lucas Collection, Selected Prints*, exhibition at the Baltimore Museum of Art, June-August 1976. On Avery see *The Diaries 1871-1882 of Samuel P. Avery, Art Dealer*, New York, 1979.

[127] Joseph Maberly, *The Print Collector: An Introduction to the Knowledge necessary for forming a Collection of Ancient Prints*, New York, 1880 (reprinted New York, 1979); this book was originally published in London in 1844. Aloys Appel, *Handbuch für Kupferstichsammler*, Leipzig, 1880. Henri Béraldi, *Les Graveurs du XIXᵉ siècle*, 12 volumes, Paris, 1885-1892.

[128] Douglas W. Druick, "Cézanne, Vollard and Lithography: the Ottawa Maquette for the Large Bathers colour lithograph," *Bulletin of the National Gallery of Canada*, No. 19, Ottawa, 1972.

[129] Douglas W. Druick, "Puvis and the Printed Image (1862-1898)," *Nouvelles de l'Estampe*, No. 34-35, July-October 1977, pp. 27-34.

[130] D.H. Kahnweiler, *Entretiens avec Francis Crémieux*, Paris, 1931.

[131] Elizabeth and Michel Dixmier, *L'Assiette au Beurre*, Paris, 1974.

[132] Jean-Michel Palmier, *L'Expressionnisme et les Arts*, Paris, 1980, Vol. 2, p. 198.

[133] Hans M. Wingler, "La Gravure au Bauhaus," supplement to the catalogue of the exhibition *Bauhaus, 1919-1969*, Musée National d'Art Moderne, Paris, and Musée d'Art Moderne de la Ville de Paris, 2 April-22 June 1969.

[134] See for example the catalogue of the exhibition *American Prints 1879-1979* by Frances Carey and Antony Griffiths, British Museum, London, 1980.

[135] *Atelier 17, A 50th Anniversary Retrospective Exhibition*, essay and catalogue by Joann Moser, Elvehjem Art Center, University of Wisconsin, Madison, Wisconsin, 1977.

[136] Michel Melot, "Henri Goetz et la gravure," in Oscar Reutersväd, Michel Melot and Denise Zayan, *Œuvre gravé de Goetz*, Paris, 1977.

CONTEMPORARY TRENDS (page 188)

[1] There are surprisingly few informative texts on recent prints; the two best were published in conjunction with exhibitions: Pat Gilmour, *The Mechanized Image, An Historical Perspective on 20th Century Prints*, London, Arts Council of Great Britain, 1978; and Riva Castleman, *Printed Art, A View of Two Decades*, New York, The Museum of Modern Art, 1980.

[2] Marshall McLuhan, *Understanding Media, The Extensions of Man*, New York, 1964; and William M. Ivins, Jr., *Prints and Visual Communication*, Cambridge, Massachusetts, 1953.

[3] E.H. Gombrich, *Art and Illusion, A Study in the Psychology of Pictorial Representation*, London, 1960. Many of Gombrich's basic thoughts could be illustrated by an analysis of Johns' work of 1956–1964.

[4] The word "technique" has several meanings. For those whose focus is principally on prints, the term refers to the chemical and mechanical process of printmaking; the image summoned up by the word is one of complex, hand-executed procedures. In this sense it is not a modern term. But there is another, more recent way this word has been employed. In this usage, the intent is to convey something far less personal; "technique" signifies an impersonal style, code, or commercial process.

[5] See Joseph E. Young, "Jasper Johns: An Appraisal," *Art International*, Vol. 13, No. 7, September 1969, pp. 50-55.

[6] Since its Cubist beginnings in 1911, collage has served to introduce bits of reality into the pictorial matrix, often by intruding them into the viewer's space. In the 1920s and 1930s the idea of photomontage–of collaging pieces of photographic realities together–joined the anti-illusionistic aspects of the Cubist collage. But it was not until the 1960s that a seamless collage of distinct media quotations made its appearance in prints.

[7] See Charles Baudelaire, "L'eau-forte est à la mode," *Revue Anecdotique*, 2 April 1862. Many reactions against so-called commercialism in printmaking were linked to the use of photographic means in the 1860s as well as the 1960s.

[8] *Estampe* designates a print executed by a skilled technician *after* a modello supplied by the artist. Although the majority of recent (French) *estampes* were manufactured to meet standards of high technical decorativeness, some works after Braque and others may well survive as significant objects.

[9] See the first volume in this series (Jean Leymarie, Geneviève Monnier, and Bernice Rose, *Drawing*, Geneva, Skira, 1979) for discussions about the roles of drawings. Our own reference quite obviously overlooks the vast sources of information provided by many kinds of diagrams, sketches and illustrations.

[10] See *Atelier 17, A 50th Anniversary Retrospective Exhibition*, Elvehjem Art Center, University of Wisconsin, Madison, 1977. Essay and catalogue by Joann Moser.

[11] The second edition of Hayter's *New Ways of Gravure* appeared in 1966, but much of the work he pioneered was set down in the text of his student, Gabor Peterdi, *Printmaking: Methods Old and New*, New York, 1959.

[12] For ideas about the collaborative process, see Michel Melot's essay in this volume, as well as Carl Zigrosser and Christa Gaehde, *A Guide to the Collecting and Care of Original Prints*, New York, 1971; and Theodore B. Donson, *Prints and the Print Market*, New York, 1977.

[13] In 1944–1945 Pollock made at least eleven engravings and drypoints in Hayter's shop; see F.V. O'Connor and E.V. Thaw, *Jackson Pollock: A Catalogue Raisonné of Paintings, Drawings, and Other Works*, New Haven, 1978, Nos. 1069-1087.

[14] Riva Castleman emphasizes the strong Surrealist current in twentieth-century printmaking; see her survey, *Prints of the Twentieth Century, A History*, New York and London, 1976.

[15] See *Tamarind: A Renaissance of Lithography*, Washington, D.C., The International Exhibitions Foundation, 1971–1972. Catalogue prepared by E. Maurice Bloch. On the history of ULAE, see Calvin Tomkins, "The Moods of a Stone," *The New Yorker*, 7 June 1976, pp. 41-76.

[16] See *The Lithographs of Jean Dubuffet*, Philadelphia Museum of Art, 1964–1965. Texts by Kneeland McNulty, N. Richard Miller and Jean Dubuffet.

[17] In addition to *21 Etchings and Poems* (Kline, de Kooning, Pereira, Lipchitz, Schrag, Racz, Martinelli, etc.) printed in 1957 but published in 1960, one de Kooning lithograph printed with friends in California, and the six screenprints by Pollock (O'Connor and Thaw, *op. cit.*, Nos. 1091-1096), there were four volumes of *The International Avant-Garde*, published by Arturo Schwarz in Milan, between 1962 and 1965.

[18] See *Druckgrafik des deutschen Informel*, 1951–1963, Nürnberg, AD Gesellschaft, 1975.

[19] See *Antoni Tápies, Das gesamte graphische Werk*, Kassel, Kassler Kunstverein, 1969.

[20] See *Contemporary American Prints from Universal Limited Art Editions / The Rapp Collection*, Toronto, Art Gallery of Ontario, 1979; or *Contemporary American Prints: Gifts from the Singer Collection*, New York, The Metropolitan Museum of Art, 1976.

[21] See Thomas Krens, *Helen Frankenthaler, Prints: 1961–1979*, New York, 1980.

[22] For a recent bibliography on Johns' prints, see Richard S. Field, *Jasper Johns: Prints 1970–1977*, Middletown, Connecticut, 1978.

[23] One of the most provocative essays on recent figure-ground developments is in Rosalind Krauss, *Line as Language: Six Artists Draw*, Princeton University, The Art Museum, 1974.

[24] The most economical and eloquent formulation of the paradoxical qualities of Johns' paintings appeared in Clement Greenberg, "After Abstract Expressionism," *Art International*, Vol. 6, No. 8, October 1962, p. 27.

[25] See *Robert Rauschenberg*, Washington, D.C., National Collection of Fine Arts, 1976. Catalogue with an essay by Lawrence Alloway and a detailed chronology.

[26] The most ambitious exhibition of relief prints was assembled by Kneeland McNulty at the Philadelphia Museum of Art in 1963; see his article, "The New Dimension in Printmaking," *Artist's Proof* 5, Vol. 3, No. 1, Spring-Summer 1963, pp. 8-17. Considerable information on the development of these prints may be found in *The Graphic Art of Rolf Nesch*, The Detroit Institute of Arts, 1969; catalogue by Jan Askeland, Ernst Scheyer, and Ellen Sharp.

[27] These methods are described by Edward A. Foster in his catalogue, *Robert Rauschenberg: Prints 1948/1970*, The Minneapolis Institute of Arts, 1970.

[28] For the development of screenprinting in painting, see Rainer Crone, *Andy Warhol*, New York, 1970. The National Serigraph Society wholeheartedly supported the restrictive notion of "the original print." The artist was to be totally responsible for all work on the "matrix" (i.e., the screen, the block, the stone, or copperplate), he was not permitted to utilize any form of photographic process, and he was personally responsible for the printing and limiting of his edition.

[29] A most revealing account of Warhol's printing habits is contained in Gerald Malanga, "A Conversation with Andy Warhol," *Print Collector's Newsletter*, Vol. 1, No. 6, January-February 1971, pp. 125-127. Norman Ives and Cy Sillman of New Haven reported (in a 1970 interview) that in 1964 Warhol had instructed them to allow the screens to clog up and print erratically.

[30] Although Warhol experimented with a few screenprints on paper in 1962 (see Crone, Nos. 601-604), his first editions date from 1963 and 1964. The portfolios already marked the beginning of standardized production, the first being *10 Marilyns* of 1967; this was followed by two *Campbell's Soup Can* portfolios of 1968, and the *Flowers* of 1970. The *Cow* wallpaper was first issued in 1966 and then again (in different colors) in 1970.

[31] A very important but still overlooked publication was E.B. Kornfeld's *1¢ Life*, 1966. The project took shape some years earlier and demonstrates, as no other publication, the transition from Abstract Expressionist to Pop. The verses (by Walasse Ting) and the images in both "styles" share an immediacy and a concern with the present, with life of the moment. The Pop images are very much drawn, that is, the vestiges of an expressionist vocabulary are turned to the service of popular imagery.

[32] The detailed history of screenprinting is yet to be written. Some of our very tentative conclusions were presented in Richard S. Field, "Silkscreen, the Media Medium," *Art News*, Vol. 70, No. 9, January 1972, pp. 40-43, 74-75. See also the Checklist for *Silkscreen: History of a Medium*, Philadelphia Museum of Art, 1971–1972; Francis Carr, *A Guide to Screen Process Printing*, New York, 1962; Wolfgang Hainke, *Siebdruck, Technik, Praxis, Geschichte*, Cologne, 1979. The best historical collection of screenprinting, so far as I know, is that built up by Carl Zigrosser and the present writer for the Philadelphia Museum of Art.

[33] The first, largely screenprinted, POP portfolios to appear in the United States were: *Ten Works by Ten Painters*, published by the Wadsworth Atheneum (Sam Wagstaff) in 1964 (Stuart Davis, Indiana, Kelly, Lichtenstein, Motherwell, Ortman, Poons, Reinhardt, Stella and Warhol); *New York Ten / 1965*, published by Tanglewood Press (Rosa Esman) included works by Anuszkiewicz, Dine, Frankenthaler, Jones, Krushenick, Levinson, Lichtenstein, Oldenburg, Rayo, and Segal. 1965–1966 marked the publication of three portfolios entitled *11 Pop Artists*, supported by Philip Morris, Inc. Each included works by D'Arcangelo, Dine, Jones, Laing, Lichtenstein, Phillips, Ramos, Rosenquist, Warhol, Wesley, and Wesselman. Other portfolios from the sixties include: *Toronto 20*, 1965; *New York International*, 1966; *Seven Objects in a Box*, 1966; *The National Collection of Fine Arts Portfolio*, 1968; *Graphics USA*, 1968; *Metropolitan Scene*, 1968; *Ten from Leo Castelli*, 1967; *Six New York Artists*, 1969; *New York Ten / 1969*; *Kunstmarkt Köln*, 1969; *The Referendum Portfolio*; *9 from Hollander* (all lithographs), 1967.

[34] See Diane Waldman, *Roy Lichtenstein, Drawings and Prints*, New York, 1970; Albert Boime, "Roy Lichtenstein and the Comic Strip," *Art Journal*, Vol. 28, No. 2, Winter 1968–1969, pp. 155-159; Richard Hamilton, "Roy Lichtenstein," *Studio International*, Vol. 175, No. 896, January 1968, pp. 20-24; and Gene Baro, "Roy Lichtenstein: Technique as Style," *Art International*, Vol. 12, No. 9, November 1968, pp. 35-38.

[35] For a formalist interpretation of Pop Art, see John Russell and Suzi Gablik, *Pop Art Redefined*, London, 1969.

[36] On serial imagery see John Coplans, *Serial Imagery*, Greenwich, Connecticut, 1968.

[37] Johns' *Ale Cans* has had a long history. Beginning with the sculpture of 1960, it has been the subject of a lithograph (1964), of an etching (1967 and 1969), of an offset lithograph (1971 and 1973), of a new series of lithographs (1975), of a painting (1972), and of many drawings.

[38] Lucy Lippard, *Six Years: The Dematerialization of the Art Object from 1966 to 1972*, New York, 1973.

[39] Ruscha's words often float in the bent space provided by "rainbow roll" inking. Although the space is strictly that of color-field painting, the technique whereby it is achieved is strictly that of the commercial screen-printing shop, and one that dates back a number of decades.

[40] See Lawrence Alloway's account in Lucy Lippard, *Pop Art*, New York, 1966, pp. 27-67, also the fine essay by Richard Morphet in the exhibition catalogue, *Richard Hamilton*, London, The Tate Gallery, 1970.

[41] Accounts of the development of Kelpra Studio are contained in the catalogue, *Kelpra Prints*, London, The Arts Council, 1970.

[42] See Rosemary Miles, *The Complete Prints of Eduardo Paolozzi*, London, The Victoria and Albert Museum, 1977. Unfortunately none of the literature has been able to decode the relationship between Wittgenstein's texts and Paolozzi's images.

[43] The most distinguished text on Hamilton is Richard Morphet's essay in the exhibition catalogue, *Richard Hamilton*, London, The Tate Gallery, 1970. See also Richard S. Field, *The Prints of Richard Hamilton*, Middletown, Conn., Wesleyan University, Davison Art Center, 1973.

[44] At this writing, the complex interplay of allusion in Kitaj's works remains pretty much unstudied; they appear closely related to the three levels of analysis described by Erwin Panofsky in the "Introductory" to his *Studies in Iconology*, Oxford, 1939.

[45] Kelly began printmaking in 1964 in response to the request of Sam Wagstaff for a contribution to the portfolio *Ten Works by Ten Painters*. In 1964 he also did a large but rather inconsequential group of lithographs for the Galerie Maeght in Paris; a serious exploration of printmaking did not take place until he began to work at Gemini in 1970. Noland, until his recent romance with paperworks, avoided prints; one or two exceptions were the rather dreary screenprints published in the late 1960s by Multiples, Inc. Olitski, on the other hand, executed two highly original and successful sets of five screenprints in 1970–1971; they were printed by Chiron Press in New York and published by Leslie Waddington of London. Each print was executed from 7-10 photoscreens made from sprayed acetate film. It was a brilliant solution to the problem of recapitulating Olitski's layers of sprayed pigment.

[46] For a thorough analysis of Stella's first lithographs (those that recapitulated the Black paintings), see Brenda Richardson with assistance from Mary Martha Ward, *Frank Stella: The Black Paintings*, The Baltimore Museum of Art, 1976.

[47] I have described this in full in my essay for *Philip Pearlstein: Prints, Drawings, Paintings*, Middletown, Conn., Wesleyan University, Davison Art Center, 1979.

[48] On Alex Katz see Irving Sandler, *Alex Katz*, New York, 1979; and Richard S. Field and Elke M. Solomon, *Alex Katz: Prints*, New York, The Whitney Museum of American Art, 1974.

[49] Many of the first graphics by the so-called "Photo-Realists" were no more than commercial, photo-offset reproductions of their paintings (producing, at times, some fairly amusing and/or confusing effects). But the *Documenta Portfolio*, published by Shorewood Atelier in New York, included only hand-drawn lithographs by Bechtle, Eddy, Gertsch, Goings, McLean, Posen, Salt, Schonzeit, and Staiger.

[50] Pearlstein conceived of the phrase "the conceptualization of realism" to describe a panel discussion at the College Art Association meetings in January 1978; see "Realism vs. Existentialism," *Allan Frumkin Gallery Newsletter*, No. 5, Spring 1978, pp. 4-6.

[51] On the structure of Chuck Close's "mezzotint" *Keith*, see my remarks in *Recent American Etching*, Middletown, Conn., Wesleyan University, Davison Art Center, 1975. An excellent discussion of Close's working methods may be found in Michael Shapiro, "Changing Variables: Chuck Close and His Prints," *Print Collector's Newsletter*, Vol. 9, No. 3, July-August 1978, pp. 69-72.

[52] See John Arthur, "Richard Estes: The Urban Landscape in Print," *Print Collector's Newsletter*, Vol. 10, No. 1, March-April 1979, pp. 12-15. For a detailed account of the role played by photographs in Estes's work see the same author's exhibition catalogue, *Richard Estes: The Urban Landscape*, Boston, The Museum of Fine Arts, 1978.

[53] See my introduction to *Recent American Etching, op. cit.*

[54] An excellent presentation of the work and comments of these artists appeared in the catalogue of Nancy Tousley's exhibition, *Prints – Bochner, LeWitt, Mangold, Marden, Martin, Renouf, Rockburne, Ryman*, Toronto, Art Gallery of Ontario, 1976.

[55] Aside from Thomas B. Hess's "Notes on Newman's 'Notes'," *Print Collector's Newsletter*, Vol. 2, No. 6, January-February 1972, pp. 121-123, there is nothing written on Newman's prints. But see Naomi Spector, "Robert Ryman: Suite of Seven Aquatints, 1972, and Nine Unique Aquatints, 1972," *Bulletin 70, Art & Project*, Amsterdam, 1973; and *idem*, "Robert Ryman: 'Six Aquatints'," *Print Collector's Newsletter*, Vol. 8, No. 1, March-April 1977, pp. 10-12.

[56] Bochner's prints have received little attention, with the exception of Tousley, *op. cit.*; the interested reader is referred to Brenda Richardson, *Mel Bochner: Number and Shape*, The Baltimore Museum of Art, 1976; to Krauss, cited above in footnote 23; and to Robert Pincus-Witten, "Mel Bochner: The Constant as Variable," *Artforum*, Vol. 11, No. 4, December 1972, pp. 28-34.

[57] Although the role of memory in the production of pictures has been prominent in art theory since the middle of the last century, a critical examination of the issues is still awaited. Similarly, there is no study of Johns' ideas on memory; yet he has encoded memory in much of his work, from his constant repetition and doubling of images, his use of photographic reproductions, to his extended experimentation with casts. I have had several occasions to refer to Johns and memory in my two catalogues of his prints (Philadelphia, 1971, and Middletown, Conn., 1978); also see Roberta Bernstein, "Jasper Johns and the Figure, Part One: Body Imprints," *Arts Magazine*, Vol. 52, No. 2, October 1977, pp. 142-144.

[58] The prints of Judd, Rockburne, Sandback, and Tuttle embody a reductiveness that makes the so-called Minimalist productions of Marden, Mangold, and Ryman appear luxurious. See John Loring, "Judding from Descartes, Sandbacking, and several Tuttologies," *Print Collector's Newsletter*, Vol. 7, No. 6, January-February 1977, pp. 165-168.

[59] See *Offset Lithography*, Middletown, Conn., Wesleyan University, Davison Art Center, 1973. Catalogue prepared by Richard S. Field and Louise Sperling. This exhibition concentrated on American work, overlooking both European offset prints and the more difficult question of reportage of artistic events and earthworks. There is a catalogue of Beuys reportage prints: Jorg Schellmann and Bernd Klüser, *Joseph Beuys Multiples*, Munich, 1977.

[60] Quite obviously this account has totally overlooked the majority of prints exhibited in the various international competitions held in Bradford, Tokyo, San Francisco, San Juan, Ljubljana, etc. Other large print exhibitions have taken place in Paris, Nürnberg, Brooklyn, The Hague, Fredrikstads, Lugano, Como, Venice, Torino, Brussels, Mulhouse, Geneva, Santiago de Chile, etc.

[61] See Thomas Krens, *Helen Frankenthaler, Prints: 1961-1979*, New York, 1980.

[62] Woodcuts seem to be enjoying a minor revival among recent painters. Aside from Frankenthaler, some of those who have tried their hand at the medium include Dine, Judd, Jennifer Bartlett, Susan Rothenberg, Sandback, Lichtenstein, Shoichi Ida, and H.C. Westerman.

[63] On paperworks see *The Handmade Paper Object*, Boston, Institute of Contemporary Art, 1977; and *Paper – Art & Technology*, San Francisco, 1979.

[64] Two recent surveys of the historical surveys of the origins and uses of medium have contained sections on contemporary applications: *Cliché-Verre: Hand-Drawn, Light Printed*, Detroit, The Detroit Institute of Arts, 1980, catalogue by Elizabeth Glassman and Marilyn F. Symmes; and *The Painterly Print: Monotypes from the Seventeenth to the Twentieth Century*, New York, The Metropolitan Museum of Art, 1980, with essays by Sue Welsh Reed, Eugenia Parry Janis, Barbara Stern Shapiro, David W. Kiehl, Colta Ives, and Michael Mazur.

GLOSSARY OF TECHNICAL TERMS

BIBLIOGRAPHY

LIST OF ILLUSTRATIONS

INDEX OF NAMES AND PLACES

Printing in the workshop of Roger Lacourière, Paris,
of etchings by André Masson for André Malraux's novel
Les Conquérants, published by Albert Skira, Paris, 1949.

242

GLOSSARY OF TECHNICAL TERMS

André Béguin

Adapted from the French
by Giulia Bartrum, Research
Assistant at the British Museum

Abbreviation. Many of the inscriptions to be found on prints, in particular old master engravings, are written or engraved in an abbreviated form. *See: lettering.*

Abrasive agent. A substance capable of wearing down and polishing the surface of a plate or lithographic stone. It is used either in powdered form, or as a type of sandpaper, or as a stone, and is rubbed over the necessary area. Different abrasives are characterized by their hardness and by the size of their grain.
See: acidic cleaning, burnishing, graining, polishing, sharpening.

Absorbency. Capacity of the support of a drawing, painting or print (usually paper) to facilitate penetration of the ink.
See: absorption, ink, paper, stone.

Absorption and adsorption. Liquids and semi-liquids penetrate absorbent materials and are therefore naturally retained by them. The process by which the same liquids are retained by non-absorbent materials, such as zinc or aluminium (in *lithography* and *offset lithography*), is known as *adsorption.*

Acid. Acid is used at many stages of printmaking, in particular for cleaning metal plates, for etching, for preparation of lithographic stones (nitric acid) and zinc plates (phosphoric acid).
See: acidic cleaning, corrosive agents, engraving, etching, lithography.

Acid wash. *See: brush etching.*

Acidic cleaning. An essential part in the preparation of metal plates and screens, it is done before the design is engraved or applied. It involves a thorough removal of stains, traces of oxidation, grease, paint, ink, etc. Detergents made from soda mixed with whiting are used on metal plates; on screens, soda detergents are also used, as well as other more specific cleaning agents for removing particular substances.

Adhesion of the ink. To ensure that a good impression is made, it is necessary for the ink to adhere properly to the support. Adhesion depends on the quality of the ink and on the absorbency of the paper.
See: ink, paper.

Aerosol. Small metal container holding a mixture of a liquid product and a propulsive gas. It can be used as a means of applying varnish, colours, solvents and various other substances used in printmaking. It produces a spray of fine droplets.

Air-brush (Aerograph). A small air-gun capable of spraying paint, ink, varnish or ground in a stream of fine droplets. It can be used in lithography and aquatint, for the application of a flat tint, and on drawings which are to be photographed in the half-tone technique.
See: aerosol, aquatint, dot work, lithography, splatter.

Albertype. *See: collotype.*

Algraphy. The treatment of an aluminium plate with the lithographic technique. The resulting print is called an *algraph.*
See: aluminium, lithography, metals.

Alignment. Operation of aligning the printing paper in the press or on the printing table.
See: impression.

Aluminium. This metal can be used in printmaking either as a plate, or as a support for an impression to be made upon. In the former case, it can be (a) engraved with the burin, (b) etched with mercuric bichloride, or (c) prepared lithographically. Impressions can be made directly onto the metal, in particular with the screenprinting technique.
See: algraphy, lithography, metals, screenprinting.

Anastatic print. A type of print produced particularly in the nineteenth century. It was made by transferring a printed image onto another piece of paper by chemical means. The image (or text) must have been originally printed with a greasy ink. The verso of the original was dampened with a gum solution added to a small amount of sulphuric acid; the recto was then inked with a greasy printing ink which only adhered to the inked parts on the original. The process was used frequently as a means of producing a lithographic transfer.
See: lithography.

Anopistographic. A term applied to incunables which are only printed on one side (antonym: opistographic).

Anti-bubble additive. A product mixed with ink in screenprinting to prevent the formation of bubbles while pulling impressions.
See: screenprinting.

Anti-static additive. A product mixed with ink in screenprinting to prevent electric currents forming. An anti-static fabric is used to neutralize electric currents on the screen.
See: base, dilutant, ink, screenprinting.

Aquatint. A process of intaglio engraving on metal. The plate is covered with a special ground made from a powdered substance through which the surface is bitten. The resulting effect is not of an engraved line, but of finely textured rings set close together. Gradated shades can be obtained between light grey and black, of varying colour tones if printed in colour. Consequently, it can produce a reasonably close representation of a wash drawing and was originally called an engraving in the wash manner (Fr. "gravure en manière de lavis"). It can be distinguished from a *brush etching* (Fr. "gravure au lavis") by the effects of the aquatint ground: the surface is indented with small dots which retain the ink, whereas the surface of a brush etching possesses an even matt appearance, since it is produced with acid alone. This distinction is disregarded by the French. The ground is traditionally obtained by shaking powdered resin or bitumen over the plate and fixing it with the application of heat. The grounded plate is then placed in a bath containing nitric acid, or an acid made from ferric

chloride, which bites the areas surrounding the particles of resin. A process initiated by André Béguin substitutes a resinous varnish vapourized in an air-brush as a means of applying the ground. The plate can also be grounded by dotting particles of resin over the surface. Aquatint plates are more fragile than those which have been line-engraved, owing to the shallow nature of their indentations. Nevertheless the prints are pulled from the same press.
See: bitumen, brush etching, dot work, dust-box, grounds, intaglio.

Aquatinter. An engraver who specializes in the aquatint process. The term dates from 1866.

Artist's proof. *See: proof.*

Autography. *See: lithography, transfer.*

Autogravure. A general term applied to all photochemical methods of making intaglio prints.
See: engraving, photogravure.

Autotype. Since the nineteenth century this term has had different meanings. Initially, it was synonymous with heliography, a photographic process; it is also the same as *line block. Autotypography* is a process which reproduces typographic designs. The black is prepared by a galvanic process.
See: galvanic processes, photogravure.

Background. 1. The part which constitutes the background of the design in a print.
2. On a relief or planographic printing element, the background is the part underneath the foreground lines of the design. On an intaglio plate, the background is engraved either on the same level or on a higher level than the foreground. In the latter case, there is greater uniformity in relation to the design.
3. Dotted background: one which is made up of more or less uniform dots.
See: dot work.
4. "A fond perdu": the French term used to describe the background of a print in which the colours reach the edge of the paper, without any border.
5. White background: where the white of the paper is conserved to form the background.

Backing. 1. Used in lithography after the stone has been inked and before the first impression is taken: the printing paper is laid on the surface of the stone; this is then superimposed with two more sheets followed by a top of compressed fibre-board which is greased with tallow—this is the backing.
2. In conservation a print is backed by another sheet of paper in order to reinforce it if it has become very fragile.
See: conservation.

Backing the block. A method of strengthening a woodcut or typographic block. Pieces of wood are cut out to correspond with the areas already cut into the block, and are glued to its reverse. By making the block thicker, more weight is given to the relief areas which consequently produce a better impression.
See: letterpress, packing, woodcut.

Badger-hair brush. A large soft brush made from badger's hair, employed in cleaning drawn or engraved surfaces, and in removing the bubbles which form on a metal plate while biting is in progress.
See: brush, bubbles, feather.

Baren. An instrument used for printing Japanese woodcuts. It is a type of *rubber* used on the back of the paper which has been applied to the inked block.
See: spoon, woodcut.

Base. 1. The product which is added to printing ink in order to obtain certain effects, e.g. *thinning varnish*, transparent varnish; used particularly in screenprinting.
2. The oxide or hydroxide contained in metals. Alkaline metals contain alkali as base.
See: corrosive agents.
3. *See: printing table.*

Bath. A term applied to the acid container used in the etching process, or the liquid container used in electroplating. It is also the receptacle used to dampen paper.
See: biting, dampening.

Beading. A greasy surface repels water and aqueous preparations by reducing them to droplets. This beading will occur if, for example, a copper plate which has not been cleaned properly is covered with Indian ink.

Bed (of press). Part of the press on which the plate or block rests during printing. In a lithographic press, the bed is a mobile element which transports the stone to a position beneath the *scraper*.
See: lithography, press.

Before lettering. *See: lettering, proof before lettering.*

Benzine. *See: solvent.*

Bevelling. The edges of intaglio plates are bevelled to ensure that they do not cut the paper in the press. A true bevel is only necessary if the plate is more than a millimetre thick, otherwise a light rounding off is sufficient.
See: press.

Biting. The process of (1) corroding a design on a metal plate in either intaglio (e.g. etching) or relief (e.g. line block); and (2) fixing the image on the stone or metal plate in lithography *(see: reinforcing).* It is done with a mordant: acid solution, salt (perchloride of iron), etc.
See: corrosive agents, mordant.

Biting with oil. When a *line* or *half-tone block* is attacked with acid, a large amount of oil is added to a protective varnish applied to the block during the final stages.

Biting with powdered substances. *Line* and *half-tone blocks* can be etched by protecting the parts to remain in relief with a resin made of powdered dragon's-blood.

Bitumen. A complex mixture of hydrocarbons existing in both solid and liquid form which may be brown or blackish in colour. Bitumen of Judea (asphaltum), mixed with oil of turpentine, is the traditional type of bitumen used in the fabrication of various grounds and varnishes. Since the invention of photography, bitumen has been used to sensitize surfaces as on exposure to light it becomes insoluble. It is also used to make lithographic crayon.
See: aquatint, grounds and varnishes, lithography, photographic processes.

Blacken. A plate or block is blackened by holding it over smoke in order to improve the visibility of the image in intaglio printing and wood engraving.
See: smoking (the plate).
Metal plates may also be blackened by submerging them in various chemical solutions (which vary according to the metal).

Blankets. Blankets may be used as the *packing* placed between the upper roller of the intaglio press and the paper when printing, in order to even out the pressure.
See: intaglio, press.

Block. The wooden element which is printed in making woodcuts and wood engraving. The word also applies to typographical printing elements.

Blockbook. A fifteenth-century relief printing process, whereby both text and images for a whole page would be cut on one block.
See: woodcut.

Blocking out. 1. "Blocking out" is the isolation of the parts which must remain in relief on a block.
See: woodcut, wood engraving.
2. In photography, "blocking out" is the process of isolating an image while covering the surrounding area.

Blow lamp. During the preparation of a lithographic stone, an image may be reinforced through the application of heat with the aid of a blow lamp.
See: lithography.

Blunt. The condition of a pointed tool which is in need of sharpening.
See: sharpening.

Blurring. An impression will receive a blurred appearance if the paper and the inked roller are not properly registered during printing.
See: ink.

"Bon à tirer". Good to print: signed on a trial proof by the artist when he wishes to indicate to the professional printer that a satisfactory state of his print has been obtained. It gives the printer the standard to which he must adhere in taking successive impressions.
See: proof, state.

Book work. In letterpress the preparation of the text in books is known as book work, as opposed to that of cards, catalogues, etc. (jobbing work). Particular kinds of inks are used for book work which are less resinous than those used in printing vignettes.

Bordering. While a plate is being etched, the borders and edges of the plate must be protected. This is done by either applying an asphalt varnish (stopping-out varnish) or by using *bordering wax*, a pure yellow wax added to a little mutton fat. It is built up around the plate as a small bank, thereby creating a saucer-shape into which the mordant can be poured.
See: biting, stopping out.

Brass. An alloy of copper and zinc sometimes used for engraving, particularly in the nineteenth century, for certain geographical maps.

Brush. The uses of the brush in printmaking include: making the drawing in lithography and applying the various substances (varnish, sugar solution, etc.) to metal plates in etching.
See: badger-hair brush.

Brush etching. A method which preceded, and is related to, the aquatint process: it aims to stimulate the light stones of a wash drawing through the application of neat acid to the plate with the aid of a brush. This creates a slight roughening of the surface which produces a tone when printed. It has been used in combination with other intaglio processes. Sulphur has also been used for the same purpose.
See: aquatint, sulphur prints.

Bubbles. While a plate is being etched, an effervescence forms on its surface which must be constantly removed throughout the procedure by brushing it with a feather.
See: biting, feather.

Burin engraving. Also known as *line engraving*, this important method of intaglio printing originated in the fifteenth century. It consists in incising lines, dots and flicks, directly onto the plate with a burin (also known as a *graver*). The incisions are filled with printing ink and the plate and paper are placed in a press between two rollers, of which the uppermost is covered with specially resilient blankets *(see: packing)* in order to even out the pressure. The paper, which has been previously dampened, penetrates the incisions and pulls out the ink.
The burin is a steel rod, of square or rectangular section, with its end bevelled to an oblique point. A mushroom-shaped handle is at the other end. It is held in the palm of the hand and pushed across the metal. Controlling the direction as well as the depth of the incision made is the most difficult

part of the technique, and the plate is placed on a cushion where it can be easily turned, so that the burin need move as little as possible when a change of direction is required. There is a tradition of working the burin in parallel lines *(see "burin rangée")*. The engraver uses these to model the form of his design, incising a shallower or deeper line to obtain a corresponding effect of relief, which may be further accentuated by cross-hatching. The line engraved by the burin has a particular clarity: lesser detail as well as areas of intense black can be achieved with equal success. It is generally done on copper; steel is also used for it has the advantage of great durability – very fine lines can be produced which do not wear down as quickly as those on copper plates.
See: impression, inking, intaglio, wiping.

"Burin rangée". The French term used to describe a method of engraving with the controlled use of parallel lines, as opposed to *free engraving or etching*.
See: burin engraving.

Burning (the block). A technique of woodcutting involving the use of burning was taken up in the nineteenth century, but it has been little used other than for printing music sheets and textile printing. The incised parts of the block were burnt out instead of being cut and a stereotype was taken with which the printing was done.

Burnishing. The operation of smoothing out the grain in the mezzotint process with the aid of the burnisher, a polished steel tool with a large round head. It is also used on metal plates where corrections are required.
See: polishing.

Burr. The cutting action of a tool across a metal plate causes rough ridges known as "burr" to be thrown up on either side of the incision. The ridges left by a *burin* are quite small and are removed with the *scraper*; the *drypoint* creates a large burr, which retains the ink and prints an area of rich tone – the particular characteristic of this technique. Burr is very fragile and, unless the plate is *steel-faced*, will rapidly wear away in the press.

Calender. A machine in which paper is glazed, by applying pressure with rollers.

Callipers. A tool resembling a pair of dividers used in making corrections on an intaglio plate. They locate the corresponding position, of the part to be corrected, on the back of the plate. The indentation caused by erasing the mistake on the front *(see: punch)* is then knocked up from behind with a hammer.

Cancelled plate. When the printing of a limited edition of prints has been completed, it is usual to deface the plates, stones, etc., to ensure that there is no possibility of their being reprinted. A "cancellation" impression is one that is taken to prove the cancellation.
See: emery.

Carbon tissue. *See: photographic processes.*

Carborundum. A very hard mixture consisting primarily of silicon carbide; it is used as an abrasive and, in powdered form, in a method of engraving invented by Henri Goetz. He used it to obtain a dotted effect by sprinkling it over a metal plate (usually duralumin) which was then pulled through a press, thereby causing the grains to penetrate the metal.

Cartogravure. Simplified technique of engraving on Bristol board. Printing is done manually and only a few impressions can be taken; it is really only of scholastic interest.

Cartouche. Ornamental design resembling the curves of a rolled-up parchment scroll. It is found at the base of old master engravings containing inscriptions (title, dedication, date, signature, etc.).

"Cat's tongue". From the French term "langue de chat" for a fine etching needle with a small furrow on its upper surface.

Celluloidograph. A nineteenth-century technique, in which a celluloid plate was engraved with a burin or an etching needle and then electrotyped. The reproduction left much to be desired.

Cellulotype. A simplified process of line engraving on a celluloid block.

Chalcography. A term that applied initially to copperplate engraving but later expanded to cover all types of line-engraved metal plates. A chalcography is a collection of engraved plates, or the place where they are kept.

"Champignon". French term for describing the handle of an engraving tool, particularly of a burin or an échoppe.

Charcoal. Charcoal (particularly of willow or lime wood) is used for polishing metal plates.
See: polishing.

"Chariot". French term for the vehicle used to transport heavy lithographic stones.

Chiaroscuro. 1. In a general sense, chiaroscuro describes the method of using contrasted light and shade as a means of illuminating and giving form to a particular subject.
2. In a specific sense, it describes a particular woodcutting process *(chiaroscuro woodcut)*, in which *tone blocks* (usually in lighter and darker tones of one colour) are overprinted and juxtaposed to obtain a coloured print. The same technique can be applied to lithography: different stones are used for the varying tones.
See: lithography, woodcut.

"Chimigramme". *See: photographic processes.*

Chinese ink. In preparing screens, a particular type of Chinese ink is sometimes used; it is opaque in colour and corrodes plastic (caustic ink).

Chisel. A flat tool used in woodcutting. It has a bevelled edge and is either pushed manually, or knocked with a mallet, over large areas to be cut away, i.e. those between the edges of the design and the sides of the block.
See: woodcut, wood engraving.

Chromium-facing. Application of a thin layer of chromium by electrolysis onto the surface of a metal plate.
See: steel-facing.

Chromolithography. In a loose manner this can mean simply printing lithographs in colour. The term was specifically applied to certain nineteenth-century colour lithographs which were reproductive in intention and imitated the appearance of oil paintings. They were printed from a large number of stones, which demands a good technical skill.
See: colour printing, lithography.

Chromotype or chromotypography. A typographical impression printed in colour.

Chromotypogravure. A nineteenth-century term for typographical colour engraving, either manually or photomechanically produced.
See: block, letterpress.

Chrysoglyph. A type of metalcut produced in the nineteenth century. The relief plate was made by electroplating a previously etched plate.
See: electroplating, metalcut.

"Cliché-verre". From the French term (it is also known as a *glass-print*). The artist draws a design with a needle on a glass plate coated with an opaque ground from which positive photographic prints are made on sensitized paper as from an ordinary negative.

Clipping. Reducing the margins of a print.

Collage. A method of preparing the screen to make a covering stencil in screenprinting.

Collagraph. The print resulting from a collage of materials glued together on a base and printed as a combined relief and intaglio plate.

Collotype. Initially called *albertype*, after its principal inventor, this process consists in pouring a layer of gelatine mixed with potassium chromate over the surface of a zinc or glass plate which is then exposed to light to receive the image. The gelatine hardens in proportion to the amount of light received, the unexposed parts remaining soft and capable of retaining moisture, and the printing can therefore be done lithographically: the plate is dampened with water and the ink is applied with a roller. It adheres to the surface in inverse proportion to the amount of moisture retained, the hard areas of gelatine printing the darkest. The reticulated grain of collotype is particularly good for reproducing watercolours, for which the process was much used during the latter part of the nineteenth century.

Colour block. Colour blocks (or *tone blocks*) print the various colours in a colour or chiaroscuro woodcut. The *key block* prints the outline.
See: chiaroscuro, colour printing.

Colour printing. In woodcuts, colour printing is done with several different colour blocks which are overprinted. Chiaroscuro woodcuts are printed in various tones of one colour and for this reason cannot be classed as true colour prints. A more unusual method of colour printing can be done from one assembled block; the various parts having been previously separated and inked with the different colours.
There are two different ways of intaglio colour printing: with several plates, i.e. one for each colour, which are overprinted or juxtaposed next to each other; or with one plate which has been inked in different parts with separate colours applied with a brush or stumps of rag (*à la poupée* or "dolly").
Several stones are used in lithographic colour printing, one or the other sometimes replaced by a zinc plate. Known as *chromolithography* (or *chromo*), it was a popular technique in the nineteenth century.
Colours can be printed side by side, or overprinted, in screenprinting, by preparing the screen in such a way that a place is reserved for each colour without the various inks smudging. In letterpress, offset lithography and photogravure several blocks/plates are also used: there are three if the base colours, blue, red and yellow, are used (by *overprinting* different colours can be obtained), or four if grey or black is added to emphasize the dark areas.
Printing with different coloured blocks, plates or stones demands exact registration involving a careful concordance of the variously coloured parts. Usually colours are printed from light to dark but often the blues are printed first. N.B. There is a difference between colour prints and impressions taken from a single colourblock, plate or stone (other than brown or black). Neither must they be confused with hand-coloured prints.
See: hand-colouring, ink, overprinting, registration.

Composuit or **comp.** Sometimes found after the name of the person who made the design on an engraving or lithograph.

Conservation. The restoration of prints aims to correct damage caused by handling, excessive exposure to light, smoke, dust, humidity or aridity, and contact with liquid or any other destructive substance. Present methods allow cleaning and repair, provided that the print has not been subjected to irreversible alterations.

Copal. A hard resin used in the production of certain grounds and in a very hard type of lithographic crayon.

Copper. The most important metal used in engraving. It is supple to work yet strong enough to endure the press, receptive to ink and wipes clean without leaving traces. It polishes well and is also sensitive to mordants. It does, however, tarnish quickly if left unprotected.
See: metals.

Copper-facing. The application of a very thin layer of copper onto a metal plate by means of electrolysis. Zinc must initially be copper-faced if a steel-facing is to be applied.
See: galvanic processes, steel-facing.

Copperplate printing. *See: intaglio.*

Copy. A print is a copy if the designer has taken the image from another artist.

Corrosive agents. Products used for cleaning and biting the various fabrics, papers, stones and metals used in printmaking are divided into three types: acids, alkalis and salts. Nitric acid is the most commonly used of the acids. It bites copper (c. 15° Baumé), zinc and steel (between 5° and 15° Baumé), in a rapid, shallow manner; it is also used for cleaning and for preparing the lithographic stone. Sulphuric acid is used for cleaning and biting steel. Hydrochloric acid attacks zinc and steel and in a diluted form is used for washing. Phosphoric acid is used for cleaning ferrous metals and aluminium as well as for preparing zinc and aluminium for the lithographic and offset techniques. Hydrofluoric acid attacks glass and ceramic. Acetic acid (vinegar) was formerly used frequently in the composition of etches. Of the alkalis, soda is the most commonly used: as a detergent for washing the screen, for cleaning metal plates, and for bleaching. It is used particularly on zinc, iron and aluminium, as well as on organic materials. Potash possesses approximately the same characteristics. Ammonia is used as a cleaning agent. The most frequently used of the salts is ferric chloride, a slow etch which penetrates in depth while preserving the form of the design. On account of these qualities it is much used in aquatint and photogravure.

Counterpart. A photographic reproduction of a negative or diapositive.

Counterproof. An impression taken from a freshly printed sheet onto another piece of paper. It shows the design in the same direction as that on the plate, stone or block; the artist uses it for assessing corrections to be made.

Counter type. In printing terminology, a counter type refers to the reproduction of a typographic block as a *stereotype* or *electrotype*.

Coverage. The ability of an ink to cover and absorb into a surface as regards the amount required for printing. It is relative to the receptivity of the support to the ink.

Covering stencil. *See: stencil.*

Crayon. Various types of crayon are used in printmaking. The greasy lithographic crayon is made with a natural grease or a chemical. A corrective crayon is used in lithography to remove lines or blemishes.

Crayon manner. A process of intaglio engraving which aims to simulate the strokes of a crayon or chalk drawing. The plate is covered with etching ground. Various tools are used on it: a type of needle possessing one or more points, much used when the technique was first employed; the *mattoir*, an instrument with a butt-end provided with irregular points; and tools of the *roulette* genus. Roulettes have a common feature in a revolving circular head with either a single serrated edge, or a wider surface dotted or lined in a variety of forms. The plate is then immersed in a mordant, as with a normal *etching*.

Cross-hatching. *See: hatching.*

Cross-line screen. A finely squared pattern engraved onto a transparent surface. It is used to reproduce tone in the photomechanical processes, by placing it in front of the image to be photographed.
See: half-tone.

Crystallography. Glass printing.
See: cliché-verre.

Cushion. A cushion is used to support the metal plate while engraving is in progress, especially if a burin is used. This facilitates turning the plate when a change of direction is required. It is made out of two saucer-shaped leather pads, stuffed with horsehair and sewn together.
See: burin engraving, wood engraving.

Cutting (wood). The cut on a wood block is made by incising obliquely away from the line, then making a second incision towards the line from the other direction, thereby disengaging the part to be removed.
See: woodcut, wood engraving.

Cutting away. The action of removing the areas on a relief block which surround the raised parts to be printed.

Cutting out. Material is cut out to make stencils and films in screenprinting.
See: knife, screenprinting, stencil.

Cylinder. A word formerly used to describe the inking roller.
See: roller.

Dabber. There are various types of dabbers used in printmaking. The inking dabber, a round tool, with a wide base, is covered in leather of fine skin; it is used for inking the incisions on an intaglio plate and the relief areas on a wood block.
See: inking, roller.
A dabber is also used for laying the ground: it is half-moon shaped, stuffed with cotton and covered in silk.
In lithography, a type of wash is applied to the stone with a dabber made of a ball of cotton covered with fine skin.

Dampening. 1. Paper is often moistened before printing as this makes it more flexible when contact is made with the block, plate, etc., and also ensures better receptivity of the ink.
See: paper.
2. In lithography and offset lithography the surface of the stone must be thoroughly dampened before the printing ink is applied. This prevents the ink from adhering to the non-greased parts.

Deckle edge. The rough uneven edge on hand-made paper and on some good quality machine-made paper which has been left untrimmed.
See: paper, squaring.

"Delineavit". Placed after the name of the artist who made the original design of the print.
See: lettering.

"Dépôt légal". In France there is a legal obligation to deposit one or more examples of any print sold or distributed publicly, with the "dépôt légal". The law dates back to Francis I and was confirmed and supplemented by Louis XIV.

"Desensitizing". The procedure necessitated by any retouching to be made on a lithographic stone, done after the trial proofs have been taken. Solvents are used over small areas of the stone and mechanical abrasives over large heavily drawn areas.
See: lithography.

Diamond. Diamond points are used to engrave very fine lines on metal. They are used directly on the surface of the plate itself, or on a ground. Ruby or sapphire points are more often used in place of diamond for reasons of economy.

Dilutant. A product used for thinning inks and varnishes.
See: grounds and varnishes, ink, oils, vehicle.

Disengaging. Passing a tool (burin, etching needle) along the inside of a line that has already been engraved.

Disintegration of paper. Printing error which occurs if paper that has been excessively dampened is put in the press. It becomes attached to the plate and disintegrates.

Division of labour. Division of labour occurs in a workshop when each stage in the production of a print (drawing, engraving, preparation of plate, printing) is done by a different specialist in order to accelerate the process and produce a better result. It was a common practice in wood engraving in the nineneeth century.

Dotted manner. A method of engraving dating from the fifteenth century. Small round holes were stamped with a punch and hammer into a metal plate which was then inked and printed as a relief block or metalcut. The stamped work appears as white dots surrounded by black and gives a crude effect of tone.
See: hammer, "opus", punch.

Dot work. A loose description of the surface of any metal plate, either relief *(see: dotted manner)* or intaglio, which has been dotted or grained in a manner such as to create an impression of tone when printed. The dots can be achieved either by working directly on the plate or by etching through a ground.
See: aquatint, crayon manner, salt, stipple, sugar.

Double image. A printing error which causes the image of the print to appear twice. It occurs if the paper falls out of alignment as a result of not being properly secured during one or, more likely, two passages through the press. The blankets may also cause the paper to move if not properly fixed.

Doubling. In lithography, a stone is doubled when it is reinforced or raised by attaching it to another, with the aid of plaster.
See: lithography.

"Dry" (processes). The methods of working directly on the surface of a metal plate with the exclusive use of tools are sometimes known as "dry"; as opposed to methods involving the intervention of a ground or varnish and the application of liquid mordants.

Drying. 1. The layer of ink on a freshly printed sheet can dry in one of three different ways: by evaporation of the solvent that maintains the ink in a liquid form; by penetration of the paper; or by oxidation on contact with the air. Inks used in relief, intaglio and lithographic printing dry by penetrating the paper and by oxidation; those used in photogravure dry by evaporation and by penetration. The greasy inks used in screenprinting dry by oxidizing and by penetrating the paper; cellulose and water-based inks also dry by evaporation and by penetration. *(See: ink.)*
2. The drying of paper: in intaglio and lithographic printing, the paper is dampened before an impression is taken. It is then flattened by laying it between sheets of cardboard and dried in a press for at least twelve hours. *(See: dampening.)*
3. Methods of drying: in most techniques, an electric drier propelling hot or cold air is used. In screenprinting, freshly printed sheets have to be placed on specially constructed racks, as it is more important for them to be kept well apart when drying than in other techniques. Usually it is sufficient to make a pile of fresh impressions with interleaving sheets.

Drying agent. A particular dilutant used in *screenprinting* to activate the drying process of the ink.
See: dilutant, drying, ink.

Drypoint. A method of intaglio engraving on metal. Marks are made on the surface of a copper, zinc or sometimes steel plate with the aid of a strong steel needle, known as a *drypoint*. Various types of drypoint are used, according to the depth and width of the line required. This may be anything between a light scoring of the plate and a deep incision which creates a larger *burr*, the ridge of metal thrown up at each side of the incision. When inked, burr prints as a rich tone, and is particularly cultivated in the drypoint technique. The medium has attracted artist engravers *(see: engraving)* in particular because it allows much freedom of expression. Drypoint plates are very fragile and only a few impressions will suffice to erase the burr and flatten the incisions; they are sometimes reinforced by *steel-facing*. The quality of an impression also depends on the skill of the printer in inking and wiping the plate, and in his interpretation of the artist's intentions as to how the impression should look.

Duralumin. A combination of copper, magnesium and manganese. It is a very light metal and is sometimes used for intaglio engraving, notably in the method of engraving with *carborundum*.

Dust-box. A large sealed box in which powdered resin is shaken over a plate for the purpose of ensuring that the aquatint ground is evenly distributed.
See: aquatint.

"Échoppe". A term adopted from the French. A type of etching needle of rectangular or triangular section and a sharpened oval end. It is used on a hard ground and creates a broader line than the usual etching needle.

Electroplating. Technique of total or partial coverage of a metal plate with a thin layer of another metal by electrolysis. In printmaking, it is used for steel-facing intaglio plates and for making relief blocks (such as electrotypes).

Electrotype. An exact duplicate of a block or plate which has been produced by electrolysis.
See: galvanic processes.

Embossing. A printmaking method in which a design is impressed into paper without the use of any ink, creating a heavily raised surface area.

Emery stick. Used to score a metal plate.
See: cancelled plate, scoring.

Emulsion. A substance which can either be a liquid, a thick paste obtained by mixing an oily substance, or a resin previously reduced into fine particles, with a liquid base, usually water.

Engraver. 1. One who practises engraving.
2. The specialist who engraved on the stone in lithographic engraving: a technique which was popular when lithography had a larger industry than it has today.
See: lithography.
3. In photogravure, the line engraver specializes in the etching process.

Engraving. In a general sense, the word covers all works of art or industry (both plate and impression) which use incision as means of marking the design. In printmaking, more specific meanings must be applied to avoid confusion. Manual engravings (e.g. burin engravings) can be differentiated from mechanical, semi-mechanical,

photomechanical, photochemical, electrochemical and, today, electronic engravings. Distinctions must also be applied to relief and intaglio engravings (the former are more usually called "cuts", except in the case of wood engravings), as well as to the type of material used: copper, zinc, aluminium, stone, glass, etc. Where the incisions are made chemically (i.e. with acid) the term "etching" should, strictly speaking, be adhered to.
See: burin engraving.

Engraving:

Artist's engraving (or etching). One which has been made by the artist of the original design as opposed to being reproduced or interpreted by a craftsman. The French term "peintre-graveur" applies to a painter who engraves or etches his own work, i.e. an artist engraver.
See: free engraving.

Broadly-spaced engraving. An engraving in which the lines are spaced well apart form each other.

Closely-spaced engraving. One in which the lines are incised (with the burin) very close to each other.

Colour engraving. Impressions from ordinary engraved plates are taken with one colour of ink. Colour engravings *(see: colour printing)* are made with several plates, one for each colour. Hand-coloured engravings are made by applying colour with a brush or a stencil directly to the impression.

Dark engraving. One in which deep wide incisions are made in order to give the impression a darker tone.

Engraving "en bois mat et de relief". A French term applied to an old type of woodcut used for printing large lettering on posters, chiaroscuro prints and painted canvases.

Engraving with sand. Metal (usually zinc) may be engraved by blasting it with sand, using a stencil as a guide.

Free engraving or etching. One made by an artist who does not follow the rigorous rules in making the lines adhered to by the engraver. Etchings have always been the preferred medium of artists who are primarily painters or draughtsmen, because of the greater freedom allowed in working the plate.
See: artist's engraving, "burin rangée".

Light engraving. One in which the lines are engraved in a shallow manner so as to produce a light appearance on the impression.

Original engraving. One which has been printed by the artist of the original design.
See: interpretative print.

Reproductive engraving. The reproduction of an original drawing or painting, through the means of an engraving made by a craftsman rather than the artist himself.
See: facsimile, interpretative print.

Etcher. An engraver who practises the etching process.

Etching. One of the most important methods of intaglio engraving. It consists in laying an acid-resistant ground over a metal plate (copper is the best, zinc is also used) on the surface of which the design is drawn so as to expose the metal. The plate is then bitten with a mordant, usually nitric acid (hence the term "eau-forte" in French), which incises the lines so that the plate can be inked and printed as an ordinary intaglio engraving.
The distinguishing characteristic of the technique is that it allows the designer much greater freedom of expression than other methods of intaglio engraving, since the laborious task of incising the plate manually is dispensed with. It has therefore been the preferred medium of artists who are primarily painters or draughtsmen. It does, however, require a certain technical experience to achieve good results, particularly in laying the ground and biting the plate.
An etching is executed in five stages: (1) The plate is polished and cleaned with chalk or whitening to ensure that the ground adheres well. (2) Laying the ground: either a ball of solid ground is melted over the plate, or a cold liquid ground is used. The former remains soft for a longer period, the latter dries rapidly and must consequently be worked more quickly than a hard ground. Different grounds are used for reworking the plate. (3) The design is cut through the ground with an *etching*

needle; the lines must remain separate in order to avoid *foul-biting*. (4) The plate is then bitten (or "etched") either by placing it in an acid bath or by covering it with the mordant. (5) The ground is removed before the plate is inked and put through the press like an ordinary intaglio engraving. The etching process is an inherent part of various other techniques, e.g. *aquatint, brush etching, soft-ground etching, sugar-lift process,* etc. It can also be combined with *burin engraving* and *drypoint*: the etched part of the design is done first.
See: biting, grounds and varnishes, impression, intaglio, techniques.
The etching process must not be confused with the "etch" used in lithography: this is a gum acid solution applied to the stone (already drawn and prepared with a resist) with the aim of reinforcing the image.
See: reinforcing (the lithographic image).
Lightly etched (plate). One which has been etched for a short period. An impression taken from such a plate is light in tone. A *light etch* refers to a weak acid or any diluted mordant.

Etching "à la plume". A method of intaglio printing in which a pen and ink drawing is made on a clean metal plate. When this has dried, the entire surface is covered with a light aquatint ground and placed in an acid bath which has the effect of removing the ground where it is to be found over the ink. The plate can then be bitten as for a normal etching. The technique is difficult to do well, and was much improved by the *sugar-lift process*.

"Excudit". Often abbreviated to *exc.* Refers to the name of the publisher after which it is placed on a print.
See: lettering.

"Ex-libris". An owner's mark placed in a book, usually on the inside of the cover. Engraved ones have been used since the fifteenth century.

Extender. Added to ink to give it a particular consistency, or to lessen the cost price. It is made from a chemically stable product such as whitening.

Eye-shade. A transparent eye-shade, usually green in colour, is used by engravers (particularly professionals) as protection against harmfully bright rays, and as a means of rendering the plate more legible.

Face (of letter). The printing surface of the type in typography.

Facsimile. 1. A print which is an exact copy of an original design, i.e. a "reproductive" print as opposed to an "original" print.
2. In a more specific sense it refers to the exact reproduction of a line drawing in wood engraving (as opposed to its interpretation in a brush or wash technique) and was particularly popular in the nineteenth century. Photomechanical processes are also used for obtaining facsimiles.
See: interpretative print, line block.

Fading. The gradation of a tint in an imperceptible manner.

False margins. A print may not have normal margins for a variety of reasons. In this case, it may be mounted on a larger sheet of paper which provides it with false margins.

Feather. A feather is used to brush away any effervescence that forms on the surface of a metal plate during the etching procedure.

"Fecit". Sometimes found after the name of the engraver at the base of a print.
See: lettering.

Feed into press. At the time of printing, the block or plate is "fed" into the press; this ensures the correct alignment.
See: alignment, press.

Feeding. The action of laying the sheet against the gauges *(see: margination).*

Felt. Woollen or cotton material used for packing round the printing rollers.
See: blankets.

Felt pen. The engraver S.W. Hayter developed a method which consisted in drawing on a clean plate with a felt pen and xylol ink, and then proceeding as in the etching process: the drawing is resistant to a short etch.

Ferric chloride. The modern name for perchloride of iron.
See: corrosive agents.

Filled in. If the application of ink or chalk on a lithographic stone has been excessive, the impression appears to be heavy and "filled in".
See: lithography.

Filling-in liquid. Used in screenprinting, it is an aqueous or cellulose solution applied with a brush or squeegee to the screen with the aim of impeding the passage of ink. It is removed with an acetone solution.
See: screenprinting.

Film. Thin translucent or transparent pellicle, manually or photographically prepared for use in screenprinting. If manually prepared, plastic film is cut out to form a stencil and glued to the underside of the screen. Photographic film is also used in lithography, offset lithography and photogravure.
See: photographic processes, screenprinting.

Film backing. In screenprinting, non-photographic film can be used as a stencil, by cutting out the design and embedding the film in the screen (as opposed to simply placing it underneath). This is done with the aid of a backing on the film which is peeled off when it is properly fixed. A similar process is used for attaching a photographic stencil to the screen. The parts of the screen through which the ink is to pass are dissolved by water.

Finger-stall. A finger-shaped rubber sheath used to retrieve the plate from the acid during the etching process.
See: biting.

Firmer. A type of chisel used in woodcutting. It has a strong, level blade with a bevelled edge and is used for levering the wood away from the block after it has been cut.

First edition. The earliest edition of a book or a print to be taken.

Flat tint. A tint which has been applied in a uniform manner.
See: gradation, grey tone, tint.

Flock. Particles of a textile material are sometimes sprinkled over a damp impression ("inked" with glue) to give it a felt-like appearance. It is used today in screenprinting; there is also a rare group of fifteenth-century woodcuts which were made in the same way, called flock prints.

Fly-leaf. Blank leaf at the beginning (and end) of a book.

Folio. *See: leaf.*

Form. In letterpress, the form is the metal frame in which the type are enclosed for printing.

Format. Plates, blocks and screens, sheets of paper, film and negatives often have current formats, which means that the dimensions of a print frequently recur.
See: imperial, royal.

"Formis". Indicates the name of the printer in the lettering of a print.
See: lettering.

Foul-biting. This occurs in etching if the acid is allowed to attack the plate indiscriminately. It is caused by any collapse of the etching ground. If, for example, two lines are drawn too close together or if the plate is immersed in the acid bath for too long, the ground will be rendered ineffective. When printed, foul-bitten lines appear enlarged, blurred or joined together.
See: biting, etching.

Frame. 1. The material forming the screen in screenprinting is stretched over and attached to a wooden or metal frame.
See: screenprinting.
2. In wood engraving, the block may be attached to a wooden frame if it is too small to be easily manipulated while engraving is in progress.

Frisket. Articulated frame which holds the paper in position during printing.
See: press.

Frontispiece. In the oldest sense of the word, the frontispiece refers to an ornate title page in a book; more recently; it has applied to an illustration placed before or opposite the title page.

Galvanic processes. All methods which include covering the surface of an object which conducts electricity (either of metal, or with a metal surface, or of a metallic mixture) with a layer of metal (electrolysis).

Galvanography. Any method which uses electrolysis to create an intaglio plate or a relief block.

Ghost image. Image of the previous drawing on a screen or stone which has not been cleaned properly.
See: lithography, screenprinting.

Gillotage. An early method of producing a line block. The line drawing was transferred, originally by autographic means and later by photography, to a zinc plate which was then etched as a relief block.
See: line block.

Glass prints. The "cliché-verre" is sometimes translated as a glass print. Completely distinct from this are certain decorative items produced in the late seventeenth and early eighteenth centuries, which are also often termed "glass prints": a mezzotint was glued face down onto glass, then rubbed from behind to remove all the paper, hand coloured, and framed.

Glazing. 1. The process in which paper is given a very smooth texture with the aid of a *calender*.
2. A thin layer of cellulose or some synthetic substance may be applied to a printing sheet with the aim of protecting and ameliorating the appearance of the surface.
3. In photogravure, a resinous powder is fixed to the plate through the application of heat, with the aim of reinforcing the protective ability of the ink. The process is known as glazing because of the change in appearance of the resin: from a whitish colour to that of a brilliant black as it mixes with the ink.

Good to print. *See: "bon à tirer".*

Gouge. A tool used for cutting wood and linoleum, specifically to clear away larger spaces of the block. Curved gouges may be obtained as well as flat ones. V-shaped gouges are used for cutting deep, angular furrows. A gouge used in linocutting resembles a pen and is attached to a pear-shaped handle.
See: linocut, woodcut.

Gradation. Gradual strengthening, or weakening, of a *tone*.
See: dot work, grey tone, tint.

Grain. 1. A loose description of aquatint ground and of its resulting effect on an impression, and of any other printing element or impression with dots or grain on its surface.
See: dot work.
2. The irreglar aspect of the surface of a stone, plate or transfer paper in the lithographic method, necessary to the firm adhesion of the marks of the crayon. It is created on the stone or plate by an initial *graining* process.
3. The irregular aspect of the surface of paper or of transparent film used in screenprinting.

Graining. 1. In lithography: a grain must be created on lithographic stone, zinc or aluminium to attain the necessary adhesion of crayon, drawing ink, gum solutions, water and printing ink. It is achieved by rubbing the surface with an abrasive powder (of sandstone or carborundum) mixed with water; this may be done with the aid of a *levigator*.
See: graining sink.
2. Graining in the collotype process: a grain is created on the sheet of glass by rubbing with emery powder mixed with water. This ensures that the layer of bichromated gelatine adheres to its surface properly.
3. A grain is created on a mezzotint plate with the aid of a rocker.
See: mezzotint.

Graining sink. 1. A sink in which the graining is done, in lithography. It is generally a wooden structure, lined with lead or fibre glass, with a rack at the bottom to support the stone. A similar apparatus is used mechanically to produce a grain on metallic plates.
2. A type of sink is also used for graining the sheets of glass in making collotypes.

Graver. *See: burin engraving.*

Grey tone. A uniform tone which appears from a distance to be grey, and which is achieved in engraving with the aid of parallel lines, crossed lines, dots, etc.

Grinding colours. The process involved in making a powdered pigment destined to be mixed with liquid in the production of inks. At one time the pigment was ground manually with a pestle on a pounding stone, but this is now performed mechanically. It is usually mixed with oil, but water, as well as other liquids such as resins, can also be used.
See: ink.

Ground, aquatint. A mixture of minute particles (of resin, bitumen, salt, sand, etc.) is deposited on the surface of the plate in aquatint and hand photogravure processes. It acts as a resist to the acid and gives a granular aspect to the surface of the plate which will print in a corresponding fashion.
See: aquatint, dot work.

Grounds and varnishes. The ground (or *stopping-out* varnish, as it is also called in liquid form), composed of various waxes, gums and resins, is the most important element in the *etching* process. It may be either melted and applied to the plate with a *dabber*, or spread on with a roller. For successive stages of biting the plate a transparent stopping-out varnish is used. A particular type of ground is used for *soft-ground etching* and *aquatint*.
There are several types of straightforward varnish used in printmaking, e.g. a protective varnish applied to prevent oxidation on metal plates, and a glazing varnish used particularly in screenprinting to strengthen the surface as well as to add gloss.
See: biting, bordering, thinning varnish.

Guard. A strip of paper stitched to the inside of a book which is used for inserting prints or fragile documents. The object is "tipped" into the guard with the aid of an adhesive.

Gum, lithographic. An abrasive gum used for erasing ink or chalk from the surface of the stone.

Gums and resins. Gums are substances to be found exuding from certain trees; they are soluble in water. Resins also secrete naturally (or upon incision) from certain trees, but may still be found in a fossilized state (hard resins). They are soluble in oil. Gum resins are a mixture of the two. Balsam is a thick resin.
In printmaking the most commonly used are: copal resin, colophony, sandarac, lacquer, mastic resin and gum Arabic for the preparation of varnishes and grounds. The latter is also used as an adhesive and in lithography. Turpentine is used in the manufacture of lithographic inks.
See: grounds and varnishes.

Gypsography. A method of producing a relief block patented in 1837 and soon superseded by other processes. It involved making a drawing through plaster mounted on a metal base, and then casting a stereotype plate in relief, using the plaster as the mould.

Half-tone. A method of reproducing a continuous tone image by placing a *cross-line screen* in front of the image to be photographed. This has the effect of breaking down the tone into a mass of dots of varying size which, when transferred to the inking surface and printed, will create the illusion of a full range of tones.

Hammer. A hammer is used for making corrections on a metal plate *(see: callipers)*, and for knocking the punch *(see: punch work)*.

Hammer impression. A method of taking an impression from a wood block manually: the sheet of paper is laid on the block and knocked on the reverse with a hammer.

Hand-colouring. Hand-coloured prints have an old tradition and must be distinguished from those printed in colour *(colour printing)*. Colouring is done in watercolour or gouache, with either a brush or a stencil cut to allow ink through over the necessary areas directly onto the impression (as opposed to the block, plate, etc.).

Hand-guard. A sheet of paper is placed under the hand while working on the plate or stone. This protects the surface from ill effects caused by the rubbing movement and by the heat of the skin.

Hand-rest. A strip of wood with blocks at either end which projects over the plate, block or stone to be worked, allowing the design to be executed without damaging the surface by unnecessary contact with the hands or instruments.

Hatching. Parallel lines which are cut close together in an engraving with the aim of giving an effect, en masse, of a grey or dark tone. The lines may be intersected by other parallel lines, a technique known as *cross-hatching*; or they may be over-hatched. Parallel marks made with a drypoint were used on geographical maps to represent water.

Heating. In aquatint and photogravure techniques the ground has to be fused to the plate by means of heating. Heat is also needed to thicken oil to a certain consistency required in making greasy inks.
See: ink, oils.

Heliography. An early name for photography (Niepce, 1826). Replaced by *daguerreotype* in 1839.

Heliotype. A nineteenth-century photomechanical process similar to *collotype*.

Hinge joints. A piece of articulated metal used in screenprinting to attach the frame of the screen to the printing table. Various types are used depending on whether the printing is performed manually or mechanically.

Homography. Term adopted from the French. A nineteenth-century method of transferring old prints onto lithographic stone.

Honey. Honey is used in an intaglio printing process which aims to create the effect of a wash drawing: it is mixed with salt, verdigris and sal ammoniac, and spread over a copper plate. The mixture is a mordant which attacks the metal, producing black or grey tones in the impression.

Hot plate. Used to warm intaglio plates prior to inking, and to fuse aquatint ground to the plate. Formerly a type of small heater or grill was used.

Hyalography. Synonym of *cliché-verre*.

Illuminated table. Use for *pricking*, especially in the nineteenth century, and for cutting out stencils in screenprinting.

Image, lithographic. The lithographic image refers to the one which appears on the surface of the stone after it has been inked. The initial design made on the stone with a greasy ink or lithographic crayon is only a part of the chemical process which produces a lithograph; it is coloured (with lamp black) only to the extent of enabling the artist to see his work.
See: lithography.

Image-maker. In printmaking, the image-maker's work of producing popular devotional figures was usually done on the wood block.

Imitation. A reproduction of an original drawing or of a particular artist's style.
See: facsimile, reproduction.

Imperial. A format of paper (762 × 559mm. or 787 × 584 mm.).

Impression. In printing terminology, an impression is any *print* taken from a particular block, plate, etc. The word may be qualified to indicate the type of impression, e.g. "natural" impression, pale impression, etc.
See: proof.

Impression:
"Cloudy". If the ink is not applied evenly in screenprinting, a "cloudy" impression will result (from the French "nuage").
Loose impression. A print on Indian or Japanese paper which has not been laid down on thicker paper (to strengthen it).

"Natural". From the French "épreuve nature": an impression taken from an intaglio plate after wiping it completely clean, as opposed to leaving a film of ink on its surface, or dragging some of the ink out of the lines to create special effects.
See: retroussage, surface tone, wiping.
"Neigeuse". The French expression for an impression taken from a badly inked or mis-printed plate which has caused white patches to appear where there ought to be lines.
Pale impression. One in which the design fails to show up sufficiently. This may be due to faulty printing; it also results from a plate with shallow incisions, such as one that has been well-used.

"Impressit" or "Imp.". Indicates the name of a printer. The artist has occasionally acted in this capacity as well as making the design.
See: lettering.

Imprint. The imprint obtained by making a mould of a relief block or an intaglio plate (in, respectively, intaglio and relief).
See: galvanic processes, printing.

"Incidit" or "Incisit" or "Inc." or "I". Indicates the name of the engraver.
See: lettering, "sculpsit".

Incunable. In a general sense, incunables are the earliest printed books, particularly those antedating 1500. They may be blockbook or typographic; the term is also occasionally extended to lithography and photography, i.e. the earliest examples of those techniques.

"India" paper. Very thin paper, of a yellowish or cream-coloured tint, which is made from the bark of bamboo. It is used for good quality impressions (usually laid down onto a thicker paper). It is made in China.

"Indian" ink. A very black ink used particularly for *sugar-lift process* and in making preparatory drawings for woodcuts. It is Chinese in origin.

Initial. A large typographical letter appearing at the beginning of texts. It can be specially engraved and decorated with figures or various ornaments.

Ink. Coloured liquid used for writing, drawing and printing. It can be thick in texture, or even solid, in which case it is dissolved. A large number of different types of ink are used in printmaking. Drawing inks are used for preparatory designs on blocks and plates. A particular type of ink is specially prepared for drawing on lithographic stone or on autographic paper.
Printing inks can either be water- or oil-based. In screenprinting cellulose-based and plastic inks are also used. Other inks are specially prepared for certain procedures, e.g. for use as a mordant, or in transfer lithography.
See: base, Chinese ink, "Indian" ink, vehicle.

Ink, length of. Inks and oils possess "length" when their flow does not stop abruptly, as in the case of liquids or pastes, but continues for a moment to form a thread. This characteristic helps it to adhere well to a support (as opposed to an ink which forms droplets) and also removes the colour from other, drier inks if placed in close contact with them.

Ink slab. A plate of marble, thick glass, metal or lithographic stone on which the printing ink is prepared, by means of spatulas, dabbers and rollers.
See: inking.

Ink, threads of. Static electricity causes threads of ink to form on a screenprint. This effect can be counteracted by mixing an antistatic product with the ink.

Inking. The process of putting the required amount of ink onto the necessary parts of the printing element, i.e. the relief areas of a block, the incised parts of an intaglio plate, the greased areas of a lithographic stone, etc. It is applied with either a *roller* or a *dabber*; on an intaglio plate pieces of muslin or a brush are also used, or it can be applied *à la poupée*. In screenprinting the ink is scraped over the screen with a *squeegee*.
See: impression, ink.

Insolation. A photographical term meaning exposure to sunlight for printing. This has been extended to indicate exposure to artificial light.
See: photographic processes.

Intaglio. Also occasionally called *copperplate printing.* Any impression in which the line has been created by the incised parts of the plate, e.g. burin engraving, etching, aquatint, crayon manner, photogravure. The other three major printmaking methods are: relief (woodcut, wood engraving, linocut, typography); planography (lithography, offset lithography); and stencil method (screenprinting).
See: engraving, impression.

Intercalation. After an impression has been taken, a sheet of paper is placed over the printed side, so that it will not mark the verso of the text to be placed on top of it. The interpolated sheets are of tissue paper.
See: drying.

Interpretative print. In contrast with the facsimile process of making an absolute transference of the lines or tones of the draughtsman's design onto a block or plate, the interpretative method is a translation of the style of another medium into the engraver's idiom, e.g. a wood engraver interprets tone made with the strokes of a brush by massing lines together on the block.
See: facsimile, reproduction.

"Invenit" or "Inv.". Accompanies the name of the artist of the original design on a print.
See: lettering.

Irisation. The colours of an impression taken from a plate on which several inks have been mixed will display an iridescent effect.

Japan paper. A good quality paper which is lightly translucent and extremely resistant. It is used for fine impressions. Imitation Japanese paper also exists.

Japanese woodcuts. A Japanese technique of woodcutting.
See: woodcut.

Justification in letterpress. Within a typographical composition, the justification refers to the length of the lines and to their alignment with the margin.

Juxtaposition. Colours are juxtaposed on prints where they are placed next to each other without mixing or overprinting.
See: mixture, overprinting, registration.

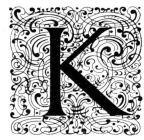

"Kakemono". Japanese prints having a long, vertical format with a bamboo stick terminating each end. It is the opposite of the type known as *makemono.*

Keepsakes. Small albums illustrated with small-scale, intimate engravings, offered as presents on such occasions as Christmas.
See: steel plates.

Key block. *See: colour block.*

Key stone. The stone on which the original drawing is made in lithography. It can be copied for transfer impressions in order to avoid damage which may be caused by over-handling.

Key transfer. The transfer of each colour from a transparency to a block for printing in several colours. The line which forms the outline of each colour on the transfer can be called the key line.
See: overprinting.

Knife. A small knife resembling a penknife is the principal tool used by the woodcutter (Fr. "canif"). In screenprinting various knives are used to cut out the stencils; the type depends on the nature of the material to be cut *(see: stylet).*

Lac. Resinous substance used in the preparation of certain varnishes and in photographic processes.

Lacquer. 1. A type of ink possessing a soluble dye that is fixed to amorphous substances, such as aluminium. White lacquer is used for lightening colours.
2. A reinforcement lacquer is used in offset lithography to prevent rubbing at the time of printing.

Laid paper. A type of hand-made paper which shows the pattern of the vertical wire-marks and the horizontal connecting chain-lines of the wires in the papermaker's *mould.*
See: paper, wove paper.

Lamp. A plate may be blackened by smoking a paraffin lamp beneath it.
See: smoking (the plate).

Leaf. Sheet of paper, with one or both sides printed, as opposed to a page which is one side of a leaf only.
See: page.

Lettering. All printed inscriptions relating to the design represented in a print. Written references on prints first appeared in the fifteenth century. In the seventeenth century the lettering took on a particular importance with the addition of dedications, mottoes, tokens of esteem, etc., to the usual titles and descriptions. In the eighteenth century it became habitual to take a proof of an engraving *before lettering,* i.e. before any writing had been engraved. Proofs were also taken with the lettering in the process of being made, e.g. with white lettering in which only the contours of the writing have been engraved, with grey lettering in which the letters have been lightly hatched, or with scratched lettering, where the writing has been deleted.
Some of the lettering concerns the fabrication of the print. The author of the design or the original painting is designated by name followed by: *delineavit, del.* (designed), *invenit* or *inv.* (invented), etc. The author of an engraving itself is described most frequently by: *sculpsit, sculp., sc., incisit, incidit* or *inc.* (engraved); or equally by: *fecit, fec., fe., ft.,* or *f.* (made) which also applies to the craftsman of a print in any other technique. *Perfecit* signifies the completion of the work, possibly by a second engraver. The name of the publisher has for a long time been accompanied by *excudit, excud.* or *excudebat,* and more recently by *chez* or the Italian version *appresso.* The name of the printer is followed by *formis* and that of the lithographic printer by *lith.* Artists who print their own prints may inscribe after their signature *imp.* or *impressit.* On some old French prints, the name of the dealer or tradesman is found preceded by *se vend chez.* Copyrights granted to engravers were expressed by *A.P.D.R.* or *C.P.R.* (French royal privileges) and by *Published According to Act of Parliament* in England (from 1735).
See: numbering of prints, proof.

Letterpress. The most important method of printing text, it dates from the middle of the fifteenth century. The principle consists in inking letters cut in relief, and then pressing paper against them to take an impression. Woodcut blocks may be incorporated with typographic letters as they can both be printed on the same press.
See: press, woodcut.

Levelling. Equalizing the height of the blocks and the type when both are used together in relief printing.

Levers. The arms of a manual typographical press.
See: press.

Levigator. A heavy metal disc equipped with a vertical handle used to grind the lithographic stone.
See: graining, lithography.

Lighting screen. Transparent paper or fine gauze is stretched over a frame and placed on the engraver's table between the plate and the source of lighting, in order to diffuse the brightness and to prevent too much reflection from the highly polished metal.

Light-staining. A print which has been exposed to the light, over a long period, without any protection, becomes dusty and dirty and acquires a stained appearance.

Line. This refers to any line as it appears on an impression, whether taken from the inked or uninked parts of the printing element; as well as to the incisions made in a plate or block, and the marks on a lithographic stone.
Lost line. A line incised too deeply into the plate for it to be inked properly.
Simple line. A single line, i.e. one that has not been strengthened by successive stages of cutting.

Line block. A photomechanical process of reproducing a line drawing. The image is made on a zinc plate which is etched in successive stages to leave the design standing in relief. The method cannot reproduce tone (for this, the *half-tone* method would be applied).
The technique was a development of Gillot's *paneiconography,* in which a relief plate was made from a drawing done by hand and later from a photographic image *(see: gillotage).* Today, metal or plastic plates are used for the purpose, and are made in a single operation, either by etching or by an electronic process.

Line engraving. A term sometimes used to specify an engraving made with the burin.

Linocut. An abbreviation of linoleum cut. The technique is a derivation of the woodcut but owing to the supple, relatively soft properties of the material, linocuts have different characteristics. The material takes all types of lines, but is most suited to large designs with contrasting dark and light flat tints. The material is cut with small pen-like tools which have a mushroom-shaped handle. The tools have a variety of forms: straight and rounded edge, double-pointed, as a chisel or a V-shaped chisel, etc. As on a woodcut, the relief parts of the block are inked. For printing a large number of important proofs, the lino is attached to a wooden block. Colour printing is done with several lino blocks.

Lith. Abbreviation of lithographer. In the nineteenth century it preceded the name of the printer at the base of numerous lithographs.
See: lettering, lithographer.

Lithochromatography, lithochromography. Rarely used synonyms of *chromolithography.*

"Lithoffset-offsetgraphie". Name given by the printer Jack Renaud to prints produced by offset lithography according to a certain procedure.

Lithographer. A printer of lithographs. The term applies equally to the artist who makes the design on the stone or lithographic plate (as opposed to the engraver or screenprinter). During the great age of lithography in the nineteenth century, there were various specialist lithographers: writers (for lettering), lithographic engravers (who produced a print in imitation of a copper-plate engraving), draughtsmen (who made the drawings on the stone, plate or transfer paper), assayers (who prepared and tested the stones) and the printers themselves who worked the presses.

Lithographic engraving. Engravings can be produced on a lithographic stone by a variety of preparations. The lines achieved slightly resemble those of a steel engraving. The technique lies half way between planographic and intaglio printing.

Lithographic etching. A polished lithographic stone can also be used for etching. The surface is covered with liquid ground such as is used for intaglio printing. After drying, the drawing is done with a blunt needle. A dilute acid is used as a mordant. N.B. This must not be confused with the "etch" used in lithography to fix the image to the stone.
See: reinforcing the lithographic image.

Lithographic mezzotint. A method which is akin to mezzotint in metal engraving although it does not attain quite the same quality. Various methods of working the stone exist of which the aim is to create the white areas by scraping away parts of a specially prepared black background.
See: scraping.

Lithographic stipple. Adaptation of the stipple process to lithography. The dots are obtained with a pen and a greasy type of ink.
See: lithography.

Lithographic wash. A process used in lithography for obtaining the effects of a wash drawing. It has also been known as a *lithotint*. It must not be confused with a lithographic aquatint in which the grain is more marked. The colour is applied with a dabber.

Lithographic woodcut, lithographic aquatint. The other techniques that lithography has simulated, as well as *lithographic mezzotint* and *lithographic engraving*.
See: lithography.

Lithography. With woodcutting and intaglio engraving, this is one of the oldest methods of printmaking. It dates from the end of the eighteenth century. It is based on the chemical fact that there is a natural antipathy between grease and water. The image is drawn on a stone with a greasy ink which is dark in colour only to aid the draughtsman with his work. The stone is then thoroughly dampened; the water remains on the ungreased areas only. The printing ink is applied with a roller: it adheres only to the greased parts. Lightly dampened paper is then placed over the surface of the image, followed by a protective sheet. Stone and paper are passed through a flat-bed *scraper* press.
Lithographic printing is a delicate operation necessitating a careful preparation of the stone and a particular kind of inking. The prints are not marked by the effect of the press as in intaglio printing, although a slight mark indicating the edge of the stone is sometimes visible.
Transfer methods can be used to avoid the difficulties involved in moving heavy stones round a studio. The drawings can be made on transfer paper which is grained, or on autographic paper which is smooth, and then transferred to the stone. Lithographic methods have also been adapted to metal plates (grained zinc and aluminium).
See: algraphy, zincography.
Lithographic colour printing is done with several stones (or metal plates), one for each colour.
See: offset lithography.

Lithostereotype. A nineteenth-century process consisting in making a drawing on autographic paper and transferring it to a stone. A relief surface is then made around the image from which a mould is produced in order to make a stereotype block.

Lithotint. *See: lithographic wash.*

Lithotypography. A nineteenth-century process consisting in transferring a typographic impression onto stone.

Loose leaf. A print which has had to be mounted on a backing for support, such as a sheet of paper or Bristol board.

Lye. Alkaline solution used for cleaning.
See: acidic cleaning.

Maculation. The stain on the verso of a new impression caused by placing it on the surface of another freshly printed sheet.

Maculature. A plate or block has to be re-inked between each impression. After an impression is taken, there may be traces of ink remaining on the plate which can be removed by printing it again on a clean sheet. Such an impression, valueless in itself, is known as a maculature.

Magnifying glass. Used for fine engraved work (particularly on steel), for dot work, for inspecting the effect of the biting procedure and the grain in paper, material, etc.

"Makemono". Certain oriental prints of a long horizontal format. The opposite of *kakemono*.

Mallet. A jointed wooden tool used for hammering chisels, punches, matting tools, etc. Some mallets are double-headed, one head being of wood or nylon and the other of steel. The head itself may be perpendicular or parallel to the handle.
See: punch work.

"Manière de peinture". A term suggested by André Béguin for a process of applying acrylic paint directly to the metal plate in the *aquatint* technique.

Manner. 1. The imitation of another technique by engraving and etching, e.g. *crayon manner*, *pastel manner*, etc. It can also describe the appearance of a method of working within a particular technique, e.g. *fine manner*, *broad manner* (engraving).
2. The personal style of an artist, engraver, etc.

Manner, fine and broad. A distinction was made by Kolloff, in 1872, between the *fine manner* (with closely worked hatching) and the *broad manner* (with widely spaced lines of parallel shading) amongst certain Italian engravings of the Quattrocento.

"Manufacture". The engraver Nanteuil applied this term to certain engravings possessing a mannered technique and an excess of calligraphy.

Margin. Unprinted parts surrounding the design. Generally the two lateral margins are of equal length; the upper and lower margins may be equal but the latter is sometimes larger in order to allow space for signature, numeration, title, etc.; at one time it may also have contained a cartouche. A larger lower margin may be kept simply to balance the print within the sheet of paper. The size of the margins also depends on the format of the paper. Margins were usually clipped until the eighteenth century, and from the beginning of the nineteenth their existence came to be regarded as an important factor in assessing the commercial value of a print. If clipped, the impression would be worth less, particularly if printed on fine quality paper. Restored margins are known as *false margins*.
See: clipping, margination, squaring.

Margin angle. In screenprinting, the material which is to be printed produces a margin angle when its horizontal and vertical edges are placed against the register tabs during the process of scraping the ink across the screen. The angle (c. 90°) must remain constant throughout the printing procedure.
See: alignment, margination, registration, screenprinting.

Margination. The margins on a print are made by laying the sheet to be printed on a *feeding table*, against gauges which ensure that the registration is correct when the impression is taken.

Mark. 1. Particular sign serving as the artist's signature on a print.
2. A vignette, sometimes accompanied by a motto, that publishers used to place either on the title page or at the end of a book.

Masking. The border which surrounds the area to be printed on the screen is masked to prevent the ink from running through. Reserve ink is kept on the masking at one end between taking impressions.
See: inking, screenprinting.

Matrix. The mould in which printer's types are cast or shaped.

Mattoir. Also known as a mace-head, it is a tool with a butt-end provided with irregular points used either on an etching ground, or directly on the plate with the aid of a hammer, to create a series of dots on the surface in the *crayon manner* process.

"Mentonnière". In the past, a lithographic draughtsman may have attached a piece of cloth to a chin-strap (known as the "mentonnière" in French) so that it covered his mouth and nose, in order to prevent his breath from condensing on the surface of the stone.

Mercury. Mercury is used in a specific lithographic process, known as "mercurographie" in French, where it plays the same role as water, i.e. in repelling greasy ink: a silver-plated copper plate receives a drawing made with a greasy ink or chalk; the surface is then steel-faced. On removing the ink, the design emerges as a silver outline which is sensitive to mercuric amalgam. When this is applied, it has the effect of making the design project in such a fashion that the plate can either be inked directly or used to make a mould from which a stereotype is produced. This process, and variants of it, were used at the end of the nineteenth and beginning of the twentieth century.

Metalcut. A method of relief printing using a metal plate.

Metal mesh. A metal mesh stretched over a frame is used in lithography for the splatter and staging out processes. The ink is rubbed through this sieve with a brush.
See: splatter.

Metallography. A term adopted from the French. In a general sense, it can mean any preparation of a metal plate with a view to printing from it. More specifically, it refers to lithographic techniques applied to metal plates.
See: algraphy, lithography, zincography.

Metals. Various types of metals are used in printmaking techniques. *Copper* is the most commonly used in intaglio printing. In the past, *brass* was sometimes used to make maps. *Steel* is used for finely worked engravings, having the advantage of great resiliency. *Zinc* is used both for intaglio and for lithographic processes. *Aluminium* is used in lithography and in offset lithography.

Duralumin is used in the method of engraving with carborundum. *Tin* was used in music printing. Other metals have also been used in the production of stereotype and electrotype plates.
See: carborundum, steel-facing.

Mezzotint. An intaglio printing process. The work is done in two stages. A metal plate is initially grained by working over it systematically with a spiked tool known as the *rocker*; this creates a multitude of fine dots all over its surface. If inked, the plate would print a rich black. The second stage of the process consists in smoothing away parts of the roughened surface with the aid of a *scraper* and a *burnisher* in order to create the white and highlighted parts of the resulting print. The scraping of the plate is a skilful job; delicate tonal transitions can be obtained if it is done well, but the flat appearance of some mezzotints is an indication of the difficulties involved. This flatness is also caused by the fact that mezzotint plates wear down very quickly. Colour mezzotints can be printed with several plates, one for each colour.

Mirror. A mirror is used for reversing the image of an original design when it is applied to the plate, stone or block, so that in the final impression it will appear the correct way round. A mirror image is an image in reverse to the original one.
See: counterproof, (in) reverse.

Mixed method. The term used to describe certain nineteenth-century prints produced from a mixture of intaglio methods, e.g. etching, drypoint, roulette work, etc.

Mixture. Combination of various products, in particular inks of different colours or properties.
See: juxtaposition, overprinting.

Monogram. A combination of letters, usually initials of a proper name, or an abbreviated signature. Many artists, and engravers in particular, have signed their work with a monogram; those whose names have remained unknown are called *monogrammists*.
See: mark.

Monotype. A method of printmaking which can be described as taking an impression from a painting. Greasy ink or paint is applied to a plate of zinc or glass with a brush or a fingertip or by some other means. A process of removing parts of a background previously applied, as in the manner of a *mezzotint*, can also be done. On completion of the image, an impression is taken by pressing a sheet of paper onto its surface. Not more than one good impression can be made.

Montage. The production of a composite image made from various elements as, for example, in the combination of photographic positives or negatives with drawn stencils in screenprinting.

Mordant. 1. A sticky substance used to attach gold-leaf.
2. Corrosive agent used to attack metal, stone or glass.
See: biting, corrosive agents.

Mould. 1. In manual papermaking, the mould is a kind of tray, consisting of crossed wires in a wooden frame, over which the paper pulp is spread.
See: paper.
2. A mould is made of a block or plate, in reverse to the original, when making a replica of it (stereotype). The mould used for casting type is known as a *matrix*.

Mount. A protective backing of cardboard or thick paper attached to a print or drawing.

Multiple tool. A type of burin, with a scored end, used in wood engravings to produce a series of parallel lines.

Muslin. A fine, delicately woven cotton fabric used for *wiping*. Tarlatan is a stiff kind of muslin used for wiping intaglio plates.

Napping. The nap of the material used in screenprinting must be prepared to ensure that the films adhere well to it (corresponding with the *graining* of a plate or stone). It is done by rubbing the surface with a slightly abrasive powder.
See: screenprinting.

Nature printing. A Victorian invention: some vegetable object such as a plant or leaf was impressed under pressure into a soft lead plate. This was then stereotyped or electrotyped, and the plate printed in intaglio.

Needle. Many different types of needles (or points) are used in printmaking. The *drypoint* is a small, fine needle, whose point can be sharpened at various angles, each producing a different type of line. Double-ended needles possess a differently sharpened point at either end. Etching needles vary in thickness and are more or less sharply pointed, according to need; *échoppes* are broader than usual etching needles and are sharpened in an oval section: they can produce variations in the width of a line according to the angle at which the point is held. Diamond, ruby or sapphire points are used for making light incisions in a metal plate or in a ground laid over it. Points made of ivory or bone (with more rounded ends than those of an ordinary needle) are used for tracing (to transfer a design), and for making marks on a ground without penetrating the metal plate beneath.

Negative. A "negative" impression produces white areas in place of the black, or vice versa, e.g. an impression taken from an intaglio plate which has been inked with a roller.

Niello. A niello is the incrustation of an engraved silver or gold plate with a metallic black enamel (Latin: "nigellum"). A niello print is an impression taken from such a plate before the enamel has been poured into the furrows, or an impression taken from a sulphur cast of such a plate.

Numbering of prints. Impressions taken from a particular edition are sometimes numbered to indicate the intrinsic value of each (i.e. the lower the total number of the edition, the higher the value). The numbers are written at the base: the number of the impression within the edition is followed by the total number printed.

Nylogravure. A method of preparing a stencil in screenprinting. The underside of the screen is coated with gum Arabic and, after drying, is engraved with a drypoint needle. It is necessary to take care that only the gum is penetrated by the needle, so that the material of the screen remains unharmed. The process was first done by François Lauvin in 1959.

Oblong. Format in which the largest dimension is the width. (Fr. "format à l'italienne".)

Offset lithography or offset. One of the four major industrial printing techniques of which the others are: *letterpress, photogravure* and *screenprinting*. It has become the most commonly used method in commercial printing, although its importance in printmaking is not very great. It is an extension of the lithographic technique: the image is picked up from the stone, or more usually plate (either zinc or aluminium which has either been grained or covered with an absorbent oxide), by a rubber roller which then reprints it onto paper. Text and image can be transferred photographically and prepared in the usual lithographic technique based on the natural antipathy between grease and water. The advantage of offset is that it enables the damping, inking and printing itself to be done by a series of rollers which enormously speeds the operation, thereby enhancing the commercial value of the technique.
See: impression, lithography, press.

Oils and greases. The principal oil used in printmaking is linseed oil. It gives the required viscosity to greasy inks since it thickens on the application of heat. Wax, tallow and glycerine are the most important greases used in lithographic preparations.

Oleograph. A nineteenth-century process whereby an ordinary colour lithograph was varnished and impressed with a canvas grain before publication in order to make it look like an oil painting.

Olive oil. A mixture of olive oil, lamp-black and oil of turpentine can be used for removing an etching ground.
See: removal solution, sulphur prints.

Opacity. A paper or an ink is said to be opaque if the light does not pass through it.
See: coverage.

"Opus". The monk Theophilus, author of a technical treatise written in the twelfth or thirteenth century, differentiated *opus punctile* (punched holes) from *opus interrasile* (marks made with a chisel). *Opus mallei* is any work done with a hammer and, equally, the punch with which it is done.
See: dotted manner, hammer.

Original. 1. The original design is the one from which a copy or tracing is made for the block, stone or plate.
2. An original print is produced when the artist himself has prepared the block, plate or stone.
See: print.

Ornament. Ornamental motifs have been frequently used in the history of printmaking to decorate the borders of prints. These types of prints must be differentiated from ornamental prints, which serve an essential purpose in themselves: they were intended to suggest patterns of decorative ornament to craftsmen in all fields of the applied arts. They played a particularly important role in German fifteenth- and sixteenth-century engraving, in French engraving (from the sixteenth to the eighteenth century), and in nineteenth-century lithography. Ornaments are also used in typography for decorative effect.
See: colophon, vignette.

Overcut. An incision made over an existing cut, in woodcuts and linocuts.
See: cutting (wood).

Overplus. That which is printed in addition to the main edition.

Overprinting. There are three methods of colour printing: by juxtaposing the colours; by mixing the colours before printing; and by printing the colours on top of each other, i.e. overprinting, to obtain gradations of tone and different colours. This latter method takes into account the principal theory that all colour is composed of red, yellow and blue, and is used particularly in photomechanical processes. Photographic negatives are made of these colours by means of filters, and when transferred to plates are overprinted to build up the image.
See: colour printing, photographic processes.

Packing. Packing is placed in the press against the printing element and over the surface which puts pressure on the paper (roller, platen, etc., according to the type of press), in order to ensure a uniform printing. It may be made of material, cardboard, paper, rubber, plastic, etc.
See: blankets.

Page. Each side of a leaf in a book is a page, whether printed or not.
See: leaf.

Pagination. Numeration of the pages in a book.

Palette. The inking palette is a flexible blade used to mix the ink on an inking table.
See: inking, ink slab.

Paneiconography. An early form of line block, paneiconography was the original nomenclature of gillotage.
See: gillotage, line block.

Pantograph. A machine by which an accurate enlargement or reduction of a print or drawing can be made.

Paper. Papermaking involves mixing vegetable fibres and water into a paste which is then drained, pressed and dried in a mould until a sheet is formed. This has to be sized with glue or gelatine to give the paper its final appearance. Linen or cotton rags are used to make good quality paper for printmaking. "India" and Japanese papers are also imported for this use on account of their high quality.
See: dampening, laid paper, mould, wove paper.
Tracing paper is used for transferring a drawing onto the plate or block. Formerly the paper with the drawing on it was covered on the verso with black or red chalk and the design was transferred to the plate by indenting its outlines on the recto. The drawing may also be pricked for transfer.
See: pricking.
Special transfer paper is used in lithography to transfer the image from the paper on which it has been drawn onto the stone. It is grained *(see: graining)* if the image has been drawn in chalk or crayon. A smooth autographic paper is used for transferring ink drawings *(see: transfer)*. Papier mâché can also be used in lithography as a replacement for the stone.
Various types of sensitized papers are used in photomechanical methods.
See: photographic processes.
Tissue paper is used for protecting freshly printed sheets and for wiping the plate after inking in intaglio printing. Blotting paper is used on sheets of dampened paper before printing, and for drying plates after they have been etched and washed before printing.

Paper, hand-made. *See: laid paper, mould, wove paper.*

Papyrography. The use of a special type of papier mâché in place of the stone or metal plate in lithography.
See: lithography.

Paste prints. A rare class of fifteenth-century woodcut. An embossed appearance was achieved by spreading a layer of paste over the sheet before impressing the cut woodblock onto it.

Pastel manner. A method of intaglio engraving developed in the eighteenth century, this technique was an extension of the crayon manner, the most important difference being that the printing was done in colour to simulate the effect of a pastel drawing.

"Peintre-graveur". *See: engraving, artist's.*

Pen. A steel pen is used for writing and drawing on the lithographic stone.

Perchloride of iron. The old denomination of ferric chloride.
See: corrosive agents.

"Perfecit" (perfected, completed). An inscription to be found on certain engravings which were completed by an engraver other than the one who commenced it.
See: lettering.

Petroleum. *See: solvent.*

Photogalvanography. A nineteenth-century term for any process whereby an electrotype plate is obtained from a positive photograph.

Photographic autography. *See: "cliché-verre".*

Photographic processes. Photographic processes are used to create an image on sensitized paper, either by means of a negative, or by exposing the paper directly to the light, having previously blocked out parts of it with various objects. The negative may also be prepared manually, as in the *cliché-verre*, a process which could be classed among the printmaking techniques. Photomechanical processes are those which involve a combination of photography with traditional printmaking methods; a positive or a negative image can be reproduced on the surface of any metal plate, stone, wood block or screen, provided that it has been sensitized beforehand. Examples of photomechanical processes are: *line block, half-tone* block, *photogravure, collotype,* and such techniques can also be applied to screenprinting and offset lithography. The artist can also make an image by combining photographic materials (i.e. sensitized paper, developer, fixative, etc.) in his own fashion; named by Pierre Cordier a "chimigramme".
For a long time, photomechanical means were rejected in the definition of original printmaking, for it was not considered true work done entirely by the artist's hand. This restriction is no longer regarded as valid, for it is now appreciated that the artist may use any photographic means at his disposal in the making of a print.

Photogravure. Sometimes known as heliogravure (particularly hand photogravure), this technique is one of the most important methods of industrial printing (the others being *letterpress* and *offset lithography*). It is an intaglio process which can be divided into two procedures: (1) Hand photogravure, a derivation of the aquatint in its method of obtaining tone. After sensitizing a copper plate and exposing it to light to form the image, resin or bitumen grain was scattered over it. The procedure continued as for a normal aquatint plate. This technique subsequently developed into a totally photomechanical process: (2) Machine photogravure, in which the tone is supplied by a *cross-line screen*. It was discovered that the plate could be bent into the form of a cylinder, a development which allowed very fast printing speeds (rotogravure). The technique is used more for magazines and catalogues than for printmaking itself.

Photolithography. A term referring to the use of photography in lithography and offset lithography.

Photozincography. A rarely used term referring to line block and half-tone methods in which a zinc plate is used.

Pigment. The constituent in ink which gives it colour.

"Pinxit" or "Pinx.". Painted. Inscribed after the name of the artist of the original design.
See: lettering.

Pitch. A residual resinous substance.
See: gums and resins.

Pitting. A fault which occurs on metal plates, particularly aluminium. Small holes are also sometimes found on the rubber roller used in offset lithography. An etching ground may also be pitted with small holes caused by an excess of heat on application of the ground. An uneven biting will result from the fault.

Place in the press. Paper which has been dampened before printing must be placed in a press in order to flatten it.
See: drying.

Planing. An operation consisting in knocking a metal plate with a hammer in order to make the surface level. A planisher is sometimes used for this purpose.

Planography. In planographic printing, as opposed to relief and intaglio processes, there is no difference in level between the inked surface and the non-inked surface.
See: lithography, offset lithography.

Plaster cast. A type of trial *proof* taken from an intaglio plate. Plaster is poured over the plate after it has been blackened with smoke, thereby producing an exact mould of the design.

Plastic (engraving on). Sheets of plastic can be engraved in the same technique as a woodcut or wood engraving. The transparency of the material greatly facilitates *registration* in colour printing.

Plate. The plate is any metal printing element, whether an intaglio, relief or planographic process is employed.

Plate coating machine. A machine possessing a revolving turn-table, at one time used for spreading a sensitized layer over a copper plate in photogravure.

Plate mark. The mark imprinted by an intaglio plate onto the paper (especially visible at the edges) caused by the pressure of the rollers in the press.
See: bevelling, pressure.

Platen. Cast iron rectangular element in the typographic press which brings the paper against the inked type or block to obtain an impression.
See: press.

Pleating (of paper). A printing error which can be caused by either initially over-dampening the paper, or by an excessive amount of pressure, or by bad registration.

Plug. A small piece of wood (or linoleum for a linocut) known as a "plug" is inserted into the block as a means of replacing a bad error or a damaged area in a woodcut. It is cut in accordance with the correction or restoration to be made.

Point. *See: needle.*

Poker work. Or pyrography: a method in which a poker is used to burn a design into wood. It has occasionally been employed in printmaking.
See: burning the block.

Polishing. The operation of smoothing and polishing is done to metal plates for engraving and to lithographic stones. Metal plates are polished with fine abrasives, dampened with water or oil, and applied either by hand or with a machine. Lithographic stones are polished with a pumice stone, into which wax has been incorporated.

"Pompon". *See: stencil.*

Portfolio. A pliable case, made of thick cardboard covered with leather, in which prints are conserved.

Positive & negative. Photographic terminology is sometimes applied to prints; i.e. a positive design is black on white, a negative one is white on black.
See: white line.

Pounce. A powdered colourant, e.g. red chalk, lamp black or crayon, applied to the surface of a drawing, the outlines of which have been pricked. It passes through the perforations and transfers an image of the drawing onto paper strategically placed beneath.
See: pricking.

"Poupée, à la". The French term used for a method of colouring an intaglio plate by hand. Contrary to usual methods of colour printing, the different colours are all applied on one plate with the aid of a stump of rag, known as a "poupée" (or dolly).
See: colour printing, inking.

Preparatory drawing. Before making an engraving, woodcut, etc., a preparatory drawing is made on the surface of the printing element. It may be a tracing or transfer of the original design, or it may be an original itself, done with ink or chalk.

Press, printing. The three most important types of press are: (1) the relief or typographic press; (2) the intaglio printing press, also used in photogravure; and (3) the planographic press used in lithography and offset lithography. Within each of these types, the manual press is generally used by artists making their own prints, and can be distinguished from the mechanical press used in industry.
1. In the relief press *(see: letterpress)*, a heavy rectangular element, the platen, is lowered over the bed of the press onto the paper and the block.
2. An intaglio printing press is comprised of two cylinders, between which the paper and the plate are pulled under great pressure.
3. In the lithographic press, the stone and the paper are transported by a mobile bed to a position beneath the scraper which supplies the pressure.
There are different models of each type of press; they vary according to the manufacturer and the period in which they were made.

Pressure. The pressure of an intaglio plate on the paper when pulled through the press results in the formation of a *plate mark*. In French, a distinction is made between the plate mark on the recto of the paper ("cuvette") and that on the verso ("foulage").
See: plate mark.

Pricking. A method of transferring a drawing, which consists in pricking with a fine needle the outlines of the design, leaving a series of small holes which may then be *pounced*. This involves shaking powdered red chalk over the dots so that a trace of the design is obtained on the paper or plate placed underneath. The process was much used in lithography for transferring drawings.

Print. The image obtained from any printing element. Originally, this was either a metal plate, engraved in intaglio, or a wood block (or metal plate) cut in relief. From the beginning of the nineteenth century, lithographic stones were included, and today screenprinting adds a further type of printing element. An impression taken planographically from a painted surface may also be termed a print *(see: monotype)*. In the past, a rigid distinction was observed between prints obtained by manual processes and *reproductions* obtained by photomechanical methods *(see: photographic processes)*. This distinction has less value today, because reproductions have been incorporated into artists' *original* prints and are therefore not solely produced, as originally intended, for mass production. A print is termed "original" if the artist of the design has worked on the printing element himself, as opposed to reproductive and *interpretative* prints which involve the use of an intermediary person to reproduce the design onto the printing element. Original prints are often only produced in small numbers; they may be numbered and signed by the artist. These distinctions between reproductions (which occasionally may also be signed and numbered) and original prints are, however, generalized. In practice the frontiers are more imprecise, particularly in commercial printing. It must be noted that some people have a much more rigorous definition of an original print than others, e.g. of a photomechanically produced original print of which only a very small number of impressions, numeration and a certificate of authenticity will make it qualify.

Printer's drawing. In reproductive printing, a drawing initially must be made after the original design. Photography is sometimes used instead. Reproduction of designs is particularly common in lithography and in screenprinting.
See: transfer.

Printing. The action of making a print on a support, whether it be of paper or of any other material, from a block, plate or stone or through a screen, in any of the printmaking procedures.
See: embossing.

Printing element. The part which is inked and produces the impression when printed, i.e. the block, plate, stone or screen.
See: impression.

Printing table or base. The surface to which the screen, placed over the paper, is attached, in screenprinting. It may be equipped with a suction device to hold the paper in position.

Proof. In a general sense, this word has been used to indicate any impression of a print. Strictly speaking, it should be limited to those impressions pulled by the artist to prove or test his work, whether before or after completion of the block, plate, etc.
See: counterproof, plaster cast.

Proof before lettering. An impression taken before the lettering (dedication, title, names of artist, engraver, etc.) has been engraved.

Proof with lettering. The lettering comprises all the writing underneath or above the design on the plate, block, etc. Impressions are sometimes taken on intaglio plates with scratched letters before the lettering is properly engraved, or with it only partly inscribed.

Proof (with remarques). A "remarque" is a scribbled sketch made by the artist outside his main design which is eliminated later for printing the main edition.

Proof:
Artist's proof. A proof reserved for the artist outside the main edition. This may be noted in the margin (E.A. on French prints means "épreuve d'artiste"). Some artists number these proofs.
"Fine" proof. A definitive proof taken with particular care, on high quality paper, with margins.
Oil proof. In the past, printers cleaned the plate with an oil-rubber and then pulled an impression from it to ensure that no ink remained in the incisions.
Printer's proof. A proof reserved for the printer.
Signed proof. One which has been signed by the artist.
Smoke proof. (Fr. fumé) A type of trial proof taken from a wood block which has been blackened with smoke. It may be taken by the woodcutter to serve as a model for the printer. More recently, the term has been used to describe a fine quality impression taken by hand from a wood block.
Trial proof. A proof taken while work is still being made on the plate, stone, etc., to test the effect of inking and from which the artist can judge the amount of additions or alterations to be made. Sometimes he may make corrections by hand on the proof itself (a "touched" proof). In the past, woodcutters pulled trial proofs by blackening the relief of the block with smoke and printing it with the aid of a burnisher or rubber. Several trial proofs may be taken until a definitive state is reached. The printer's proof is often a trial proof.
Wax proof. A type of trial proof taken from an intaglio plate. The incisions are blackened with smoke and an impression is taken onto a sheet of paper covered with white wax which picks up the design.

Provenance. A history of ownership. The provenance of some prints can be traced back to the time that they were made.

Pulling angle. The angle that it is necessary to maintain between the squeegee and the screen (c. 50°) during the process of pulling impressions.
See: screenprinting.

Pumice stone. A light volcanic stone used for grinding and polishing surfaces. It may also be used in a powdered form.
See: abrasive agent, graining, polishing.

Punch. A tool with a sharp point, or points, that is used directly on a metal plate with the aid of a hammer or mallet. It may be obtained in a variety of forms e.g. dotting punch (with a single point) and matting punch (with a flattened head, hatched in the manner of a file).

See: mattoir, punch work, ring punch, roulette. For making corrections on a metal plate, an ordinary flat punch is used, or one possessing a rounded head (cocking punch) if the plate is particularly thick.
See: dotted manner, punch work, stipple.

Punch work. A method of dotting a metal plate with a punch and hammer. The punches can be obtained in various shapes and sizes to vary the shape.

Pyrography. *See: poker work.*

Ream. Twenty quires or 480 sheets of paper.

Rebiting. Rebiting an etched plate, in order to accentuate the indentations. A stopping-out varnish is used to protect the parts sufficiently etched.

Receptivity. In printing terminology, a surface is said to be receptive if it retains the ink well. The word is applied to the rollers, the paper, or the plates to be inked. Too much ink makes the impression heavy and thick, too little will render it pale and irregular. Receptivity is also applicable to the rubber rollers used in offset lithography, as well as to a freshly glued surface in its "receptivity" of the other surface which is to adhere to it.
See: collage, inking.

Registration. Owing to the number of plates or blocks, etc., used in colour printing, a careful registration is required to ensure that each element prints in the correct position. The method of doing it varies according to the technique. In intaglio printing and lithography, needles are pierced through the paper into holes, specially placed for this purpose in the plate or stone.
See: colour printing.

Reinforcing (the lithographic image). A lithographic "etch" is used to reinforce the image after it has been drawn on the stone: powdered resin or bitumen is scattered over it, then heated so that it adheres to the stone and is finally bitten with acid. This has the effect of giving an imperceptible relief to the image which will clarify and intensify the impression.

Relief. As opposed to intaglio and planographic printing, the black areas of an impression taken from a block cut in relief are made by inking the raised parts, thereby leaving the furrows to print white.
See: letterpress.

Remarques. *See: proof (with remarques).*

Removal solution. While preparing the lithographic stone a removal solution (washout) can be used to aid elimination of the previous design from the surface.
See: lithography.
During the etching process, a removal solution is used on areas of ground and stopping-out varnish when protection of those parts of the plate is no longer required.
See: grounds and varnishes, olive oil.

Reproduction. Before the introduction of photography, a work was reproduced by either copying it identically, or interpreting it as closely as possible if a different technique to that of the original was used. Engraving, wood engraving and lithography were the most common methods of reproduction. A print is therefore termed reproductive if it is made by someone other than

the artist of the original design, as opposed to an *original print* which is made by the artist himself.
See: interpretative print.

Resin. *See: gums and resins.*

Restraining agent. A product which is mixed with ink (or vapourized on its surface) in order to delay the drying procedure.

Retroussage. A method of wiping the plate in intaglio printing. A fine muslin was passed over the already inked and wiped plate in order to pull some of the ink out of the indentations. This gave the lines a softer appearance in the impression. The English term sometimes used is "dragging up".
See: impression, "natural", and wiping.

Reverse, in. 1. The design of a print is always drawn in the reverse sense on the block, plate or stone, so that it will print the correct way round.
2. An image is reversed in all printing procedures except screenprinting. The engraver, lithographer or woodcutter must, accordingly, always work in reverse to his original design; a mirror is sometimes employed as an aid.

Rework. When part of the printing element has been corrected or touched up.

Ring punch. A small punch with a hollow circular head. In the past, it was used by engravers to incise circles to represent towns, etc., on maps.

Rocker. The tool used for preparing (or "grounding") a mezzotint plate. It has a thick blade with a serrated, semicircular cutting edge. When moved backwards and forwards across the plate, it creates a surface uniformly indented with a grain which retains ink and prints as pure black.
See: graining, mezzotint.

Roller, inking. Cylinder made of metal, or sometimes wood, and covered with a more pliable material, such as skin, rubber or gelatine. It is used for inking relief blocks, lithographic stones and metal plates used in lithography. It is held by handles situated at each side, or by a single central handle the teeth of which constitute the axle of the roller.

Roller, printing. The rollers of an intaglio printing press are two steel cylinders between which the paper and the plate together are pulled. A similar arrangement of rollers is used for glazing paper *(see: calender, glazing)*. One of the earliest types of lithographic presses to be developed made use of a cylinder to push forward the bed of the press.
See: bed, press.

Roller, varnishing. Varnish can be applied with either a *dabber* or a roller. The latter is made of rubber or of some synthetic material. The roller used for revarnishing or stopping out is traditionally covered with a fine skin.

Rotogravure. *See: photogravure.*

Rough-polishing. The first stage in the preparation of a lithographic stone before grinding.
See: graining, lithography.

Roulette. An engraver's tool, having a revolving circular head, with either a single serrated edge (the simple roulette), or a wider surface dotted or lined in a variety of forms. It is used in some of the dot processes *(see: stipple, crayon manner)* with the aim of creating areas of tone on an impression; may be used either directly on the metal plate or through the intervention of an etching ground. A tool similar to the simple roulette was used, particularly in the nineteenth century, to perforate drawings *(see: pricking, pounce)*; and, in letterpress, to make dotted lines on sheets destined to be detached.

Royal. A format of paper (620 × 500 mm.).

Rubber, leather. The tool used in hand-printing from a wood block. It is made from horsehair stuck together with strong glue, covered with leather and fitted with a handle.

Rubbing. A method of taking an impression from a relief block with a leather rubber or a burnisher used manually on the verso of the paper.
See: impression.

Rubbing in lithography. 1. Rubbing ink is a soft ink applied directly to the stone with the fingertip when drawing the design.
2. A crayon or ink drawing may be rubbed with a stump or a brush to create a soft effect.

Rubbing up. An image is "rubbed up" in lithography in order to renew its original intensity after a number of impressions have been taken.

Ruby. Ruby points are used to make very fine lines, either directly on a metal plate or through the intervention of a ground.
See: diamond, needle, sapphire.

Rule. In typography, the rule is a thin line separating text, diagrams, etc.

Salt. Salt may be used to produce a grain on the surface of a metal plate in the same manner as *sugar*. Granules of salt are scattered over a plate previously covered with stopping-out varnish. This is then submerged in water which causes the particles of salt to swell and remove any varnish immediately surrounding them thereby exposing those parts as bare metal. When etched, an irregular grain is formed on the surface of the plate.

Sapphire. Sapphire points are used for making fine lines on a metal plate or lithographic stone.
See: diamond, needle, ruby.

Scoring (the plate). The surface of a metal plate can be scratched with bunches of needles or emery stone pencils to produce fine tones of grey in the print.

Scorper. A tool used for metal and wood engraving. It has the appearance of a fine *échoppe*, with an oval section and a bevel resembling a small finger-nail (Fr. "onglette").

Scraper. 1. A scraper in the form of a knife is used for removing ink from the printing roller when it is being cleaned.
2. The scraper used in intaglio printing is a finely sharpened steel blade, used to remove *burr* from the plate.
3. The scraper used for clearing the backgrounds in woodcuts and wood engravings is a strong steel blade with a hooked appearance.
4. Lithographic scraper: a wooden bar, cut along its length into a V-sharped blade which is covered with leather. It is used to press the paper against the stone during printing.
5. Mezzotint scraper: the tool used to smooth away those parts of the grained mezzotint plate which are to print white *(see: mezzotint)*. It has two cutting edges, a different shape from the ordinary scraper described above (2).

Scraperboard or scratchboard. Invented about 1865 by the Austrian, Karl Angerer. He covered cardboard with a coating consisting of kaolin, gelatine and glycerine. This created a surface which for the engraver was very easy to work, and from which the same effects could be obtained as from wood. After completion, the design was photographed, transferred to zinc and etched (i.e. as a *line block*). The technique was used for illustrating cheap books.
See: line block.

Scraping. 1. Removal of the burr produced by the burin, or any other tool, when it is not to be retained for printing. It is done with the *scraper*, an instrument possessing a finely sharpened steel blade.
See: burr.
2. Scraping is done to make corrections on a plate or stone, by means of a scraper, burnisher, abrasive chalk or needles.

3. A special type of scraper is used in wood engraving to remove areas of wood.
4. In lithography, a drawing process resembling mezzotint can be made, by scraping away parts of a stone already covered with black ink to create the white areas when printed. It is done with various needles.
See: lithographic mezzotint.
5. Scraperboard technique.
See: scraperboard.

Scraping the ink. In screenprinting, the ink is scraped through the screen to make an impression. If it is to be done manually, great experience is required from the printer to ensure that an even, steady movement is made; this is essential if a good impression is to be obtained.
See: screenprinting, squeegee.

Scratched work. (French: "manière eraillée"; Italian: "sgraffio"). A method of scratching sometimes done on the surface of metalcut plates (fifteenth century).

Screen. The printing element in screenprinting. It is made by stretching material (silk, nylon, metal mesh, etc.) over a frame.
See: screenprinting.

Screenprinting. An ancient method of oriental printmaking which, considerably modified and ameliorated, has become one of the four most important methods of modern printing. Contemporary artists have made much use of it as a printmaking technique.
The principle of screenprinting consists in applying *stencils* to a screen (constructed of silk or of some synthetic or metallic material), in such a way that when ink is applied it is prevented from passing through some parts while penetrating the rest of the screen, thereby printing an image on paper placed underneath. The screen is stretched across a frame and attached to a base in such a manner that it can readily move up and down, so that paper can be easily placed and removed as required. For each impression, the paper is placed against registration tabs to ensure that the printing is done in the correct position. The ink is poured over the *masking* at one end of the screen and when this has been lowered into position, the ink is scraped across the screen with the aid of a *squeegee*. The most important part of the process is the preparation of the screen. Stencils may be applied in a variety of ways, including the use of *filling-in liquid, varnish* or *plastic film*. A drawing can be made directly on the surface with a special ink which is removed in readiness for printing after the rest of the screen has been blocked out. A photographic stencil is made by initially sensitizing the screen.
See: stencil.

Screen washer. Used for cleaning the screen after pulling an impression.
See: screenprinting.

"Sculpsit". Or the abbreviated form, *sculp. sc., s.*, denotes the name of the engraver on a print.
See: lettering.

Sensitized plate. A sheet of glass covered with sensitized emulsion used in photography instead of film.

Serration. The appearance of the edges of a screen loaded with ink, under strong magnification.
See: screenprinting.

"Sgraffio". *See: scratched work.*

Shade. 1. Shade, in a print, refers to the darkest parts, as opposed to highlighted or lighter areas.
See: hatching.
2. The depth of hue in a tint, tone or colour. The shade is appreciable in a print whether it be in colour or in black and white.
See: colour, tint, tone.

Shade card. Or colour chart: a catalogue of the different colours distributed by ink manufacturers.

Sharpening. The action of sharpening the pointed end or blade of a tool or instrument used for working the plate. The abrasives used for sharpening burins, gouges, etching needles, etc., are usually made of stone possessing a fine ground.
See: abrasive agent, burin, knife, stone.

Side-sticks. Wedges of wood or metal used in typography to hold the type in position.

Signature. *See: lettering.*

Silkscreen. The term usually used in America for *screenprinting*.

Small sheet (of paper). A sheet which is printed with narrow margins, as opposed to being clipped. A large sheet of paper which is printed with wide margins can also perhaps signify that it is of fine quality.

Smoking (the plate). After the ground has been laid in the etching technique, the plate is blackened by holding it over some lighted tapers; and consequently the lines drawn with the etching needle can be easily seen as shining exposed metal. *See: grounds and varnishes.*

Soap. At one stage during the nineteenth century, electrotypes were made from casts taken from engravings done on soap.

Soft-ground etching. One of the etching processes which aims to simulate the effects of a chalk or crayon drawing *(see: crayon manner)*. The plate is initially covered with a soft ground. The drawing is made with a hard crayon on paper which has been pressed to the surface of the grounded plate; the ground adheres to the back of the paper where the crayon has left indentations in it, thereby creating an impression on the plate of the marks of the crayon. The paper with the attached ground is carefully removed and the plate is bitten. It is possible to reproduce any kind of texture with this method: textiles (taking impressions of silk is called "procédé à la cravate" in Fr.), rough papers, netting or leather can be pressed into a soft ground in a similar fashion.

Solvent. The liquid product used to dissolve and maintain in solution the solid components in inks, varnishes and the various other preparations used in printmaking. It is to be distinguished from the *dilutant*, a thinning agent, although a product may be both solvent and dilutant at the same time. The different solvents used are: water, oil of turpentine, benzine, acetone, carbon tetrachloride, alcohols and light oils.

Spatula. A type of knife with a flexible steel blade used for scraping ink.

Splatter. A method of applying the ink in lithography. It is sprayed through a metal mesh onto the stone with the aid of a stiff brush. Areas which are to remain white or be very lightly splattered are protected with gum Arabic *(staging out).*

Spoon. This can be used in printing from a relief block. The paper is pressed to the inked surface and rubbed on the reverse with the back of a spoon. *See: woodcut.*

Spout. A small opening in the form of a pouring spout is built into the wall of wax surrounding a plate when it is to be etched using this method. *See: bordering.*

Square. 1. A paper format.
2. The engraved outline determining the shape of the design of the print.
3. A type of incision made at right angles.

Squaring. The angles of machine-made paper are squared up when it is cut, unless a *deckle edge* is to be maintained (as in the case of hand-made paper).

Squeegee. The essential tool of screenprinting. It is a rubber or plastic blade with a wooden or metal handle, and is used for scraping the ink across the screen. *See: screenprinting.*

Staging out. Another term for *stopping out.* *See: splatter.*

Stamp. A type of punch having a letter or a sign in relief at one end, used in intaglio printing.

Stamping press. A typographic screw-press. *See: press.*

State. The proofs taken while the artist is working on the plate, stone, etc. to check different stages of his progress are known as states; each one showing additional working constitutes a different state. The last one is said to be the difinitive state (or proof).

Steel-facing. A process consisting of depositing, by electrolysis, a very thin layer of iron onto a copper plate in order to reinforce it. Copper, the most commonly engraved metal, can become scratched and worn down through use. Furthermore, the wheels of the press tend to flatten out the indentations, removing the finest ones altogether, and rub away the idiosyncratic burr on plates engraved with the drypoint. In this respect steel-facing is an added protective and allows a greater number of impressions to be made while maintaining a constant quality. The steel-facing can be removed if reworking on the plate is required. Zinc must be faced with copper before being steel-faced. Chromium is sometimes used instead of steel, generally in photogravure, to strengthen the printing drums. It has the advantage of preventing oxidation (it is necessary to varnish or grease a steel-faced plate), and of producing a surface that facilitates wiping at the time of printing. *See: chromium-facing, steel plates.*

Steel plates. Iron plates are known to have been used before the sixteenth century and Dürer made several etchings on this metal. Steel, made from a mixture of iron and a slightly larger proportion of carbon, did not become generally used until the end of the eighteenth century, and this was particularly in England. It can either be etched or engraved: frequently the indentations on the plate are first made with acid and then finished off with the burin. A steel plate has a particularly clean, sharp line that can be extremely fine; it also produces many more impressions than a copper plate. It is used in particular for book illustrations, stamps, book-plates, vignettes and greeting cards. *See: burin, etching, keepsakes, metals, steel-facing.*

Stencil. 1. Stencils are an essential part of screenprinting: they are attached to or incorporated with the screen to ensure that the ink passes through in the correct places. They can be made in many different forms, e.g. as a simple masking or covering stencil; as a "wash-out" stencil, which involves drawing the design on the screen in a greasy substance, then covering the whole screen with filler or gum, and finally dissolving the greasy image in turps, thereby forming a "positive" stencil; or as a photo-stencil, whereby photographic images are incorporated into the screen. *See: screenprinting, wax stencil.*
2. Stencils are also used for colouring prints by hand. Stencils of the areas to be coloured are cut out in zinc or aluminium; the colours are dabbed on with a large brush (known as a "pompon" in French); they may be juxtaposed or superimposed over each other. The method was much used in the colouring of maps, topographical prints and devotional woodcuts. It is still used today for book illustration and on greeting cards. *See: hand-colouring, image-maker, registration.*

Stencil brush. A particular brush which may be used in applying colour with a stencil.

Stereotype. A metal cast made, especially from wood engravings, by means of a mould.

Stipple. A method of intaglio printing which dates from the end of the eighteenth century. Its aim is to render tone by means of a conglomeration of dots and short strokes (or flicks). It is done by dotting and flicking the plate with a special type of curved burin (stipple graver) which may be aided by the *roulette*, various etching needles and the *drypoint*. Both etching and engraving without the intervention of a ground are employed in the process. *See: dot work.*

Stone. Stones are used as the printing element in lithography, and as a means of sharpening printmaking tools.

Stopping out. Protecting, with a varnish, any part of a metal plate which is not to be etched, during the biting procedure. *Stopping-out varnish is* used for this purpose. It is applied with a roller or a dabber. *See: bordering, grounds and varnishes.*

Stump. Stumps are used for blending the colours of the lithographic crayon.

Stylet. A slender pointed instrument, used especially for cutting out stencils in screenprinting.

Sugar. Sugar may be used to create tone in intaglio printing. It is scattered over a plate covered with stopping-out varnish which, when dry, is immersed in water. This causes the granules of sugar to swell, displacing the varnish immediately surrounding them and exposing the metal underneath at these points. When etched, an irregular grain is formed on the surface of the plate.

Sugar-lift process. A method of defining drawn areas on an intaglio plate. The necessary area is painted directly onto the metal surface with Indian ink in which sugar has been dissolved. This is covered with a stopping-out varnish and, when the latter has dried, submerged in water which causes the sugar mixture to swell, removing the varnish and exposing the metal at the parts where the drawing has been made.

Suite. A set of prints dealing with the same subject, or by the same artist, which are published as a whole. It can also refer to a series of prints taken apart from an illustrated book.

Sulphur print. There are various ways in which sulphur is involved in printmaking. (1) A mixture of flowers of sulphur and olive oil can be applied directly to the surface of a metal plate to produce a tone similar to that of an aquatint. Some engravers spread the oil on first, and then apply the powdered sulphur. (2) A sulphur proof may be taken onto a sheet covered with sulphur, from an intaglio plate in which the incisions have been previously filled with lamp black. (3) *See: niello.*

Support. The material on which an impression is made, e.g. paper, textiles, metal sheets, etc.

Surface tone. If a plate is not wiped properly before printing, "surface tone" is created by the films of ink left on its surface. *See: wiping.*

Surround. The border, frame or margin of a print. It can also refer to the design surrounding a printed text. *See: margin, square.*

Tail piece. A vignette on a blank page at the end of a chapter in a book.

Tank. 1. A tank is used for soaking paper prior to printing. It can be of metal, wood, glass, rubber or porcelain.
2. A tank filled with a mordant, in which the plate is immersed, can be used for the etching process and for acidic cleaning.
3. Special tanks are used for electrolysis.

Techniques, combination of. The use of several different techniques in the production of one print. *See also mixed method.*

Textured (effect). The appearance of an impression which gives an effect of the texture of the element from which it has been printed.

Thinning varnish. A liquifying substance which is mixed with the ink in order to make it more fluid; it can also add a sheen to the surface.
See: base, grounds and varnishes, ink.

Thread-counter. A small instrument used for examining details of engraved work or the weave of materials used in screenprinting.
See: magnifying glass.

Tin. Tin was used in the nineteenth century for printing music by means of a punch and hammer.
See: punch work.

Tint. Generally speaking, a tint can be any colour; more specifically it is a variant shade obtained by mixing one colour with another, particularly white. The delicate series of lines used to denote areas of shade (as opposed to those representing line) in wood engravings, were at one time known as "tints"; hence *tint tool*, the type of burin used to produce them.

Tone. The particular shade of a colour. In printing terminology, tone is opposed to *line*. It refers to non-linear techniques, such as wash or paint, etc., and its interpretation into prints is effected by the tonal processes, e.g. *aquatint, brush etching, dotted manner, stipple.*
See: dot work.

Tone block. *See: colour block.*

Tracing point. An instrument used for making preparatory tracings on the surface of metal, wood or stone printing elements.

Transfer. A process of transferring an image onto the lithographic stone. The drawing is made initially on transfer (or autographic) paper so that it can be easily removed from this surface to the stone.
See: lithography, paper.

Transparent ground. A ground, either solid or liquid, which is used when reworking an etched plate, so that the lines already incised show through.
See: grounds and varnishes.

Type-high. To set the type at the correct height to print with accompanying type, blocks, etc.
See: letterpress, packing, underlay.

Typographic block. Block in which the design is entirely made up of typographic letters.

Vehicle. One of the main constituents of ink with which the pigment is covered. The vehicle of greasy inks is oil; it may be either crude or refined.
See: ink.

Vice. A particular kind of vice is used for holding hot metal plates: it has lip-shaped edges so as not to cut into the metal and is made of wood so as not to be affected by the heat of the plate.

Viscosity. The viscosity of ink prevents the liquid from separating when it is applied to the roller, spatula, etc. An ink base must possess a certain viscosity to enable it to retain any varnishes which may be incorporated with it.
See: ink, oils and greases.

Washing. Washing of materials is frequent in printmaking. A screen is washed during and especially after printing. Metal plates must be cleaned after biting. The resilient *blankets* used in the presses to even out the pressure must also be washed.

Water-bath. When heating liquid or semi-liquid substances, they are placed in a water-bath if they are unable to withstand a naked source of heat. A receptacle holding the substance is placed in a container of water under which the heat is applied. The method ensures a temperature of constant regularity.

Watermark. Manufacturer's mark made in the paper. It is recognizable by its transparency.

Wax stencil. Used in screenprinting: the screen is blocked out with a layer of wax from which the stencil is created by pressing it out, or working directly on it with various instruments.
See: screenprinting, stencil.

White. 1. White in prints: the uninked area of the sheet. In this case, the design can be either positive (i.e. black on white), as in woodcuts or line engravings; or negative (white on black), as in mezzotints or white-line woodcuts. It can also be obtained by superimposing opaque white ink over a darker colour, as in chiaroscuro woodcuts, or in screenprints, which make particular use of covering ink. Transparent white ink and transparent white lacquer are also used to lighten tinted areas.
See: chiaroscuro woodcuts, etching, ink, screenprinting, woodcuts.
2. White in letterpress: In printing language in general, the white is the area which is not printed. To "whiten" means to increase the proportion of white. The French term "tirer en blanc" means to print one side of the sheet only.
3. White products: Two types of white products are used in printmaking: pigments (white lead, zinc white and barium white), for the constitution of ink; and powders possessing a chemical stability (whiting made from powdered chalk), which can be used as a thickening agent in the production of ink and as light abrasives. (*See: cleaning, polishing*).

White line. Any design in which the image shows as white on black. The most usual type are *white-line cuts*, principally woodcuts or wood engravings; in the nineteenth century they were also produced by etching zinc in relief.
See: woodcut.

White manner. From the French "manière blanche". A method of working an engraving, lithograph or screenprint with the aim of obtaining a white design on a black background.
See: white, white line.

White mark. An absence of ink or of pressure on a certain place on the printing element will appear as a white mark in the impression.

Widening. The width of a line is increased by widening or deepening it on the plate, stone, etc.
See: line.

Wiping (the plate). In all intaglio printing methods the plate is wiped after it has been inked; the white areas of a print will not appear clean unless this is done very thoroughly. It is wiped initially with three pieces of muslin, each cleaner than the last, and finished with either the palm of the hand or tissue paper. Some ink may be purposefully left on the plate to create *surface tone*, or some may be dragged out of the lines for further effect.
See: impression, "natural", and retroussage.

Wood engraving. A technique which appeared towards the end of the eighteenth century. It is essentially a woodcut made from wood cut across the grain (Fr. "bois de bout"). Small cubes of wood are stuck together to make up the block; this helps to create a very hard surface on which a much finer line can be produced than on a woodcut. It is cut with a burin; various types of burins are used to obtain close cross-hatching, dots, etc., and gouges and chisels for the larger spaces to be removed.

Woodburytype. A nineteenth-century photomechanical process, it was an antecedent of the *collotype*, patented in England.

Woodcut. One of the oldest and most important techniques in printmaking (*see: letterpress*). The principle consists in cutting a design, in relief, on a hard, polished block of wood. The relief areas take the ink and print the design in reverse. It can be either cut so that the design is produced by the relief areas (positive), or so that the furrows are treated as the design (negative), seen in a *white-line* woodcut. The blocks are cut along the grain of the block (Fr. "bois de fil") with various tools: the woodcutter's knife, gouges, chisels, scrapers, etc. The design must be large enough to ensure that the parts left in relief, which appear as small banks with sloping edge, are strong enough to withstand the pressure of the tools and the press. Woodcuts printed in graduated colour tones are known as *chiaroscuro woodcuts* and have been made since the sixteenth century. They are made by printing the different tones on separate blocks: the first for the outline of the design (*key block*), and as many consecutive blocks as are necessary for each tone (*tone blocks*). The characteristic effect of the technique is achieved by superimposing the various tone blocks.
In the East, woodcut is a traditional method of printmaking and has its specialized techniques. Japanese woodcuts are produced by making an initial drawing on semi-transparent paper which is reversed and attached to the block so that the image is the right way up in the print. Gouges and chisels are used for cutting away the wood. Water-based inks are applied with a brush. Printing is done manually by rubbing the back of the paper (placed on the block) with a *baren*, a disc made of wound hempen cord covered with a bamboo leaf.
Linocuts are related to woodcuts in that they are cut in relief but they possess their own particular technique.
See: linocut.
Today, plastic is often used instead of wood to make woodcut (and wood-engraved) blocks. It is inked with a roller, and printed either manually, by pressing paper onto the block and rubbing it with the back of a spoon, a folding stick or leather rubber (Fr. "frotton"); or in a mechanical press of which there exist many examples.
See: press, wood engraving.

Wove paper. A type of hand-made paper produced from a *mould* with a mesh so tightly woven as to leave no visible pattern.
See: laid paper, paper.

Zincography. A term sometimes adopted from the French, meaning the use of lithography on a zinc plate. As zinc may also be etched, it is best to avoid use of the term without specification, since it could be taken to imply this different technique as well.
See: algraphy, lithography.

Bibliography

STANDARD WORKS ON THE ARTS AND TECHNIQUES OF THE PRINT PUBLISHED FROM THE 17th TO THE 19th CENTURY

M. ALVIN, *Les nielles de la Bibliothèque royale de Belgique*, Brussels, 1857. – A. ANDRESEN, *Der deutsche Peintre-Graveur. 1560–1800*, 5 vols., Leipzig 1864–1878 (reprint. New York 1969). – A. APELL, *Handbuch für Kupferstichsammler*, Leipzig 1880.
F. BALDINUCCI, *Cominciamento e progresso dell'arte dell'intagliare in rame, colle vite di molti de' più eccellenti maestri della stessa professione*, Florence 1686; 2nd ed., annotated by D.M. Manni, Florence 1767. – A. BARTSCH, *Catalogue raisonné des estampes gravées à l'eau-forte par Guido Reni et de celles de ses disciples...*, Vienna 1795; *Le Peintre-Graveur*, 21 vols., Vienna 1803–1821; *Anleitung zur Kupferstichkunde*, Vienna 1821. – P.-F. BASAN, *Dictionnaire des graveurs anciens et modernes*, Paris 1767. – P. de BAUDICOUR, *Le peintre-graveur français continué, ou catalogue raisonné des estampes gravées par les peintres et les dessinateurs de l'Ecole Française nés dans le XVIIIe siècle. Ouvrage faisant suite au peintre-graveur français de Robert Dumesnil*, 2 vols., Paris 1859–1861. – E. BAYARD, *L'art de reconnaître les gravures anciennes*, Paris, n.d. – R.Z. BECKER, *Gravures en bois des anciens maîtres allemands...*, Gotha 1808. – H. BERALDI, *Les graveurs du XIXe siècle. Guide de l'amateur d'estampes modernes*, 12 vols., Paris 1885–1892. – BERTHIAUD, *Nouveau manuel complet de l'imprimeur en taille douce*, Paris 1837. – L. BINYON, *Dutch Etchers of the Seventeenth Century*, London 1895. – C. BLANC, *Manuel de l'amateur d'estampes*, 4 vols., Paris 1854–1889. – E. BOCHER, *Les gravures françaises du XVIIIe siècle*, 6 vols., Paris 1875–1882. – A. BONNARDOT, *Essai sur la restauration des anciennes estampes et des livres rares...*, Paris 1846; *Histoire artistique et archéologique de la gravure en France*, Paris 1849. – L. BONNET, *Le pastel en gravures*, Paris 1769. – A. BOSSE, *Traicté des manières de graver en taille-douce sur l'airain...*, Paris 1645; *Traité des manières... Revu et augmenté d'une nouvelle manière de se servir des dites eaux-fortes par M. Le Clerc*, Paris 1701; *De la manière de graver à l'eau-forte et au burin. Et de la gravure en manière noire... Nouvelle édition revue, corrigée et augmentée du double,...*, Paris 1745; *De la manière de graver à l'eau-forte et au burin... Nouvelle édition, augmentée de l'impression qui imite les tableaux, de la gravure en manière de crayon, et de celle qui imite le lavis...*, Paris 1758 (reprint, Melsungen 1979). – H. BOUCHOT, *Le Cabinet des estampes de la Bibliothèque nationale*, Paris 1895; *La Lithographie*, Paris 1895; *Exposition d'œuvres du XVIIIe siècle à la Bibliothèque Nationale. Cent estampes (manière noire et pointillé) choisies parmi les plus remarquables ayant figuré à l'exposition*, Paris 1906. – G. BOURCARD, *Les estampes du XVIIIe siècle, Ecole Française*, Paris 1885; *Dessins, gouaches, estampes et tableaux du XVIIIe siècle. Guide de l'amateur*, Paris 1893. – C. de BROU, *Quelques mots sur la gravure au millésime de 1418*, Brussels 1846. – BRULLIOT / A. LOCHERER, *Copies photographiques des plus rares gravures criblées, estampes, gravures en bois, etc., des XVe et XVIe siècles...* Munich 1854–1855. – A. BRY, *L'imprimeur lithographe...*, Paris 1835. – P. BURTY, *L'Eau-forte en 1874 et 1875*, 2 vols., Paris 1874–1875. – J.J. BYLAERT, *Neue Manier Kupferstiche von verschiedenen Farben zu verfertigen nach Art der Zeichnungen*, Amsterdam 1773.
J. CHELSUM, *A history of the Art of Engraving in Mezzo Tinto from its Origin to the Present Times*, Winchester 1786. – P.P. CHOFFARD, *Notice historique sur l'art de la gravure en France*, Paris 1804. – T. CHON, *Lehrbuch der Kupferstecherkunst, der Kunst in Stahl zu stechen, in Holz zu schneiden, Chalcographie, Siderographie und Xylographie...*, Ilmenau 1831 . – L. CICOGNARA, *Dell'origine, composizione e decomposizione dei nielli*, Venice 1827. – H. COHEN, *Guide de l'amateur de livres à vignettes du XVIIIe siècle...*, Paris 1870 (reprint, 1912). – CUNDALL, *A Brief History of Wood-Engraving*, London 1895.
E. DAVID, *Discours historique sur la gravure en taille-douce et sur la gravure en bois*, Paris 1808. – H. DELABORDE, *La gravure. Précis élémentaire de ses origines, de ses procédés et de son histoire*, Paris, n.d. – P. DELESCHAMPS, *Des mordants, des vernis et des planches dans l'art du graveur...*, Paris 1836. – A. DEMBOUR, *Description d'un nouveau procédé de gravure en relief sur cuivre...*, Metz 1835. – DESPRÉAUX, *Note détaillée sur l'invention de la gravure en relief*, Paris 1836. – J. DUCHESNE, the Elder, *Essai sur les nielles, gravures des orfèvres florentins du XVe siècle*, Paris 1826; *Notice des estampes exposées à la Bibliothèque Royale, formant un aperçu historique des produits de la gravure*, Paris 1841. – R. DUMESNIL, *Le peintre-graveur français, ou catalogue raisonné des estampes gravées par les peintres et les dessinateurs de l'école française. Ouvrage faisant suite au peintre-graveur de M. Bartsch...*, 11 vols., Paris 1835–1871. – G. DUPLESSIS, *La gravure au salon de 1855*, Paris 1855; *Les graveurs sur bois contemporains*, Paris 1857; *Histoire de la gravure en France*, Paris 1861; *Essai de bibliographie contenant l'indication des ouvrages relatifs à l'histoire de la gravure et des graveurs*, Paris 1862; *Le Cabinet du Roi, collection d'estampes commandées par Louis XIV*, Paris 1869; *Les merveilles de la gravure*, Paris 1869; *Histoire de la gravure en Italie, en Espagne, en Allemagne, dans les Pays-Bas, en Angleterre et en France...*, Paris 1880. – G. DUPLESSIS / AMAND-DURAND, *Eaux-fortes et gravures des maîtres anciens*, 10 vols., Paris 1872–1878. – G. DUPLESSIS / H. BOUCHOT, *Guide du collectionneur. Dictionnaire des marques et monogrammes des graveurs*, Paris 1886–1887. – E. DUTUIT, *Manuel de l'Amateur d'estampes. Ecoles flamande et hollandaise*, 3 vols., Paris and London 1885.
G. ENGELMANN, *Rapport sur la lithographie introduite en France...*, Mulhouse, n.d. [1815]; *Manuel du dessinateur lithographe*, Paris 1824; *Traité théorique et pratique de la lithographie*, Mulhouse 1840. – J. EVELYN, *Sculptura: or the History and Art of Chalcography and Engraving in Copper... To which is annexed a new manner of engraving, or mezzo tinto communicated by His Highness Prince Rupert to the authour of this Treatise*, London 1662.
W. FAITHORNE, *The Art of Graveing and Etching...*, London 1662 (reprint, New York 1968). – FAUCHEUX, *Catalogue des œuvres de maîtres, peintres et graveurs, vendus depuis plus de cent ans*, Brussels 1860. – T. H. FIELDING, *The Art of Engraving with the Various Modes of Operation...*, London 1844. – A. FIRMIN-DIDOT, *Essai typographique et bibliographique sur l'histoire de la gravure sur bois...*, Paris 1863. – A. FISCHER von ZICKWOLFF / W. FRANKE, *Das Kupferstichkabinett. Nachbildungen von Werken der graphischen Kunst vom Ende des XV. bis zum Anfang des XIX. Jahrhunderts*, 5 vols., Berlin 1897–1901. – FOURNIER, the Younger, *Dissertation sur l'origine et les progrès de l'art de graver en bois...*, Paris 1758; *De l'origine et des productions de l'imprimerie primitive en taille de bois*, Paris 1759. – G. FRAIPONT, *Les procédés de reproduction en creux et de la lithographie...*, Paris, n.d. – G. FRITZ, *Handbuch der Lithographie*, Halle a. S. 1898. – J.C. FUESSLI, *Raisonirendes Verzeichnis der vornehmsten Kupferstecher und ihrer Werke...*, Zurich 1771.
J. GARNIER, *Nouveau manuel complet du ciseleur contenant la description des pro-*

cédés…, Paris 1859. – M. GAUCHER, Lettre à M. Quatremère de Quincy sur la gravure, n.p. [1791]. – J. GAUTIER D'AGOTY, Lettre concernant le nouvel art de graver et d'imprimer les tableaux, Paris 1749; Observations sur la peinture et sur les tableaux anciens et modernes, Paris 1753 (reprint, Geneva 1972). – J. GRAND-CARTERET, Vieux papiers, vieilles images. Carton d'un collectionneur, Paris 1896. – R. GRAUL, Die Radierung der Gegenwart in Europa und Nordamerika, Vienna 1892.
S. HADEN, About Etching, London 1878. – P. G. HAMERTON, Etching and Etchers, London 1868; The Graphic Arts, A Treatise on the Varieties of Drawing, Painting and Engraving…, London 1882. – E. HAMILTON, The Engraved Works of Sir Joshua Reynolds. A Catalogue Raisonné of the Engravings made after his Painting from 1755–1822, London 1884 (reprint, Amsterdam 1973). – J. HAUCK-WITZ, An Essay on Engraving and Copper-plate Printing…, London 1732. – R. HECQUET, Catalogue des estampes gravées d'après Rubens…, Paris 1751. – C. H. de HEINECKEN, Idée générale d'une collection complète d'estampes avec une dissertation sur l'origine de la gravure et sur les premiers livres d'images, Leipzig and Vienna 1771; Dictionnaire des artistes, dont nous avons des estampes, avec une notice détaillée de leurs ouvrages gravés, 4 vols., Leipzig 1778–1790. – J. HELLER, Geschichte der Holzschneidekunst von den ältesten bis auf die neuesten Zeiten…, Bamberg 1823; Praktisches Handbuch für Kupferstichsammler…, 2 vols., Bamberg 1823–1836. – F. HERBET, Les Graveurs de l'école de Fontainebleau, Paris 1896–1902 (reprint, Amsterdam 1969). – T. HIPPERT / J. LINNIG, Le Peintre-graveur hollandais et belge du XIXᵉ siècle, 2 vols., Brussels 1874–1879. – G. HIRTH / R. MUTHER, Meisterholzschnitte aus vier Jahrhunderte, Munich 1893. – J. R. HITCHCOCK, Etching in America, New York 1886. – M. HUBER, Notices générales des graveurs divisés par nations et des peintres rangés par écoles, Dresden 1787 (reprint, Geneva 1972); Handbuch für Kunstliebhaber und Sammler über die vornehmsten Kupferstecher und ihre Werke…, 9 vols., Zurich 1796–1808. – M. HUBER / C.C.H. ROST, Manuel des curieux et des amateurs d'art, contenant une notice abrégée des principaux graveurs…, 9 vols., Paris and Zurich 1797–1808. – A. von HUMBERT, Abrégé historique de l'origine et des progrès de la gravure et des estampes en bois et en taille-douce, Berlin 1752.
J.B. JACKSON, An Essay on the Invention of Engraving and Printing in Chiaroscuro, London 1754. – J.B. JACKSON / W.A. CHATTO, A Treatise on Wood-engraving, historical and practical, London 1839; A Treatise on Wood-engraving, …with a new chapter on the artists of the present day by H.G. Bohn, London 1861 (reprint, Detroit 1969). – H. JANSEN, Essai sur l'origine de la gravure en bois et en taille-douce, 2 vols., Paris 1808. – F.E. JOUBERT, Manuel de l'amateur d'estampes…, 3 vols., Paris 1821. – C.F. JOULLAIN, Réflexions sur la peinture et la gravure…, Metz and Paris 1786 (reprint, Geneva 1973).
N. KINDLINGER, Nachricht von einigen noch unbekannten Holzschnitten, Kupferstichen und Steinabdrücken aus dem fünfzehnten Jahrhundert, Frankfurt 1819. – S.R. KOEHLER, Etching, Boston 1885. – P. KRISTELLER, Early Florentine Woodcuts with an Annotated List of Florentine Illustrated Books, London 1897; Kupferstich und Holzschnitt in vier Jahrhunderten, Berlin 1905. – T. KUTSCHMANN, Geschichte der deutschen Illustration, vom ersten Auftreten des Formschnittes bis auf die Gegenwart, 2 vols., Berlin 1899.
L. de LABORDE, Essais de gravure pour servir à une histoire de la gravure en bois, Paris 1833; Histoire de la gravure en manière noire, Paris 1839. – M. LALANNE, Traité de la gravure à l'eau-forte, Paris 1866. – J.C. LE BLON, Coloritto; or the Harmony of Colouring in Painting…, London, n.d. [between 1723–1726?]; L'art d'imprimer les tableaux (gravure en couleurs)…, edited by J. Gaultier de Montdorge, Paris 1756 (reprint, Geneva 1973). – J.-B. LE BRUN, Almanach historique et raisonné des architectes, peintres, sculpteurs, graveurs et ciseleurs, 2 vols., Paris 1776–1777 (reprint, Geneva 1972). – J.A.L. (de LEUTRE), Opinion d'un bibliophile sur l'estampe de 1418, conservée à la Bibliothèque royale de Bruxelles, Brussels 1846. – W.J. LINTON, The Masters of Wood-Engraving, New Haven and London 1889. – F. LIPPMANN, Kupferstiche und Holzschnitte alter Meister in Nachbildungen, 10 vols., Berlin 1889–1899; Der Kupferstich, Berlin 1893. – G. LONGHI, La calcografia, propriamente detta, ossia l'arte d'incidere in rame coll'acqua forte, col bulino e colla punta, Milan 1830. – A. de LOSTALOT, Les procédés de la gravure, Paris n.d. [1886]. – F.G.H. LUCANUS, Vollständige Anleitung zur Erhaltung, Reinigung, und Wiederherstellung der Gemälde, zur Bereitung der Firnisse, so wie auch zum Aufziehen, Bleichen, Reinigen und Restauriren der Kupferstiche, Leipzig 1812. – W. von LÜDEMANN, Geschichte der Kupferstich-Kunst und der damit verwandten Künste, Holzschneide- und Steindruck-Kunst, Dresden 1828. – C. von LÜTZOW, Die Vervielfältigende Kunst der Gegenwart. I der Holzschnitt, II der Kupferstich, III die Radierung, IV die Lithographie, 4 vols., Vienna 1887–1903.
J. MABERLY, The Print Collector: An Introduction to the Knowledge necessary for forming a Collection of Ancient Prints…, London 1844; new ed., New York 1880 (reprint, New York 1979). – M. de MARCENAY de GHUY, Idée de la gravure, n.p., n.d. [Paris 1756]. – M. de MAROLLES, Catalogue de livres d'estampes…, Paris 1666; Le livre des peintres et des graveurs, Paris n.d. [c. 1677]; new ed. by G. Duplessis, Paris 1855. – A.P. MARTIAL, Nouveau traité de la gravure à l'eau-forte pour les peintres et les dessinateurs, Paris 1873. – MAYER, Scelta collezione di stampe della metà del secolo XV, sino a tutto il XVIII…, Padua 1837. – A. MELLERIO, La Lithographie originale en couleurs, Paris 1898. – G.C. MEZGER, Augsburgs älteste Druckdenkmale und Formschneiderarbeiten nebst Geschichte der Bücherdruckes und Buchhandels in Augsburg, Augsburg 1840. – D.J. MORENO de TEJADA, Excelencias del pincel y del buril…, Madrid 1804. – C. MOTTEROZ, Essai sur les gravures chimiques en relief, Paris 1871. – C.G. von MURR, Beyträge zur Geschichte der ältesten Kupferstiche, Augsburg 1804. – J.C.L. M(USSEAU), Manuel des amateurs d'estampes, Paris 1821.
R. NAUMANN / R. WEIGEL, Archiv für die zeichnenden Künste mit besonderer Beziehung auf Kupferstecher und Holzschneidekunst und ihre Geschichte, 6 vols., Leipzig 1855–1862. – NIEPCE de SAINT-VICTOR, Mémoire sur la gravure héliographique sur acier et sur verre, Batignolles [Paris 1854]; Traité pratique de la gravure héliographique sur acier et sur verre, Paris 1856.
W.Y. OTTLEY, An Inquiry into the Origin and Early History of Engraving upon Copper and in Wood…, 2 vols., London 1816; A Collection of Fac-similes of Scarce and Curious Prints…, London 1826.
J.B. M. PAPILLON, Traité historique et pratique de la gravure en bois, 2 vols., Paris 1766. – J.D. PASSAVANT, Le peintre-graveur; contenant l'histoire de la gravure sur bois, sur métal et au burin jusque vers la fin du XVIᵉ siècle…, 6 vols., Leipzig 1860–1864. – G. PEIGNOT, Recherches historiques et littéraires sur les danses des morts et sur l'origine des cartes à jouer, Dijon and Paris 1826. – J. and E. PENNELL, Lithography and Lithographers, London 1898 (reprint, 1915). – A.M. PERROT, Manuel du graveur, ou Traité complet de la gravure en tous genres…, Paris 1830; Nouveau manuel complet du graveur. Nouvelle édition très augmentée par F. Malepeyre, Paris 1844. – B. PICART, Impostures innocentes. Recueil d'estampes d'après divers peintres illustres, tels que Rafael, le Guide… gravées à leur imitation par Bernard Picart…, Amsterdam 1734. – R. de PILES, Abrégé de la Vie des peintres avec réflexions sur leurs ouvrages… et de l'utilité des estampes, Paris 1699. – A.W. POLLARD, Early Illustrated Books, London 1893. – R. PORTALIS / H. BERALDI, Les graveurs du XVIIIᵉ siècle, 3 vols., Paris 1880–1882. – A. POTÉMONT, Lettre sur les éléments de la gravure à l'eau-forte, Paris 1864.
J.G. von QUANDT, Entwurf zu einer Geschichte der Kupferstecherkunst…, Leipzig 1826. – QUATREMÈRE de QUINCY, Réflexions nouvelles sur la gravure, Paris 1791.
Baron de REIFFENBERG, La plus ancienne gravure connue avec une date, Brussels 1845. – J. RENOUVIER, Des types et des manières des maîtres graveurs, pour servir à l'histoire de la gravure en Italie, en Allemagne, dans les Pays-Bas et en France, 4 vols., Montpellier 1853–1856; Une passion de 1446. Suite de gravures au burin: les premières avec date, Montpellier 1857; Des gravures en bois dans les livres d'Antoine Vérard, maître libraire, imprimeur, enlumineur et tailleur sur bois, de Paris, 1485–1512, Paris 1859; Histoire de l'origine et des progrès de la gravure dans les Pays-Bas et en Allemagne jusqu'à la fin du XVᵉ siècle, Brussels 1860; Histoire de l'art pendant la Révolution considéré principalement dans les estampes, Paris 1868. – Duc de RIVOLI, Etudes sur l'art de la gravure sur bois à Venise. Les missels imprimés à Venise de 1481 à 1600…, Paris 1896. – K. ROBERT, Traité pratique de la gravure à l'eau-forte, Paris 1891. – A. ROSENBERG, Der Kupferstich in der Schule und unter dem Einfluss des Rubens, Vienna 1893. – G.B. de ROSSI, Dell' origine della stampa in tavole incise e di una antica e sconosciuta edizione zilografica, Parma 1811. – C.F. von RUMOHR, Zur Geschichte und Theorie der Formschneidekunst, Leipzig 1837. P.-N. SALIÈRES, Gravure diaphane. Nouveau procédé à la portée de tous les peintres et de tous les dessinateurs, Montpellier 1853. – J.F. van SAMERAN, Essai d'une bibliographie de l'histoire spéciale de la peinture et de la gravure en Hollande et en Belgique (1500–1875), Amsterdam 1882. – W.L. SCHREIBER, Manuel de l'amateur de la gravure sur bois et sur métal au XVᵉ siècle, 8 vols., Berlin and Leipzig 1891–1911 (German ed., Leipzig 1926–1930). – A. SENEFELDER, Vollständiges Lehrbuch der Steindruckerey, Munich 1818; L'Art de la lithographie…, Paris 1819 (reprint, 1974); A Complete Course of Lithography, London 1819 (reprint, New York 1968, with introduction by Hyatt Mayor). – A. SIRET, La gravure en Belgique, sa situation, son avenir, Ghent 1852. – J.C. SMITH, British Mezzotint Portraits, 5 vols., London 1878–1883. – STAPART, L'art de graver au pinceau, nouvelle méthode mise au jour, Paris 1773 (German ed., Nuremberg 1780). – J. STRUTT, A Bibliographical Dictionary of All the

Engravers, 2 vols., London 1785–1786 (reprint, Geneva 1972).
L. TISSIER, Historique de la gravure typographique sur pierre et de la tissiérographie, Paris 1843.
A.E. UMBREIT, Über die Eigenhändigkeit der Malerformschnitte, 2 vols., Leipzig 1840–1843.
A. VILLON, Nouveau manuel... du graveur en creux et en relief, Paris 1894 (reprint, 1914, Manuel Roret). – C.G. VOORHELM SCHNEEVOOGT, Catalogue des estampes gravées d'après P.P. Rubens avec l'indication des collections où se trouvent les tableaux et les gravures, Haarlem 1873.
R. WEIGEL, Holzschnitte berühmter Meister, Leipzig 1851–1854. – T.O. WEIGEL, Verzeichniss der Xylographischen Bücher des XVen Jahrhunderts, Leipzig 1856. – J.E. WESSELY, Anleitung zur Kenntnis und zum Sammeln der Werke des Kunstdruckes, Leipzig 1876. – A. WHITMAN, The Masters of Mezzotint, the Men and their Work, London 1898; Nineteenth Century Mezzotinters, London 1903–1904. – W.H. WILLSHIRE, An Introduction to the Study and Collection of Ancient Prints, London 1877 (reprint, Ann Arbor 1971). – G.E. WOODBERRY, A History of Wood Engraving, New York 1883 (reprint, Detroit 1969).
A. ZANETTI, Le premier siècle de la chalcographie, ou catalogue raisonné des estampes du cabinet du comte Léopold Cicognara, Venice 1837. – D.P. ZANI, Materiali per servire alla storia dell'origine e de' progressi dell'incisione in rame e in legno..., Parma 1802.

GENERAL WORKS

J. ADHÉMAR, L'estampe française... Le bois gravé en France jusqu'à la fin du XIXᵉ siècle, n.p., n.d. – J. ADHÉMAR / M. BARBIN / M. MELOT / F. PORTELETTE / R.-A. WEIGERT / F. WOIMANT, La Gravure, Paris 1972. – J. ADHÉMAR / M. HÉBERT / J. LETHÈVE, Les Estampes, Paris 1973. – M.F. ANDREWS, Creative Printmaking, Englewood Cliffs, N.J., 1964. – P.J. ANGOULVENT, La Chalcographie du Louvre. Catalogue général, Paris 1933. – R. AVERMAETE, La gravure sur bois moderne de l'Occident, Vaduz 1977.
A. BARTSCH, Le Peintre-Graveur illustré, Philadelphia 1971 – New York 1980 (reprint of A. Bartsch, Le Peintre-Graveur, Vienna 1803–1821): 1. Netherlandish Artists (edited by L.J. Slatkes, intr. by W. Koschatzky, 1978); 2. Netherlandish Artists (M.C. Leach, P. Morse, 1978); 3. Netherlandish Artists: Hendrick Goltzius (W.L. Strauss, 1980); 4. Netherlandish Artists: Matham, Saenredam, Muller (W.L. Strauss, 1980); 5. Netherlandish Artists (preface by F. Robinson, 1979); 7. Netherlandish Artists (O. Naumann, 1978); 11. Sixteenth Century German Artists: Hans Burgkmair, Hans Schäufelein, Lucas Cranach (T. Falk, 1980); 14. Early German Masters: Albrecht Altdorfer, Monogrammists (R.A. Koch, 1978); 25. Early Italian Masters (M. Zucker, 1980); 26. The Works of Marcantonio Raimondi and of his School I (K. Oberhuber, 1978); 27. The Works of Marcantonio Raimondi and of his School II (K. Oberhuber, 1978); 32. Italian Artists of the Sixteenth Century School of Fontainebleau I (H. Zerner, 1979); 33. Italian Artists of the Sixteenth Century School of Fontainebleau (H. Zerner, 1979). – D. BAUD-BOVY, Les Maîtres de la gravure suisse, Zurich 1935. – K.F. BEALL, Kaufruhe und Strassenhändler. Cries and Itinerant Trades, Hamburg 1976. – A. BÉGUIN, L'aquatinte à

l'aérographe: nouveau procédé de gravure au grain, Brussels 1975; Dictionnaire technique de l'estampe, 3 vols., Brussels 1977. – J.E. BERSIER, La gravure: les procédés, l'histoire, Paris 1947 (reprint, Paris 1963/1974); Introduction à l'estampe, Geneva 1959. – L. BINYON, Masterpieces of Etching, 2 vols., London 1914. – D.P. BLISS, A History of Wood Engraving, London 1928 (reprint, London 1964). – E. BOCK, Die Deutsche Graphik, Munich 1922; Geschichte der graphischen Kunst..., Berlin 1930. – H. BOCKHOFF / F. WINGER, Das Grosse Buch der Graphik, Brunswick 1968. – R. BONFILS, Initiation à la gravure, Paris 1939. – K.G. BOON / J. VERBEEK, Dutch and Flemish Etchings, Engravings and Woodcuts, ca. 1450–1700, Van Ostade-de Passe, Amsterdam 1964. – G. BOURCARD, A travers cinq siècles de gravures, 1350–1903, Paris 1903 (reprint, Amsterdam 1970); Graveurs et Gravures. France et Etranger. Essai de Bibliographie 1540–1910, Paris 1910; La cote des estampes des différentes écoles anciennes et modernes de 1900 à 1912, Paris 1912. – C.M. BRIQUET, Les filigranes, dictionnaire historique des marques du papier dès leur apparition vers 1282 jusqu'en 1600, 4 vols., Paris 1907. – W. BRÜCKNER, Imagerie populaire allemande, Milan 1969. – F. BRUNNER, Manuel de la Gravure / A Handbook of Graphic Reproduction Processes / Handbuch der Druckgraphik, Teufen, (Aargau, Switzerland) 1962. – J. BRUNSDON, The Technique of Etching and Engraving, London 1965. – M. BRYAN, Dictionary of Painters and Engravers. New ed. under the supervision of George C. Williamson, 5 vols., Port Washington, N.Y., 1964. – M. BUCHERER, Der Originalholzschnitt, Zurich 1946. – J. BUCKLAND-WRIGHT, Etching and Engraving, London 1953.
A. CALABI, La Gravure italienne, Paris 1931. – Cent ans d'affiches dans le monde, Bibliothèque Nationale, Paris 1972. – Le choix d'un amateur d'estampes: gravures sur cuivre de la coll. Robert Stehelin. Palais Rohan, Cabinet des Estampes, Strasbourg 1977. – Clairs-obscurs. Gravures sur bois imprimées en couleur de 1500 à 1800 provenant des collections hollandaises. Institut néerlandais, Paris 1965. Museum Boymans-van Beuningen, Rotterdam 1965/66. – J. CLEAVER, A History of Graphic Art, New York 1963. – S. COBLENTZ, La Collection d'estampes Edmond de Rothschild au Musée du Louvre, Paris 1954. – H. COLAS, La gravure sur bois, bois de fil, bois de bout, bois en couleurs et la lithographie, crayon, lavis..., Paris 1952. – P. COLIN, La Gravure et les graveurs, répertoire des ouvrages à consulter, 2 vols., Brussels 1916–1918. – F. COURBOIN, L'Eau-forte, Paris 1906; L'estampe française. Essais. Graveurs et marchands, Brussels 1914; La gravure en France, des origines à 1900, Paris 1923; Histoire illustrée de la gravure en France, 4 vols. 8°., 3 vols. folio, Paris 1923–1929. – F. COURBOIN / M. ROUX, La Gravure française, essai de bibliographie, 3 vols., n.p. 1927–1928. – H. CURWEN, Processes of Graphic Reproduction in Printing, London 1924.
E. DACIER, La Gravure française, Paris 1944. – H. DANIELS, Printmaking, London 1971. – A.J.J. DELEN, Histoire de la gravure dans les anciens Pays-Bas & dans les provinces belges, des origines jusqu'à la fin du XVIIIᵉ siècle, 3 vols., Paris and Brussels 1924–1925. – L. DIMIER, La Gravure, n.p. 1930. – B. DISERTORI, L'incisione italiana, Florence 1931 (reprint, Milan 1974). – Dizionario enciclopedico Bolaffi dei pittori e degli incisori italiani, Turin 1973. – A. DONJEAN, Initiation à la gravure: eau-forte, pointe sèche, aquatinte,

burin, Paris 1975. – T.B. DONSON, Prints and the Print Market, New York 1977. – Duitse grafiek, 1450–1700. (Gravures allemandes, 1450–1700), Museum Boymans-van Beuningen, Rotterdam 1973. – P. DURUPT, Les procédés originaux d'illustration. La gravure sur cuivre... suivis de l'héliogravure au grain de résine et de l'impression en taille-douce en noir et couleurs, Paris 1951.
F. EICHENBERG, The Art of the Print: Masterpieces, History, Techniques, London 1976. – H. and M. EVANS, Sources of Illustration: 1500–1900, Bath 1971.
J. FARLEIGH, Engraving on Wood, Leicester 1954. – O. FISCHER, Geschichte der deutschen Zeichnung und Graphik, Munich 1951. – A. FLOCON, Traité du burin, Geneva 1954. – H. FOCILLON, Maîtres de l'estampe, Paris 1930 (reprint, Paris 1969); De Callot à Lautrec, Paris 1967. – J. FRIBOURG / W. SPEISER / R. GOEPPER, Arts de la Chine, peinture, calligraphie, estampages, estampes, Fribourg (Switzerland) 1973. – M.J. FRIEDLÄNDER, Der Holzschnitt, Berlin 1917 (revised ed. by H. Mähle, Berlin 1970).
A. GARRETT, A History of British Wood Engraving, Tunbridge Wells 1978. – E. GLASSMAN / M.S. SYMMES, Cliché-Verre: Hand-Drawn, Light Printed, The Detroit Institute of Arts, Detroit 1980. – The Golden Age of the Woodcut: 1450–1550. The Woodcut Revival: 1800–1925, Museum of Art, Lawrence, Kansas 1968. – Grafische Techniken. Eine Ausstellung des Neuen Berliner Kunstvereins in den Räumen der Kunstbibliothek, Kunstbibliothek, Berlin 1973. – M.H. GRANT, Dictionary of British Etchers, London 1953. – Graphic Art Exhibitions at the National Gallery of Art, National Gallery of Art, Washington 1965. – Gravure. Choix d'œuvres significatives du langage de la gravure en creux des origines à nos jours, présenté par l'Atelier de Saint-Prex, Château de La Sarraz, near Lausanne. 1974. – La gravure sur bois en Suisse. Der schweizerische Holzschnitt, Musée d'Art et d'Histoire, Fribourg 1970. – A. GRIFFITHS, Prints and Printmaking, London 1980. – A. GROSS, Etching, Engraving and Intaglio Printing, London 1970. – J. GUIBERT, Le Cabinet des Estampes..., histoire des collections, Paris 1926. – P. GUSMAN, La gravure sur bois et d'épargne sur métal, du XIVᵉ au XXᵉ siècle, Paris 1916; L'Art de la gravure. Gravure sur bois et taille d'épargne. Historique et technique, Paris 1933.
S. HAMILTON, Early American Book Illustrators and Wood Engravers 1670–1870, Princeton 1958. – E.H. van HEURCK / G.J. BOEKENOOGEN, L'imagerie populaire des Pays-Bas, Belgique-Hollande, Paris 1930. – A.M. HIND, A Short History of Engraving and Etching, London 1908 (3rd ed., 1923); A History of Engraving and Etching from the 15th Century to the Year 1914, 3rd revised ed., London 1923 (reprint, New York 1963); Catalogue of Drawings by Dutch and Flemish Artists preserved in the Department of Prints and Drawings in the British Museum, London 1926; British Museum. A Guide to the Processes and Schools of Engraving, British Museum pamphlet, 3rd ed., London 1933 (reprint, 1952). – R. HOBERG, Die Graphischen Techniken und ihre Druckverfahren, Berlin 1922. – H. HOFER, The Artist and the Book, Harvard University Press, Cambridge 1961. – D. HOFFMANN, Die Welt der Spielkarte, eine Kulturgeschichte, Leipzig 1972. – F. HOLLENBERG, Radierung, Ätzkunst und Kupferstichdruck, Ravensburg 1962. – F.W.H. HOLLSTEIN, German Engravings, Etchings and Woodcuts ca. 1400–1700, 18 vols., Amsterdam 1955–1978 (in progress); Dutch and Flemish Etchings, Engravings and

Woodcuts ca. 1450–1700, 20 vols., Amsterdam 1949–1978 (in progress). – C. HOLME, *Modern Etching and Engraving, European and American*, London 1902. – S. HOUFE, *The Dictionary of British Book Illustrators and Caricaturists: 1800–1914*, London 1978. – T. HUGHES, *Prints for the Collector: British Prints from 1500 to 1900*, London 1970. – A. HYATT MAYOR, *Prints and People. A Social History of Printed Pictures*, New York 1971. – A. HYATT MAYOR / R.V. WEST, *Language of the Print*, New York 1971. – *Incisioni dal XV al XIX secolo*, Gabinetto delle stampe, Milan 1976. – *International Colour Woodcuts*, Victoria and Albert Museum, London 1954–1955.
W.M. IVINS, Jr., *Notes on Prints*, New York 1930; *How Prints Look*, New York 1943 (reprint, Boston 1958); *Prints and Visual Communication*, Cambridge, Mass., 1953 (reprint, New York 1969).
A. JACQUEMIN / J. BERSIER, *Technique de la gravure*, n.p. 1937.
N. KEIL, *Die Graphischen Verfahren vom 15. bis 20. Jahrhundert*, Albertina, Vienna 1963. – F.D. KLINGENDER, *Art and the Industrial Revolution*, New York 1947 (revised ed. by A. Elton, New York 1968). – W. KOSCHATZKY, *Die Kunst der Graphik. Technik, Geschichte, Meisterwerke*, Salzburg 1972. – W. KOSCHATZKY / A. STROBL, *Die Albertina in Wien*, Salzburg 1970.
J. LARAN, *L'estampe*, 2 vols., Paris 1959. – E. LAVAGNINO, *Gli artisti italiani in Germania. Vol. 3: i pittori e gli incisori*, Rome 1943. – J. LAVER, *A History of British and American Etching*, London 1929; *Stampe popolari inglesi*, Milan 1973 / *Imagerie populaire anglaise*, Milan 1976. – C. LEIGHTON, *Wood-Engraving*, London 1932. – J. LEISCHING, *Schabkunst, ihre Technik und Geschichte*, Vienna 1913; *Die Graphischen Künste*, Vienna and Leipzig 1926. – R. LEPELTIER, *Restauration des dessins et estampes*, Fribourg (Switzerland) 1977. – H. LEPORINI, *Der Kupferstichsammler*, Berlin 1924. – *Les plus belles gravures du monde occidental, 1410–1914*, Haus der Kunst, Munich 1966 / Bibliothèque Nationale, Paris 1966 / Rijksmuseum, Amsterdam 1966. – H.C. LEVIS, *A Bibliography of American Books relating to Prints...*, London 1910; *A Descriptive Bibliography of the Most Important Books in the English Language relating to... Engraving*, London 1912, supplement 1913. – J. LEWIS, *Anatomy of Printing. The Influences of Art and History on its Design*, London 1970. – J. LIEURE, *La gravure dans le livre et l'ornement*, Paris and Brussels 1927. – R. LIGERON, *La gravure originale en couleurs*, Paris 1923. – K. LINDLEY, *The Woodblock Engravers*, Newton Abbot, Devon 1970. – F. LIPPMANN, *Der Kupferstich*, Berlin 1926 (revised ed., 1963). – R. LOCHE, *La Lithographie (Les métiers d'art) / Die Lithographie (Das Kunsthandwerk)*, Geneva 1971. – F. LUGT, *Les marques de collections de dessins et d'estampes*, revised ed., 2 vols., The Hague 1956. – E.S. LUMSDEN, *The Art of Etching*, New York 1922.
N. MALENFANT, *L'Estampe, La Documentation Québécoise*, Quebec 1980. – R. MARSH, *Monoprints for the Artist*, London 1969. – L. MASON, *Print Reference Sources: A Selected Bibliography 18th-20th Centuries*, compiled by L. Mason assisted by J. Ludman, Millwood, N.Y. 1975. – E. MAURIANGE, *Musée national des arts et traditions populaires: guide de la galerie d'étude, arts populaires graphiques*, Paris 1974. – J. MEDER, *Technische Entwicklung der Graphik*, Albertina, Vienna 1908. – *Meister europäischer Graphik aus der Kunstsammlung der Universität Lüttich*, Rheinisches Landesmuseum,

Bonn / Museen der Stadt, Nuremberg 1974. – *Meisterwerke europäischer Graphik 15.-18. Jh. aus dem Besitz des Kupferstichkabinetts Coburg*, Kunstsammlungen der Veste Coburg, Coburg 1975–1976. – M. de MEYER, *Imagerie populaire des Pays-Bas: Belgique, Hollande*, Milan 1970. – B.F. MORROW, *The Art of Aquatint*, New York 1935. – *Musée du Louvre, catalogue de la Chalcographie du Musée du Louvre*, Paris 1954. – H.T. MUSPER, *Der Holzschnitt in fünf Jahrhunderten*, Stuttgart 1944 (reprint, 1964).
F. O'DONOGHUE / H.M. HAKE, *Catalogue of Engraved British Portraits preserved in the Department of Prints and Drawings in the British Museum*, 6 vols., London 1908–1925. – *Original Printmaking in Britain, 1600–1900*, London 1972. – *The Painterly Print: Monotypes from the Seventeenth to the Twentieth Century*, Metropolitan Museum of Art, New York 1980.
R. PASSERON, *L'estampe originale: ses secrets, les différents procédés des grands maîtres contemporains*, Paris 1972. – G. PAULI, *Inkunabeln der Deutschen und Niederländischen Radierung*, Berlin 1908. – P. PELLIOT, *Les Débuts de l'imprimerie en Chine*, Paris 1953. – J. PENNELL, *Etchers and Etching*, London 1920 and New York 1931. – B. PEPPIN, *Fantasy Book Illustration*, London 1975. – G. PETERDI, *Printmaking Methods Old and New*, New York 1959 (reprint, 1971). – A.M. PETRIOLI TOFANI, *Stampe italiane dalle origini all'ottocento*, Florence 1975. – C.A. PETRUCCI, *Catalogo generale delle stampe tratte dai rami incisi posseduti dalla Calcografia Nazionale*, Rome 1953. – G. PILTZ, *Deutsche Graphik*, Leipzig-Jena-Berlin, 1968. – V. PIONTELLI, *Indice bibliografico degli incisori italiani dalle origini fino al XVIII secolo / Bibliographical Index of Italian Engravers from the Fifteenth to the Eighteenth Century*, Milan 1978. – G. POMMERANZ-LIEDTKE, *Der graphische Zyklus...*, Berlin 1956; *Die Weisheit der Kunst. Chinesische Steinabreibungen*, Frankfurt 1963. – R.T. PORTE, *Dictionary of Printing Terms*, Salt Lake City 1941. – V. PREISSIG, *Zur Technik der farbigen Radierung und des Farbenkupferstichs*, Leipzig 1909. – S.T. PRIDEAUX, *Aquatint Engraving*, London 1909. – *Prints 1400-1800. A Loan Exhibition from Museums and Private Collections*. Minneapolis Institute of Arts, Cleveland Museum of Art, Art Institute of Chicago, 1956/1957. – G. PROFIT, *Procédés élémentaires de la gravure d'art, eau-forte, burin, pointe-sèche*, Paris 1913.
H. RASMUSEN, *Printmaking with Monotype*, Philadelphia 1960. – G.N. RAY, *The illustrator and the book in England from 1790 to 1914*, New York 1976. – L. RÉAU, *La gravure d'illustration*, Paris and Brussels 1928. – I. REINER, *Holzschnitt-Holzstich*, St. Gall 1947. – E.H. RICHTER, *Prints, a Brief Review of their Technique and History*, London – Boston – New York 1914. – L. ROSENTHAL, *La gravure*, Paris 1909 (revised ed. by H. Focillon, Paris 1939). – J. ROSS, *The Complete Printmaker*, New York 1972. – M. ROTHENSTEIN, *Linocuts and Woodcuts*, New York 1962; *Holzschnitt und Linolschnitt heute*, Ravensburg 1964; *Frontiers of Printmaking. New Aspects of Relief Printing*, London 1966; *Relief Printing*, with contributions by T. Allen, B. Cheese, S. Nankivell, London 1970. – E. ROUIR, *L'estampe valeur de placement. Conseils aux amateurs et collectionneurs*, Paris 1970. – R. RUMPEL, *La Gravure sur bois (Les métiers d'art) / Der Holzschnitt (Das Kunsthandwerk)*, Geneva 1972.
P.J. SACHS, *Modern Prints and Drawings*, New York 1954. – M.C. SALAMAN, *The Great Etchers from Rembrandt to Whistler*,

in *Studio*, winter number, London 1913–1914; *The Graphic Arts of Great Britain: Drawing, Line Engraving, Etching, Mezzotint, Aquatint, Lithography, Wood Engraving, Colour Printing*, London 1917; *British Book Illustration Yesterday and To-day*, London 1923. – A. SCHEIDEGGER, *Graphische Kunst*, Berne and Stuttgart, 1972; *Die schweizer Künstlergraphik*, Berne 1975. – J. SCHULTZE / A.M. WINTHER, *Der Kupferstich vom 15. Jahrhundert bis zur Gegenwart*, Kunsthalle, Bremen 1975. – W. SCHÜRMEYER, *Holzschnitt und Linolschnitt*, Ravensburg 1964. – J.P. SEGUIN, *La carte à jouer, donation faite à la Bibliothèque Nationale par Paul Marteau, maître-cartier*, Bibliothèque Nationale, Paris 1967; *Le jeu de cartes. Histoire des cartes, le dessin des figures, les techniques...*, Paris 1968. – B. SEIDEL, *Printmaking*, London 1965. – L. SERVOLINI, *Problemi e aspetti dell'incisione*, Forlì 1939. – F. SHORT, *Etchings and Engravings. What they are, and are not, with some notes on the care of prints*, London 1912, revised ed. with notes on woodcuts and wood engravings by M. Osborne, London 1952. – H. SIMON, *Five Hundred Years of Art in Illustration: from Albrecht Dürer to Rockwell Kent*, New York 1954 (reprint, 1978). – H.W. SINGER, *Der Kupferstich*, Leipzig 1904; *Die moderne Graphik*, Leipzig 1914; *Handbuch für Kupferstichsammler...*, Leipzig 1923. – M.R. SLYTHE, *The Art of Illustration, 1750–1900*, London 1970. – A. SMITH, *Concerning the Education of a Print Collector...*, Harlow, Keppel, c. 1920. – K. SOTRIFFER, *Die Druckgraphik, Entwicklung, Technik, Eigenart*, Vienna and Munich 1966; *Printmaking, History and Technique*, New York 1968. – C. SPENCER, *A Decade of Printmaking*, London 1973. – *Spielkarten aus aller Welt, vom Mittelalter bis zur Gegenwart*, Staatsgalerie Stuttgart, Graphische Sammlung, Stuttgart 1968. – H. STRUCK, *Die Kunst des Radierens, Ein Handbuch*, Berlin 1908.
J. TAYLOR ARMS, *Handbook of Printmaking and Printmakers*, New York 1934. – *Les techniques traditionnelles et contemporaines de la gravures en creux*, Musée d'Art Moderne, Paris 1967. – N. TEDESCHI, *La Stampa degli Artisti, L'Aquaforte*, Verona 1971. – M. TERRAPON, *Le Burin (Les métiers d'art) / Der Kupferstich (Das Kunsthandwerk)*, Geneva 1974; *L'eau-forte (Les métiers d'art) / Die Radierung (Das Kunsthandwerk)*, Geneva 1975. – *La Terre et son image. 100 chefs-d'œuvre de la cartographie de Marco Polo à La Pérouse*, Bibliothèque Nationale, Paris 1971. – R. TILLEY, *A History of Playing Cards*, London 1973. – P. TOSCHI, *Stampe popolari d'Italia*, Milan 1973. – *Tre secoli di incisione dal '500 al '700*, Libreria Marsilio, Padua 1971. – J. TREVELYAN, *Etching: Modern Methods of Intaglio Printmaking*, New York 1963.
A. de VESME, *Le peintre-graveur italien. Ouvrage faisant suite au «peintre-graveur» de Bartsch*, Milan 1906 (reprint, Turin 1963). – J. VEYRIN-FORRER, *Hommage aux premiers imprimeurs de France, 1470–1970*, Bibliothèque Nationale, Paris 1970. – *Vom Handdruck zum Poster*, Wallraf-Richartz-Museum, Cologne 1973/1974.
A. WAGNER, *Als das Papier kam, enstand die Kunst der Graphik*, Munich 1969. – H.J. WECHSLER, *Great Prints and Printmakers*, New York 1967; *La gravure, art majeur. Des maîtres inconnus à Picasso. Guide pratique de l'amateur d'estampes*, Paris 1969. – F. WEDMORE, *Etchings*, London 1911. – W. WEGNER, *Fünf Jahrhunderte europäischer Graphik*, Munich 1966. – F. WEITENKAMPF, *How to Appreciate*

Prints, New York 1942. – F.L. WIDLER, How to Identify Old Prints, London 1969. – W.H. WILLSHIRE, A Descriptive Catalogue of Playing and Other Cards in the British Museum, London 1876 (reprint, Amsterdam 1975). – A. de WITT, La collezione delle stampe [alla] R. Galleria degli Uffizi, Rome 1938. – F. van WYCK, Gleanings from Old Engravings, Boston 1936; Hours with Old Engravings, Boston 1936. C. ZIGROSSER, Six Centuries of Fine Prints, New York 1937; The Book of Fine Prints, New York 1956; The Appeal of Prints, Philadelphia 1970. – C. ZIGROSSER (editor), Prints, Thirteen Essays on the Art of the Print, New York 1962. – C. ZIGROSSER / C.M. GAEHDE, A Guide to the Collecting and Care of Original Prints, New York 1965.

15th and 16th centuries

J. ADHÉMAR, Les graveurs français de la Renaissance, Paris 1946. – Anfänge der Graphik. Holzschnitte, Kupferstiche und Zeichnungen des 15. Jahrhunderts, Kupferstichkabinett der Öffentlichen Kunstsammlung, Basel 1970. G.G. BERTELÀ / A.M. PETRIOLI TOFANI, Feste e apparati medicei da Cosimo I a Cosimo II. Mostra di disegni e incisioni, Galleria degli Uffizi, Gabinetto Disegni e Stampe, Florence 1969. – Bibliothèque Nationale. Inventaire du fonds français du Cabinet des Estampes. Graveurs du XVIe. Vol. I, A. Linzeler, Paris 1932; Vol. II, J. Adhémar, Paris 1938. – A. BLUM, Les Origines de la Gravure en France, Paris and Brussels 1927 / The Origin and Early History of Engraving in France, New York 1930 (reprint, New York 1978); La route du papier, Grenoble 1946; Les nielles du Quattrocento, Paris 1950; Les primitifs de la gravure sur bois. Etude historique et catalogue des incunables xylographiques du Musée du Louvre, Cabinet des Estampes, collection Edmond de Rothschild, Paris 1956. – R. BRUN, Le livre français illustré de la Renaissance. Etude suivie du catalogue des principaux livres à figure du 16e siècle, Paris 1969. – Buchillustrationen von Gutenberg bis Dürer, von der Handschrift zum Wiegendruck, Kunstmuseum, Berne 1977. M. BUSSET, La technique moderne du bois gravé, et les procédés anciens des xylographes du XVIe siècle et des maîtres graveurs japonais…, Paris 1925. CAMPBELL DODGSON, Catalogue of Early German and Flemish Woodcuts preserved in the British Museum, London 1903–1911. – W.M. CONWAY, The Woodcutters of the Netherlands in the Fifteenth Century, Hildesheim 1961. – S. COSACCHI, Makabertanz. Der Totentanz in Kunst, Poesie und Brauchtum des Mittelalters, Meisenheim am Glan 1965. S. DAMIANI / G. PANAZZA, Mostra di stampe francesi del 500 e del 600, Civica Pinacoteca Tosio-Martinengo, Brescia 1968. – Dieux et Héros, Musée d'Art et d'Histoire, Cabinet des Estampes, Geneva 1978. – L. DONATI, Incisori fiorentini del Quattrocento, Bergamo 1944. L'Ecole de Fontainebleau, Grand Palais, Paris 1972–1973 – Estampes de l'Ecole de Fontainebleau, Musée des Beaux-Arts, Lyons 1973. C. FERGUSON / D.S. STEVENS SCHAFF / G. VIKAN, Medieval and Renaissance Miniatures, National Gallery of Art, Washington 1973. – S. FERRARA / G.G. BERTELÀ, Catalogo generale della raccolta di stampe antiche della Pinacoteca Nazionale di Bologna, Gabinetto delle Stampe. Incisori bolognesi ed emiliani del XVI secolo. Appendice ai volumi Incisori bolognesi ed emiliani del XVII e XVIII

secolo, Bologna 1975; Catalogo generale della raccolta di stampe antiche della Pinacoteca Nazionale di Bologna, Gabinetto delle Stampe. Incisori toscani dal XV al XVII secolo, (coll. R. d'Amico), Bologna 1976; Incisori liguri e lombardi dal XV al XVIII secolo (coll. P. Bellini, R. d'Amico), Bologna 1977. – R.S. FIELD, Fifteenth Century Woodcuts and Metalcuts, National Gallery of Art, Washington 1965–1966; The Fable of the Sick Lion: A Fifteenth Century Blockbook, Middletown, (Conn.) 1974; Fifteenth Century Woodcuts, Metropolitan Museum of Art, New York 1977. – L. FISCHEL, Bilderfolgen im frühen Buchdruck. Studien zur Inkunabel. Illustration in Ulm und Strassburg, Constance 1963. – M. FOSSI, Mostra di chiaroscuri italiani dei secoli XVI, XVII, XVIII, Gabinetto disegni e stampe degli Uffizi, Florence 1956. M. GEISBERG, Die Anfänge des Kupferstiches, Leipzig n.d.; Der deutsche Einblatt-Holzschnitt in der ersten Hälfte des 16. Jahrhunderts, Munich 1924–1930; Der Buchholzschnitt im XVI. Jahrhundert in deutschen, schweizer, niederländischen, französischen, spanischen und italienischen Drucken des XVI. Jahrhunderts, Olten 1937; The German Single-Leaf Woodcut 1500–1550, revised ed. by W.L. Strauss, 4 vols., New York 1974. – F. GELDNER, Die deutschen Inkunabeldrucker: ein Handbuch der deutschen Buchdrucker des XV. Jahrhunderts nach Druckorten, 2 vols., Stuttgart 1968–1970. – C. GLASER, Gotische Holzschnitte, Berlin 1923. – J. GOLDSMITH PHILIPS, Early Florentine Designers and Engravers, Cambridge 1955. – H. GOLLOB, Der Wiener Holzschnitt in den Jahren von 1490 bis 1550, seine Bedeutung für die nordische Kunst, seine Entwicklung, seine Blüte und seine Meister…, Vienna 1926. – E. GRADMANN, Meisterholzschnitte des 15. und 16. Jahrhunderts, Print Room, Eidgenössische Technische Hochschule, Zurich 1959. J.F. HAYWARD, Virtuoso Goldsmiths 1540–1620, London 1976. – E.H. van HEURCK, Les Drapelets de pèlerinage…, Antwerp 1922. – A.M. HIND, Catalogue of Early Italian Engravings preserved in the Department of Prints and Drawings in the British Museum, 2 vols., London 1909/1910; An Introduction to a History of Woodcut with a detailed survey of work done in the fifteenth century, London 1935 (reprint, 2 vols., New York 1963); Early Italian Engraving. A critical catalogue with complete reproduction of all the prints described, London 1938/1948 (reprint, 1970). – A.M. HIND / M. CORBETT / M. NORTON, Engraving in England in the Sixteenth and Seventeenth Centuries, 3 vols., Cambridge 1952–1964. – E. HODNETT, English Woodcuts 1480–1535, New York and London 1973. – H. HYMANS, L'Estampe de 1418 et la validité de sa date, Brussels 1903. – Les Incunables de la collection Edmond de Rothschild: la gravure en relief sur bois et sur métal, Musée du Louvre, Paris 1974. P. JEAN-RICHARD, Maîtres de l'eau-forte des XVIe et XVIIe siècles, Musée du Louvre, Collection Edmond de Rothschild, Paris 1980. D. KUHRMANN, Die Frühzeit des Holzschnitts, Staatliche Graphische Sammlung, Munich 1970. – H. KUNZE, Geschichte der Buchillustration in Deutschland: das 15. Jahrhundert, 2 vols., Leipzig 1975. L. LEBEER, L'Esprit de la gravure au XVe siècle, Brussels 1943. – M. LEHRS, Geschichte und kritischer Katalog des deutschen, niederländischen und französischen Kupferstichs im XV. Jahrhundert, 9 vols. and 9 albums, Vienna 1908–1934 (reprint, 9 vols. and 1 vol. ill., Nendeln, Lichtenstein 1969; English ed., New York 1970). – P.-A. LEMOISNE, Les Xylographes du XIVe et du XVe siècle au

cabinet des estampes de la Bibliothèque Nationale, 2 vols., Paris and Brussels 1927–1930. – J.A. LEVENSON / K. OBERHUBER / J.L. SHEEHAN, Early Italian Engravings from the National Gallery of Art, National Gallery of Art, Washington 1973. – K. LINDLEY, The Woodblock Engravers, Newton Abbot, Devon 1970. – Mannerism and North European Tradition. Prints from c. 1520 to c. 1630, London 1974. E. MONGAN / C.O. SCHNIEWIND, The First Century of Printmaking: 1400–1500, Art Institute of Chicago, Chicago 1941. – R. MORTIMER, Italian 16th Century Books, Cambridge, Mass. 1974. – R. MUTHER, Die deutsche Bücherillustration der Gothik und Frührenaissance, 1460–1530, Munich 1922. A.M. NAGLER, Theatre Festivals of the Medici 1539–1637, New Haven 1964. O. PANKOK / R. SCHRÖDER, Deutsche Holzschneider, Düsseldorf 1958. – A. PETRUCCI, Il Cinquecento. Panorama della incisione italiana, Rome 1964. – M. PITTALUGA, L'incisione italiana nel cinquecento, Milan 1928. – P. POIRIER, Un siècle de gravure anversoise. De Jérôme Cock à Jacques Jordaens. Du dessin à l'estampe, 1550–1650, Brussels 1967. – L. PONOMA-RENKO / A. ROSSEL, La gravure sur bois à travers 69 incunables et 434 gravures, Paris 1970. C.E. RAVA, Supplément à M. Sander: le livre à figures italien de la Renaissance, Milan 1969. – A. REICHEL, Die Clair-Obscur Schnitte des XVI., XVII. und XVIII. Jahrhunderts, Zurich 1926. – E. ROUIR, La gravure des origines au XVIe siècle, Paris 1971. M. SANDER, Le livre à figures italien depuis 1467 jusqu'à 1530. Essai de sa bibliographie et de son histoire (reprint, 5 vols., Nendeln, Lichtenstein 1969). – A. SCHRAMM, Der Bilderschmuck der Frühdrucke, 23 vols., Leipzig 1920–1943. – M.J. SCHRETLEN, Dutch and Flemish Woodcuts of the Fifteenth Century, n.p., n.d. [New York 1925] (reprint, New York 1969). – J.P. SEGUIN, L'information en France avant le périodique. 517 canards imprimés entre 1529 et 1631, Paris 1964. – L. SERVOLINI, La Xilografia a chiaroscuro italiana nei secoli XVI, XVII, XVIII, Lecco 1928. – A. SHESTACK, Fifteenth Century Engravings of Northern Europe, National Gallery of Art, Washington 1968. – A. STIX, Meisterwerke der Graphik im XV. bis XVII. Jahrhundert, Vienna 1921. – W.L. STRAUSS, Chiaroscuro. The Clair-Obscur Woodcuts by the German and Netherlandish Masters of the XVIth and XVIIth Centuries. A Complete Catalogue, New York 1973; The German Single-Leaf Woodcut 1550–1600, 3 vols., New York 1975. E. TIETZE-CONRAT, Die französischen Kupferstiche der Renaissance, Munich, c. 1930. – La ville au Moyen Age. Gravure allemande du XVe siècle, Musée d'Art et d'Histoire, Cabinet des Estampes, Geneva 1974–1975. L. VOET, The Golden Compasses, A History and Evaluation of the Printing and Publishing Activities of the Officina Plantiniana at Antwerp, 3 vols., Amsterdam 1969. E. WALDMANN, Die Nürnberger Kleinmeister, Leipzig 1910. – W. WORRINGER, Die altdeutsche Buchillustration, Munich and Leipzig 1912. H. ZERNER, Ecole de Fontainebleau. Gravures, Paris 1969.

17th and 18th centuries

J. ADHÉMAR, La gravure originale au 18e siècle, Paris 1963, New York 1964. – D. ALEXANDER, The German Single-Leaf

Woodcut 1600–1700: A Pictorial Catalogue, with W.L. Strauss, 2 vols., New York 1977. – R. d'AMICO, Incisori d'invenzione romani e napoletani del XVII secolo, Bologna 1978. – M. AUDIN, Essai sur les gravures de bois en France au dix-huitième siècle, Paris 1925. – Bibliothèque Nationale. Inventaire du fonds français du Cabinet des Estampes. Graveurs du XVIIe siècle, R.A. Weigert and M. Préaud, 14 vols., Paris 1940–1979. – Bibliothèque Nationale. Inventaire du fonds français du Cabinet des Estampes. Graveurs du XVIIIe siècle, M. Roux. E. Pognon, Y. Bruand, M. Hébert, Y. Sjöberg, F. Gardey, 13 vols., Paris 1931–1974. A. BLUM, La gravure en Angleterre au XVIIIe siècle, Paris 1930. – E. BOUVY, La gravure en France au XVIIe siècle. La gravure de portraits et d'allégories, Paris and Brussels, 1929. – Das Buch als Kunstwerk. Französische illustrierte Bücher des 18. Jahrhunderts aus der Bibliothek Hans Fürstenberg, Ludwigsburg, Schloss, 1965.
A. CALABI, La gravure italienne au XVIIIe siècle, Paris 1931.
E. DACIER, La gravure en France au XVIIIe siècle. La gravure de genre et de mœurs, Paris and Brussels 1925. – E. DACIER / A. VUAFLART / J. HEROLD, Jean de Julienne et les graveurs de Watteau au XVIIIe siècle, 4 vols., Paris 1929–1932. – S. DAMIANI, Mostra di stampe italiane del seicento, Civica Pinacoteca Tosio-Martinengo, Brescia 1972. – L. DELTEIL, Manuel de l'amateur d'estampes du XVIIIe siècle, Paris 1911. – J. DUPORTAL, La gravure en France au XVIIIe siècle: la gravure de portraits et de paysages, Paris 1926.
Entwurf und Ausführung. Italienische Druckgraphik und ihre Vorzeichnungen von Barocci bis Piranesi, Staatliche Museen, Kupferstichkabinett, Berlin 1964.
S. FERRARA / G.G. BERTELÀ, Catalogo generale della raccolta di stampe antiche della Pinacoteca Nazionale di Bologna, Gabinetto delle Stampe. Incisori bolognesi ed emiliani del secolo XVII, Bologna 1973; Incisori... del secolo XVIII, Bologna 1974. – J. FRANKAU, Eighteenth Century Colour Prints, London 1900. – Französische Farbstiche 1735–1815, aus dem Kupferstichkabinett der Veste Coburg, Kunstsammlung der Veste Coburg, Coburg 1965. – French Prints Drawings and Books of the XVII–XVIII Centuries, Philadelphia Museum of Art, Philadelphia 1954. – J. FURSTENBERG, La gravure originale dans l'illustration du livre français au dix-huitième siècle / Die Original-Graphik in der französischen Buch-Illustration des achtzehnten Jahrhunderts, Hamburg 1975.
D. GIOSEFFI, Pitture, disegni et stampe del 700 dalle collezioni dei Civici Musei di Storia ed Arte di Trieste, Museo Sartorio, Trieste 1972. – E. and J. GONCOURT, L'art du XVIIIe siècle. 3 vols., Paris 1912–1914. – E.W. GOSSE, British Portrait-Painters and Engravers of the 18th Century, Paris 1906.
H. HAMMELMANN, Book Illustrators in Eighteenth Century England, New Haven 1975. – J. HEROLD, Gravure en manière de crayon. Jean-Charles François, 1717–1769. Catalogue de l'œuvre gravé, Paris 1931; Louis-Marin Bonnet, 1743–1793. Catalogue de l'œuvre gravé, Paris 1935. – O.E. HOLLOWAY, French Rococo Book Illustration, London 1969. – L'incisione bolognese nel secolo XVII, Galleria degli Uffizi, Gabinetto disegni e stampe, Florence 1953.
H. LEHMANN-HAUPT, An Introduction to the Woodcut of the Seventeenth Century, New York 1977.
R.M. MASON, Vues vénitiennes du XVIIIe siècle, Musée d'Art et d'Histoire, Cabinet des Estampes, Geneva 1973. – A. MASSON, Estampes du XVIIIe siècle, Rouen 1925; La

gravure française au XVIIe siècle, Bibliothèque de la Ville, Rouen 1926. – J. MODEL / J. SPRINGER, Der Französische Farbenstich des 18. Jahrhunderts, Stuttgart and Berlin, 1912.
R. PALLUCCHINI, Mostra degli incisori veneti del settecento, Venice 1941. – T. PIGNATTI, Venedig in Kupferstichen des 18. Jahrhunderts, Mainz 1968; Gli incanti di Venezia rivisti con Canaletto, Guardi..., Milan 1974. – E.C. PIRANI, Il libro illustrato italiano, secoli XVII–XVIII, Rome 1956. – M. PITSCH, La vie populaire à Paris au XVIIIe siècle d'après les textes contemporains et les estampes, 2 vols., Paris 1949; Essai de catalogue sur l'iconographie de la vie populaire à Paris au XVIIIe siècle, Paris 1952. – M. PITTALUGA, Acquafortisti veneziani del Settecento, Florence 1953. – M. PRAZ, Studies in Seventeenth Century Imagery, Rome 1964.
E. ROUIR, La gravure originale au XVIIe siècle, Paris 1974.
M.C. SALAMAN, Old English Colour-Prints, London 1909; Old English Mezzotints, ed. by Charles Holmes, London and New York 1910. – Schwarze Kunst: englische Schabkünstler des 18. Jahrhunderts, Staatliche Kunsthalle, Karlsruhe 1976. – F. SHORT, British Mezzotints, London 1925.
D. TERNOIS, L'art français du 17e siècle vu à travers l'estampe. La formation du Classicisme, Bibliothèque de la Ville, Lyon 1965. – Venezianische Veduten des 18. Jahrhunderts. Radierung aus dem Museo Correr, Venedig, Germanisches Nationalmuseum, Nuremberg 1964.
L. VOET, Antwerp, The Golden Age, Antwerp 1973.

19th century

J. ADHÉMAR, Les Lithographies de paysage en France à l'époque romantique, Paris 1937; L'estampe française. La lithographie en France au XIXe siècle, n.p., n.d. [Paris 1942].
J. BAILLY-HERZBERG, L'eau-forte des peintres au dix-neuvième siècle. La Société des Aquafortistes, 1862–1867, 2 vols., Paris 1972. – J.E. BERSIER, La Lithographie en France: L'Epoque du romantisme, Mulhouse 1947; Petite histoire de la lithographie originale en France, Paris 1970. – Bibliothèque Nationale. Departement des estampes. Un siècle d'histoire de France par l'estampe, 1770–1871. Collection de Vinck. Inventaire analytique, Paris 1938; Bibliothèque Nationale. Inventaire du fonds français du Cabinet des Estampes. Après 1800, J. Laran, J. Adhémar, J. Lethève, F. Gardey, 14 vols., Paris 1933/1967. – Bild vom Stein, die Entwicklung der Lithographie von Senefelder bis heute, Staatliche Graphiche Sammlung, Munich 1961. – E. BINNEY, Delacroix and the French Romantic Print, Smithsonian Institution, Washington 1974.
A. CALABI, Saggio sulla litografia, Milan 1958. – CAMPBELL DODGSON, French Etching from Meryon to Lepère, London 1922. – E. CHASE, The Etchings of the French Impressionists and their Contemporaries, Paris 1946. – B. CIRKER, 1800 Woodcuts by Thomas Bewick and His School, New York 1962. – H. CLIFFE, Lithography, London and New York 1965; Lithographie heute. Technik und Gestaltung, Ravensburg 1968.
DAVIS / BURKE / R. KING, The World of Currier and Ives, New York 1968. – Delacroix et la gravure romantique, Bibliothèque Nationale, Paris 1963. – L. DELTEIL, Manuel de l'amateur d'estampes des XIXe et XXe siècles (1801–1924), 2 vols., Paris 1925–1926; 700 reproductions d'estampes des XIXe et XXe siècles pour servir de complément au Manuel

de l'amateur d'estampes, 2 vols., Paris 1926; Le peintre-graveur illustré. XIXe et XXe siècles, 31 vols., Paris 1906/1930; Le peintre-graveur illustré. The Graphic Works of Nineteenth and Twentieth Century Artists. An Illustrated catalogue, 31 vols., reprint, New York 1969; Vol. 32: Appendix and glossary. – F. DÖRNHÖFFER, Die Lithographie..., Vienna 1903. – J. M. DUMONT, Les maîtres graveurs populaires, 1800–1850, Epinal 1965. – D. DURBÉ, I macchiaioli, Rome 1978. – L. DUSSLER, Die Inkunabeln der Deutschen Lithographie 1796–1821, Berlin 1929 (reprint, 1955).
R.K. ENGEN, Victorian Engravings, London and New York 1975. – L'Estampe impressionniste, Bibliothèque Nationale, Paris 1974–1975.
French Printmakers of the Nineteenth Century. Selected Works from the Collection of the Art Gallery of Ontario, New York Cultural Center, New York 1972 / Art Gallery of Ontario, Toronto 1972. M.J. FRIEDLÄNDER, Die Lithographie, Berlin 1922.
C. GLASER, Die Graphik der Neuzeit vom Anfang des 19. Jahrhunderts bis zur Gegenwart, Berlin 1922. – P. GUSMAN, La gravure sur bois en France au XIXe siècle, Paris 1929. – L.W. GUTBIER, Katalog internationaler Graphik des XIX. Jahrhunderts, Dresden 1911. A.S. HARTRICK, Lithography..., London 1932. – U. HEIDERICH / J. SCHULTZE / A.M. WINTHER, Die Lithographie von den Anfängen bis zur Gegenwart..., Kunsthalle, Bremen 1976. – F. HICKLIN, Bewick: Wood Engravings, London 1978. – Hommage à Senefelder. Künstlerlithographien aus der Sammlung Felix H. Man, Aargauer Kunsthaus, Aarau (Switzerland) 1971. – B. HUNNISETT, Steel-Engraved Book Illustration in England, London 1980. – R. HUTCHINSON, 1800 Woodcuts by Thomas Bewick and his School, New York 1962. – A. HYATT MAYOR, A. Senefelder. A Complete Course of Lithography New York 1968 (reprint of the London ed. of 1819). – Idylle, Klassizismus und Romantik. Deutsche Druckgraphik zu Wallrafs Zeiten, Wallraf-Richartz-Museum, Cologne 1974.
C.F. IVES, The Great Wave: The Influence of Japanese Woodcuts on French Prints, Metropolitan Museum of Art, New York 1974.
U.E. JOHNSON, Ambroise Vollard, éditeur: Prints..., New York 1944 (reprint, 1977). – W.M. JOHNSON, French Lithography. The Restauration Salon, 1817–1824, Agnes Etherington Center, Kingston, Ontario 1977. – E. JUSSIM, Visual Communication and the Graphic Arts, Photographic Technologies in the Nineteenth Century, Rochester, N.Y., 1974.
L. LANG, La lithographie en France: des origines au début du Romantisme, Mulhouse 1946; Godefroy Engelmann imprimeur-lithographe..., Colmar 1977. – J. LETHÈVE, La Vie Quotidienne des artistes français au XIXe siècle, Paris 1968. – J. LIEURE, La Lithographie artistique et ses diverses techniques, n.p. 1939.
F.H. MAN, 150 Years of Artist's Lithography, 1803–1953, London 1954. – R. MICHALIK, Der frühe Steindruck in Regensburg, Regensburg 1971. – L. MONTAGNER, Incisori italiani dell'Ottocento, Padua 1976.
R. PASSERON, La gravure impressionniste: origines et rayonnement, Fribourg (Switzerland) 1974. – H.T. PETERS, Currier and Ives: Printmakers to the American People, New York 1942.
C. RATTA, L'Arte della litografia in Italia, Bologna 1928. – C. de RENDINGER, L'Affiche d'intérieur, le poster, Paris 1977. – C. ROGER-MARX, La gravure originale en France de Manet à nos jours, Paris 1939; La

gravure originale au XIXe siècle, Paris 1962; English ed., New York 1962.

E. SCHAAR, *Von Delacroix bis Munch: Künstlergraphik im 19ten Jahrhundert*, Hamburg 1977. – R. SÖDERBERG, *French Book Illustration, 1800–1905*, Stockholm 1977. – B. STEWART, *Prints of the Impressionists, Estampes des impressionnistes*, National Gallery of Canada, Ottawa 1979.

C. THON, *Französische Plakate des 19. Jahrhunderts in der Kunstbibliothek Berlin*, Berlin 1970. – M. TWYMAN, *Lithography 1800–1850. The Techniques of Drawing on Stone in England and France and their Application in Works of Topography*, London 1970.

A. VOLLARD, *Souvenirs d'un marchand de tableaux*, Paris 1937.

P. WEAVER, *The Technique of Lithography*, New York 1964. – W. WEBER, *Saxa loquuntur. Steine reden. Geschichte der Lithographie.* 2 vols., Heidelberg 1961–1964; *Histoire de la lithographie*, Paris 1967; German ed., 1961–1964; English ed., 1968. – R.A. WINKLER, *Die Frühzeit der deutschen Lithographie: Katalog der Bilddrucke von 1796–1821*, Munich 1975.

20th century

J. ADHÉMAR, *La gravure originale au XXe siècle*, Paris 1967. – *Atelier Lacourière*, Maison des Arts et Loisirs, Montbéliard 1972. – K.W. AUVIL, *Serigraphy: Silk Screen Techniques for the Artist*, Englewood Cliffs, N.J. 1965. – R. AVERMAETE, *Le graveur sur bois moderne de l'Occident*, n.p. 1928 (reprint, Vaduz, Lichtenstein 1977).

K. BACHLER, *Bruckmann's Handbuch der modernen Druckgraphik*, Munich 1973. – *Bauhaus, 50 Jahre Bauhaus Ausstellung. Sonderkatalog Bauhaus Graphik*, Kunstgebäude am Schlossplatz, Stuttgart 1968; *Bauhaus 1919–1969*, Musée d'Art Moderne de la Ville de Paris, Paris 1969. – *Bibliothèque Nationale: Cinq cents gravures contemporaines. Récents enrichissements du Cabinet des Estampes*, Bibliothèque Nationale, Paris 1969; *L'Estampe contemporaine à la Bibliothèque Nationale*, Bibliothèque Nationale, Paris 1973; *L'Estampe aujourd'hui, cinq années d'enrichissement du Département des Estampes et de la Photographie*, Bibliothèque Nationale, Paris 1978. – B. BIDAULT, *Manuel pratique de sérigraphie pour l'initiation à l'impression sur tous supports*, Paris 1971. – J.I. BIEGELEISEN, *The Complete Book of Silkscreen Printing Production*, New York 1963; *Screen Printing: A Contemporary Guide*, New York 1971. – H. BIRKNER, *La sérigraphie sur papier et sur étoffe*, Paris 1971. – *British International Print Biennale*, City Art Gallery and Museum, Cartwright Hall, Bradford 1972 / Museum and Arts Centre, Durham 1972 / Oxford Gallery, Oxford 1972. – L.G. BUCHHEIM, *Der Künstlergemeinschaft Brücke. Gemälde, Zeichnungen, Graphik, Plastik, Dokumente*, Feldafing 1956; *Graphik des Deutschen Expressionismus*, Feldafing 1959.

CAMPBELL DODGSON, *Contemporary English Woodcuts*, London 1922. – F. CARR, *A Guide to Screen Process Printing*, London 1961. – R. CASTLEMAN, *Contemporary Prints*, New York 1973 / *Modern Prints since 1942*, London 1973; *Prints of the Twentieth Century, A History with Illustrations from the Collection of the Museum of Modern Art*, New York 1976; *Printed Art, A View of Two Decades*, New York 1980. – M. CAZA, *La technique de la sérigraphie*, Paris 1963; *La sérigraphie*, Geneva 1973. – C. CHIEFFO, *Silk Screen as a Fine Art*, New York 1967.

A. DÜCKERS, *Druckgraphik der Gegenwart 1960–1975 im Berliner Kupferstichkabinett*, Staatliche Museen, Kupferstichkabinett, Berlin 1975.

The Engravings of S.W. Hayter, Victoria and Albert Museum, London 1967. – *L'estampe en Suisse. Son édition et son impression*, Musée des Arts décoratifs, Lausanne 1970. – *The Exhibition (36th) of the Japan Print Association. Special Exhibition: Swiss Contemporary Prints*, Japan Print Association, Tokyo 1968. – *Exposition de la gravure... italienne contemporaine*, Bibliothèque Nationale, Paris 1930. – *The Expressionist Print: the Kaerwer Collection*, Elvehjem Art Center, University of Wisconsin, Madison 1972.

R.O. FOSSETT, *Techniques in Photography for the Silk Screen Printer*, Cincinnati 1959. P. GILMOUR, *Modern Prints*, London 1970; *The Mechanized Image, an Historical Perspective on 20th Century Prints*, London 1978. – A. GLEIZES / J. METZINGER, *Du cubisme. Gravures originales par Marcel Duchamp, Albert Gleizes, M. Laurencin, J. Metzinger. F. Picabia...*, Paris 1947. – R.T. GODFREY, *Printmaking in Britain*, London 1971. – C. GOERG, *Stanley William Hayter, 40 ans de gravure*, Cabinet des Estampes, Geneva 1966. – C.J. GOODMAN, *A Study of the Marketing of the Original Print based on a Study of the Marketing of Fine Prints...*, Los Angeles 1973. – *Graphik von 1890 bis heute*, Ulmer Museum, Ulm 1964. – *Graphik des XX. Jahrhunderts. Neuerwerbungen des Berliner Kupferstichkabinetts, 1958–1968*, Staatliche Museen, Kupferstichkabinett, Berlin 1968. – *Graphik der Welt, Internationale Druckgraphik der letzten 25 Jahre*, Kunsthalle, Nuremberg 1971. – *Graveurs anglais contemporains*, Musée d'Art et d'Histoire, Cabinet des Estampes, Geneva 1974. – *Graveurs vaudois contemporains*, Musée d'Art et d'Histoire, Cabinet des Estampes, Geneva 1966; *La jeune gravure vaudoise*, Cabinet des Estampes, Geneva 1964. – K.M. GUICHARD, *British Etchers, 1850–1940*, London 1977.

G.F. HARTLAUB, *Die Graphik des Expressionismus in Deutschland*, Stuttgart 1947. – S.W. HAYTER, *New Ways of Gravure*, London 1949 (reprint, London and New York 1966); *About Prints*, London 1962. – J. HELLER, *Printmaking Today*, New York 1958. – H.H. HOFSTÄTTER, *Peinture, gravure et dessin contemporains*, Paris 1972. B. JACOBSEN, *Fourteen Big Prints*, London 1972.

D. KARSHAN, *Language of the Print*, New York 1968. – M. KNIGIN, *The Contemporary Lithographic Workshop around the World*, New York 1974. – M. KNIGIN / M. ZIMILES, *The Technique of Fine Art Lithography*, New York 1970. – E. KOLLECKER / W. MATUSCHKE, *Der moderne Druck – Handbuch der grafischen Techniken*, Hamburg 1956. – A. KOSLOFF, *Photographic Screen Process Printing*, Cincinnati 1968. – C. KRUCK, *Technik und Druck der künstlerischen Lithographie*, Frankfurt 1962. – O. KRÜGER, *Die Lithographischen Verfahren und der Offsetdruck*, Leipzig 1949. – *Künstler sehen sich selbst: graphische Selbstbildnisse unseres Jahrhunderts Privatsammlung*, Städtisches Museum, Braunschweig 1976–1977. – D. KUNZLE, *The Early Comic Strip, Narrative Strips and Picture Stories*, Berkeley – Los Angeles 1973.

N. LALIBERTE, *Twentieth Century Woodcuts: History and Modern Techniques*, New York 1971. – N. LALIBERTE / A. MOGELON, *The Art of Monoprint*, New York 1974. – L. LANG, *Expressionistische Buchillustration in Deutschland, 1907–1927*, Lucerne 1975; *Malerei und Graphik in der DDR*, Lucerne 1979. – L.E. LAWSON, *Offset Lithography*,

London 1963. – J. LEWIS, *The Twentieth Century Book. Its Illustration and Design*, London 1967. – *Lithographies anglaises contemporaines*, Musée d'Art et d'Histoire, Cabinet des Estampes, Geneva 1953.

J. MOSER, *Atelier 17, A 50th Anniversary Retrospective Exhibition*, Elvehjem Art Center, University of Wisconsin, Madison 1972. – F. MOURLOT, *Souvenirs et portraits d'artistes*, Paris 1973; *Gravés dans ma mémoire: cinquante ans de lithographie avec Picasso, Matisse, Chagall, Braque, Miró*, Paris 1979.

C. NEWTON, *Photography in Printmaking*, Victoria and Albert Museum, London 1979.

H. OHFF, *Galerie der neuen Künste: Pop, Happening, Hard-Edge*, Gütersloh 1971.

R. PASSERON, *La gravure française au XXe siècle*, Fribourg 1970; *French Prints of the 20th Century*, New York 1970; *L'estampe originale: ses secrets, les différents procédés des grands maîtres contemporains*, Paris 1972. – H. PLATTE, *Farbige Graphik unserer Zeit*, Stuttgart 1960. – *Prints from the Mourlot Press. Exhibition... circulated by the Travelling Exhibition Service of the National Collection of Fine Arts, Smithsonian Institution, 1964/1965* (introduction by J. Adhémar), Paris 1964.

K.A. REISER, *Deutsche Graphik der letzten hundert Jahre aus der Sammlung Karl August Reiser, Bonn*, Rheinisches Landesmuseum, Bonn 1968. – J. RUSSELL / S. GABLIK, *Pop Art Redefined*, London 1969.

P.J. SACHS, *Modern Prints and Drawings*, New York 1954. – M.C. SALAMAN, *Modern Woodcuts and Lithographs by British and French Artists*, London 1919; *The Woodcut of To-day at Home and Abroad*, London 1927; *The New Woodcut*, London 1930. – L. SERVOLINI, *Dizionario... degli incisori italiani moderni...*, Milan 1955. – M. SEVERINI, *Grafica italiana contemporanea nel Gabinetto disegni e stampe dell'Istituto di storia dell'arte dell'università di Pisa*, Venice 1961. – H. SHOKLER, *Artist's Manual for Silk Screen Print Making*, New York 1960. – J. SIBLIK, *La gravure contemporaine*, Paris 1971. – *Silk-Screen: History of a Medium*, Philadelphia Museum of Art, Philadelphia 1971–1972. – *Société des peintres graveurs français*, periodic exhibitions since 1899, Bibliothèque Nationale, Paris. – K. SOTRIFFER, *Expressionismus und Fauvismus*, Vienna 1911. – W. STUBBE, *Die Graphik des zwanzigsten Jahrhunderts*, Berlin 1962; *Graphic Arts in the 20th Century*, New York 1963. – *Swiss Concrete Art in Graphics*, University Art Museum, Austin, Texas 1975. – *Unmittelbar und unverfälscht: frühe Graphik des Expressionismus*, Wallraf-Richartz-Museum und Museum Ludwig, Cologne 1976–1977.

S. von WIESE, *Graphik des Expressionismus*, Teufen, Aargau (Switzerland) 1976. – H.M. WINGLER, *Graphic Work from the Bauhaus*, New York Graphic Society, Greenwich, Conn. 1969.

C. ZIGROSSER, *The Expressionists. A Survey of their Graphic Art*, London 1957.

United States, 20th century

Amerikanische Druckgraphik 1913–1963, Graphische Sammlung Albertina, Vienna 1976. – *Amerikanische Graphik seit 1960*, Bündner Kunsthaus, Chur, Switzerland 1972 / Kunstverein, Solothurn 1972 / Musée d'Art et d'Histoire, Geneva 1972. – G.Z. ANTREASIAN, *The Tamarind Book of Lithography: Art and Techniques*, Los Angeles 1971. – *Artists USA 1972–1973. A guide to contemporary American Art*, 1972.

G. BARO, *30 Years of American Printmaking, including the 20th National Print Exhibition*, Brooklyn Museum, New York 1976–1977. – M.W. BASKETT, *American Graphic Workshops: 1968*, Cincinnati Art Museum, Cincinnati, 1968. – K.F. BEALL, *American Prints in the Library of Congress*, Baltimore 1970. – M. BLOCH, *Tamarind: A Renaissance of Lithography*, travelling exhibition of the "Tamarind Lithography Workshop" International Exhibitions, 1971–1972. – A. BLOCH / K.A. SMITH Foundation, *Made in California. An Exhibition of Five Workshops*, Grunwald Graphic Arts Foundation, Dickson Art Center, University of California, Los Angeles 1971. – E. BRYANT, *Graphics '68. Recent American Prints*, University of Kentucky Art Gallery, Lexington, Kentucky, 1968.
F. CAREY / A. GRIFFITHS, *American Prints: 1879–1979*, The British Museum, Department of Prints and Drawings, London 1980. – R. CASTLEMAN, *Technics and Creativity: Gemini G.E.L.*, Museum of Modern Art, New York 1971; *American Prints: 1913–1963*. travelling exhibition, International Council of the Museum of Modern Art, New York, 1976 (Brussels, Leeds, Vienna). – P.A. CHEW, *American Artists as Print Makers*, The Westmoreland County Museum of Art, Greensburg, Pennsylvania 1963. – H. CLOVER, *Contemporary Graphics Published by Universal Limited Art Editions*, Dayton's Gallery 12, Minneapolis 1968. – *Contemporary American Prints: Gifts from the Singer Collection*, Metropolitan Museum of Art, New York 1976. – *Contemporary American Prints from Universal Limited Art Editions, The Rapp Collection*, Art Gallery of Ontario, Toronto 1979. – P. CUMMINGS, *A Dictionary of Contemporary American Artists*, New York 1966.
A. DESHAIES, *Graphics 'Sixty Two*, University of Kentucky Art Gallery, Lexington, Kentucky 1962.
J.M. FARMER, *New American Monotypes*, Smithsonian Institution Traveling Exhibition Service, Washington 1978. – R.S. FIELD, *Recent American Etching*, National Collection of Fine Arts, Smithsonian Institution, Washington, and Wesleyan University, Middletown, Conn., 1975. – R.S. FIELD / L. SPERLING, *Offset Lithography*, Middletown, Conn., 1973. – J.A. FLINT, *New Ways with Paper*, National Collection of Fine Arts, Smithsonian Institution, Washington 1977–1978. – K.A. FOSTER, *American Drawings, Watercolors and Prints*, New York 1980.
Gravures américaines d'aujourd'hui, Centre Culturel Américain, Paris 1969.
The Handmade Paper Object, Institute of Contemporary Art, Boston 1977. – H. HARTMANN, *Amerikanische Graphik seit 1960*, Kunstmuseum, Kupferstichkabinett, Basel 1972. – J. HELLER, *Printmaking Today*, New York 1972. – T. HEYMAN, *Prints California. Profile of an Exhibition*, Oakland Museum, Oakland, California 1975. – T. HEYMAN / D. BEALL, *Contemporary Prints from Northern California*, Oakland Museum, Oakland, California, 1966.
D. JOHNSON, *Contemporary Graphics from the Museum's Collection*, Museum of Art, Rhode Island School of Design, Providence 1973.
D. KELDER, *Graphics in Long Island Collections from the Studio of Universal Limited Art Editions*, Hofstra University, Emily Low Gallery, Hempstead, Long Island 1970.
P. LARSON, *Johns, Kelly, Lichtenstein, Motherwell, Nauman, Rauschenberg, Serra, Stella, Prints from Gemini G.E.L.*, Walker Art Center, Minneapolis 1974. – J. LEERING, *Experiment in Grafiek. Gemini Graphic Editions Limited*, Van Abbemuseum, Eindhoven, Holland 1971. – W.S. LIEBERMAN, *London-New York-Hollywood: A New Look in Prints*, Museum of Modern Art, New York 1966; *Manhattan Observed. Selections of Drawings and Prints*, Museum of Modern Art, New York 1968. – W.S. LIEBERMAN / R. RAUSCHENBERG, *Lithographies d'artistes américains: Lee Bontecou, Jim Dine, Fritz Glarner, Jasper Johns, Robert Rauschenberg, Larry Rivers*, Galerie Gérald Cramer, Geneva 1965. – W.S. LIEBERMAN / V. ALLEN, *Tamarind: Homage to Lithography*, Museum of Modern Art, New York 1969. – N. LYNTON, *Order and Experience. Prints by Agnes Martin, Sol LeWitt, Robert Ryman, Robert Mangold, Brice Marden, Edda Renouf, Dorothea Rockburne*, Arts Council of Great Britain, 1975.
Modern Art in the United States: A Selection from the Collections of the Museum of Modern Art, New York, Tate Gallery, London 1956. – K. McNULTY, *A Decade of American Printmaking*, Philadelphia Museum of Art, Philadelphia 1952. – *Multiples-U.S.A.. (Josef Albers, Jasper Johns, Roy Lichtenstein, Claes Oldenburg, etc.)*, Fourth National Print Biannual, Western Michigan University, Kalamazoo, Michigan 1970.
The Painterly Print: Monotypes from the 17th to the 20th Century, Metropolitan Museum of Art, New York 1980. – *Paper Forms: Hand-Made Paper Projects*, The Visual Arts, Massachusetts Institute of Technology, Cambridge, Mass. 1978.
D.S. RUBIN, *Paper Art*, Galleries of the Claremont Colleges, Claremont, California, 1977.
W. SHADWELL, *American Printmaking: The First 150 Years*, Museum of Graphic Art, New York 1969. – K.L. SPANGENBERG, *San Francisco Area Printmakers*, Cincinnati Art Museum, Cincinnati 1973.
G. THIEM, *Amerikanische und Englische Graphik der Gegenwart aus der Graphischen Sammlung der Staatsgalerie Stuttgart*, Staatsgalerie Stuttgart, Stuttgart 1974. – N. TOUSLEY, *Prints. Bochner, LeWitt, Mangold, Marden, Martin, Renouf, Rockburne, Ryman*, Art Gallery of Ontario, Toronto 1975–1976. – *Twenty-eight Contemporary American Graphic Artists*, Rijksakademie van Beeldende Kunsten, Amsterdam 1968.

Print Magazines

L'Amateur d'Estampes, Paris 1921–1933. – *L'Eau-forte*, Paris 1903–1904. – *L'Estampe*, Paris 1881–1902. – *L'Estampe et l'Affiche*, Paris 1897–1899. – *L'Estampe moderne*, Paris 1897–1899. – *The Fine Art Circular and Print-Collector's Manual*, London 1857. – *Graphics, The Magazine of Original and Fine Arts Prints*, Hollis, New Hampshire, since 1977. – *Graphis*, Zurich, since 1945. – *Die Graphischen Künste*, Vienna 1879–1932; new series, Vienna 1936–1938. – *Journal of the Print World*, Meredith New Hampshire, since 1976. – *Lithographe, Journal des Artistes et des Imprimeurs*, Paris 1838–1848. – *La Lithographie, Organe mensuel des artistes lithographes*, Paris 1897–1901. – *Le Livre et l'Image*, Paris 1893–1894. – *Maso Finiguerra, Rivista della stampa incisa del libro illustrato*, Rome 1936–1938. – *Les Nouvelles de l'Estampe*, Paris, since 1963. – *The Print Collector's Quarterly*, London 1911–1939. – *The Print Collector's Newsletter*, New York, since 1970. – *The Print Connoisseur*, New York 1921–1931. – *Print Review*, New York, since 1973. – *Prints*, New York, 1930–1937; *Print*, since 1940. – *I Quaderni del conoscitore di stampe*, Milan since 1970. – *L'Ymagier*, Paris 1894–1896.

List of Illustrations

271

275

Index of Names and Places

DESIGN AND LAYOUT BY SYLVIA SAUDAN-SKIRA

PRODUCED BY THE TECHNICAL STAFF OF
EDITIONS D'ART ALBERT SKIRA S.A., GENEVA

TEXT FILMSET BY TYPELEC, GENEVA
COLOUR FILMS MADE BY LITH-ART, BERNE
COLOUR FILMS AND HELIO-OFFSET
ILLUSTRATIONS IN BLACK AND WHITE
AND TEXT PRINTED BY ROTO-SADAG, GENEVA
BINDING BY ROGER VEIHL, GENEVA

PUBLISHED SEPTEMBER 1981

PRINTED IN SWITZERLAND

HISTORY OF AN ART

PRINTS